国家出版基金项目
NATIONAL PUBLICATION FOUNDATION

THE CHINESE PATH 中国道路

GREEN MANUFACTURING

The Rise to Power of China's
Manufacturing Industry in the Future

ZHAO JIANJUN

Translated by
HE SHAN, XU JIN, ZENG PING

Proofread by
LI WEIBIN, ZHANG JIE

中国财经出版传媒集团
经济科学出版社
Economic Science Press

图书在版编目（CIP）数据

绿色制造：中国制造业未来崛起之路 ＝ Green
Manufacturing: The Rise to Power of China's
Manufacturing Industry in the Future：英文/赵建
军著；何姗，胥瑾，曾苹译. --北京：经济科学出版
社，2022. 3
　　（《中国道路》丛书）
　　ISBN 978-7-5218-3559-5

Ⅰ.①绿…　　Ⅱ.①赵…②何…③胥…④曾…　　Ⅲ.
①制造工业—产业发展—研究—中国—英文　　Ⅳ.
①F426.4

中国版本图书馆 CIP 数据核字（2022）第 053304 号

责任编辑：李　宝
责任校对：易　超
责任印制：王世伟

绿色制造：中国制造业未来崛起之路
Green Manufacturing: The Rise to Power of China's
Manufacturing Industry in the Future
赵建军　著
何　姗　胥　瑾　曾　苹　译
经济科学出版社出版、发行　新华书店经销
社址：北京市海淀区阜成路甲 28 号　邮编：100142
总编部电话：010-88191217　发行部电话：010-88191522
网址：www.esp.com.cn
电子邮箱：esp@esp.com.cn
天猫网店：经济科学出版社旗舰店
网址：http://jjkxcbs.tmall.com
北京季蜂印刷有限公司印装
787×1092　16 开　14.5 印张　360000 字
2022 年 5 月第 1 版　2022 年 5 月第 1 次印刷
ISBN 978-7-5218-3559-5　定价：69.00 元
（图书出现印装问题，本社负责调换。电话：010-88191510）
（版权所有　侵权必究　打击盗版　举报热线：010-88191661
QQ：2242791300　营销中心电话：010-88191537
电子邮箱：dbts@esp.com.cn）

Editorial Board of *The Chinese Path Series*

Preface

The Chinese path refers to the path of socialism with distinctive Chinese characteristics. As Chinese President Xi Jinping points out, it is not an easy path. We are able to embark on this path thanks to the great endeavors of reform and opening up over the past 30 years and more, and the continuous quest made in the 60-plus years since the founding of the People's Republic of China (PRC). It is based on a thorough review of the evolution of the Chinese nation over more than 170 years since modern times and carrying forward the 5,000-year-long Chinese civilization. This path is deeply rooted in history and broadly based on China's present realities.

A right path leads to a bright future. The Chinese path is not only access to China's development and prosperity, but also a path of hope and promise to the rejuvenation of the Chinese nation. Only by forging the confidence in the path, theory, institution and culture can we advance along this path of socialism with Chinese characteristics. With this focus, *The Chinese Path Series* presents to readers an overview in practice, achievements and experiences as well as the past, present and future of the Chinese path.

The Chinese Path Series is divided into ten volumes with one hundred books on different topics. The main topics of the volumes are as follows: economic development, political advancement, cultural progress, social development, ecological conservation, national defense and armed forces building, diplomacy and international policies, the Party's leadership and building, localization of Marxism in China and views from other countries on the Chinese path. Each volume on a particular topic consists of several books which respectively throw light on exploration in practice, reform process, achievements, experiences and theoretical innovations of the Chinese path. Focusing on the practice in reform and opening up with the continuous exploration since the founding of the PRC, these books summarize on the development and inheritance of China's glorious civilization, which not only display a strong sense of the times, but also have profound historical appeal and future-oriented impact.

The series is conceived in its entirety and assigned to different authors. In terms of the writing, special attention has been paid to the combination of history and reality, as well as theory and practice at home and abroad. It gives a realistic and innovative interpretation of the practice, experience, process and theory of the Chinese path. Efforts are made on the distinctive and convincing expression in a global context. It helps to cast light on the "Chinese wisdom" and the "Chinese approach" that the Chinese path has contributed to the modernization of developing countries and solutions to human problems.

On the basis of the great achievements in China's development since the founding of the PRC, particularly since the reform and opening up, the Chinese nation, which had endured so much and for so long since the modern times, has achieved tremendous growth—it has stood up, become prosperous and grown in strength. The socialism with distinctive Chinese characteristics has shown great vitality and entered a new stage. This path has been expanded and is now at a new historical starting point. At this vital stage of development, the Economic Science Press of China Finance & Economy Media Group has designed and organized the compilation of *The Chinese Path Series*, which is of great significance in theory and practice.

The program of *The Chinese Path Series* was launched in 2015, and the first publications came out in 2017. The Series was listed in a couple of national key publication programs, the "90 kinds of selected publications in celebration of the 19th CPC National Congress", and National Publication Foundation.

Editorial Board of The Chinese Path Series

Contents

Chapter 1
The Rise of China's Green Manufacturing Industry

Producing is the perpetual motion of human beings. It is through the capability of producing that human beings can evolve from nature. In the 19th century, the invention of the steam engine marked the beginning of modern industrial manufacturing, which opened a new era for production. From then on, production has shifted from manual labor to mechanized manufacturing. Therefore, the manufacturing industry is a reflection of national productivity and a watershed that defines the developed and developing countries. A major problem facing the manufacturing industry is that the manufacturing industry is notorious for emitting pollution. As environmental protection has increasingly become a major issue concerning the future of humanity, all walks of life are faced with changes, and manufacturing is the first to bear the brunt. Green manufacturing was born in the context of the intense discussion of the end of the industrial age and the transformation of our minds, lives, and behaviors, and it is closely linked to our creation of a prosperous world and a genuinely harmonious future.

1.1 The green manufacturing orientation

Resources, environment, and manufacturing industry are equally crucial to humans, and problems in either of them can cause serious consequences. Since the Second World War, all countries in the world have recovered from a social upheaval and restored production and the global economy has witnessed a period of unprecedentedly rapid development. On the one hand, the manufacturing industry has created a large amount of material wealth for humankind, and has dramatically advanced the progress of human civilization; on the other hand, it also brings over-exploitation and waste of resources, massive emissions of pollutants and destruction of the ecological environment, resulting in global resource shortages, environmental pollution and ecosystem imbalances. These problems have posed threats to the survival and development of human being, triggered great conflicts among resources, environment, and manufacturing, and have exposed the various drawbacks of traditional industrial development. Therefore, it is urgent to solve the problems brought by the development of the manufacturing industry.

1.1.1 Disadvantages of traditional manufacturing

The world today is still faced with new challenges as follows, including the rise of global temperature within the 2 ℃, the risk of resource shortage due to excessive resource consumption, and the continuous increase of global environmental pollution. The world is still in the dilemma of environment and development; global ecology service function continues to decline as the "ecological deficits" accelerates.

The traditional manufacturing industry relies too much on the exploitation and utilization of energy, resources and raw materials and emphasizes the quantity for efficiency. As a result, this mode of production has high investment but low output. World Resources Report (1996-1997) states: From 1950 to 1997, the output value of the manufacturing and service industries worldwide increased nearly 5 times, but at the same time, global timber consumption increased by 8 times, paper consumption increased by six-folds, and fossil fuels increased by 5.5 times.[1] From the specific situation of China, industrial energy consumption accounts for more than 70 percent of total energy consumption. In 2012, China's total primary energy consumption was equivalent to 3.62 billion tons of standard coal, accounting for 21.3 percent of the world's total energy consumption, but it only created 11.6 percent of the world's GDP. The energy consumption per unit of GDP is twice that of the international level and four times that of the United States. Due to the pressure of resources, the resource-dependent manufacturing model is inevitably unsustainable. Therefore, China's manufacturing industry must change its concepts, innovate technology, and take a new path of energy conservation and consumption reduction. For a long time, China's manufacturing industry has followed the path of low-end, assembly, OEM, repeated investment, and overcapacity for decades. On the one hand, the drawbacks cannot be eliminated, but more serious; on the other hand, the enterprises lack technological innovation, and the products are difficult to compete with the world's advanced manufacturing enterprises, which will inevitably affect the long-term development of the overall national economy.

In the traditional industrial production mode, the manufacturing of products is the

---

[1] Xi Junjie et al., "From Traditional Production to Green Manufacturing and Circulation Economy", *Forum on Science and Technology in China*, 2005(9), p.95.

main focus of attention. Generally, the manufacturing process is only implemented from the perspective of economic efficiency. In the product design, the function and quality of the products are mainly taken into consideration, but industrial emissions and resource shortages, environmental damage and other issues are often neglected. According to statistics, the pollutants emitted by the manufacturing industry account for 70 percent of the global total, generating about 5.5 billion tons of non-hazardous waste and 700 million tons of hazardous waste each year. [1] In the national economy, the final products needed by the society only account for 20 percent to 30 percent of the raw material consumption, and 70 percent to 80 percent of the resources eventually become environmental waste, causing environmental pollution and ecological damage. [2] Traditional manufacturing generally adopts "end-of-pipe" treatment to solve the environmental pollution problems of wastewater, waste gas and solid waste generated in production, but this method cannot fundamentally solve the environmental pollution generated by manufacturing and its products. Besides, the problem of large investment and high cost will further consume resources. Therefore, how to do our best to save resources and make proper use of them to the best, and to minimize the emission of harmful substances and protect the ecological environment has become one of the hot issues of concern to governments, enterprises, and academia. A sustainable society is becoming an important theme in the wave of social reforms in the 21st century. Since the 1990s, green manufacturing technology has risen rapidly under the impetus of sustainable development and green waves and has been widely used in developed countries.

Besides, even emerging industries in recent years may fall into the old path of traditional manufacturing. According to reports, there are more than 2,000 robot companies in China, and they are still taking the old road of expanding production capacity and importing core components. Other industries, such as smart manufacturing, biomedical engineering, new energies and so on, due to the competitive layout of various regions, introduced foreign equipment, components at high prices, or exchanged technology with the market. After they have the corresponding technology and capabilities, there may be overcapacity. They have to sell their products to foreign countries, which may incur the punishment of anti-dumping. It can be seen that some

---

[1] Li Wenbin, Li Changhe, Sun Wei, *Advanced Manufacturing Technology*, Wuhan: Huazhong University of Science & Technology Press, 2014, p.216.

[2] Ren Xiaozhong, *Advanced Manufacturing Technology* (*Second Edition*), Wuhan: Huazhong University of Science & Technology Press, 2013, p.123.

emerging industries are not fundamentally different from traditional manufacturing industries, and they are still limited to low value-added links such as assembly, processing, and manufacturing. They are in a weak position in the value chain and continue to pay a heavy price for resource consumption and environmental pollution. For example, the environmental protection and energy conservation of the photovoltaic industry determines that it must be an emerging industry. However, due to the lack of unified energy consumption, land occupation and environmental protection standards, most polysilicon production enterprises in China are difficult to compete with foreign companies in production cost and product quality. According to the report of the US investment agency Maxim Group, China's top ten photovoltaic (PV) companies' loans have amounted to US$17.5 billion, about RMB110 billion. China's PV industry is on the verge of bankruptcy.

Generally speaking, although China is already a large manufacturing country, it is "large but not strong". There are still a big gap and many problems compared with other manufacturing powers. The essential problem is to change the traditional manufacturing development model that is labor intensive, resource and energy consumption, and even at the expense of the environment. It is necessary to reshape the core competitive advantage of China's manufacturing industry and blaze a trail for smart transformation and green development. Thereby, the transition from low-cost competitive advantage to quality-efficiency is realized, as well as the transition from high-energy consumption and high-polluting extensive development to green development.

1.1.2 The rise of green manufacturing

Research on green manufacturing can be dated back to the 1980s, but it was not until 1996 that the definition, meaning, and content were fully presented by the Society of Manufacturing Engineers (SME). The above expression is included in SME's Blue Book *Green Manufacturing*. In 1998, SME published a report on the future forecast of green development through the Internet. The academic leader of the green manufacturing team of the Michigan State University is Professor Steven A. Melnyk, who collaborated with Richard T. Smith in 1996 and wrote the *Green Manufacturing* of SME. He has long been engaged in researches on green manufacturing, and his primary research directions include green supply chain management, green MRP, environmentally responsible manufacturing and total quality management, environmental management systems and ISO14000.

The University of California, Berkeley specializes in the design and manufacturing industry that combines organizational research and resource conservation and has developed an Internet portal—Greenmfg—for precise understanding and inquiry of green manufacturing. AT&T also published a number of research papers on green manufacturing in the enterprise technology journal. The International Institution for Production Engineering Research (CIRP) has published many research papers on environmentally conscious manufacturing and multi-lifecycle engineering in recent years. More than a dozen research projects reported at the conference for the National Science Foundation funded projects in 1999 were related to green manufacturing. At this conference, Dr. Martin Vega, director of the Design and Manufacturing Department of the National Science Foundation, pointed out six challenging issues facing the manufacturing industry in his keynote speech in 2000, among which the issues of environmental compatibility are closely related to green manufacturing. Later, he defined "Waste Minimization Processing Technology" as green manufacturing technology in his "Ten Key Technologies" in the future. New York University has a project focusing on global green development and environmental protection. It proposes that "greening" is a change in enterprise's understanding, thinking and action in the environment, development, and protection. And the greening of a company can be calculated by calculating the area of the triangle formed by the above three factors.

There are also many research teams in Europe that conduct in-depth researches on green manufacturing. For example, the sustainable manufacturing research team of the University of Cambridge is dedicated to research and development of material conversion technologies that do not emit greenhouse gases, avoid the use of non-renewable materials, and reduce waste generation. The research areas include advanced green technology, paper recycling, recycling of polymeric plastics and waste textiles, knowledge and technology management for sustainable production, and reverse logistics supply chain. The School of Life Cycle Engineering at the University of Stuttgart in Germany has also conducted several researches related to green manufacturing. Its research content includes: life cycle assessment and life cycle engineering, environment-oriented designing, environmental management, life cycle work environment and so on. Since 1992, according to customer demands, they have developed in cooperation with PE Europe GmbH for the Gabi software system and database, which are mainly used for product lifecycle evaluation and have been globally used in the automotive, chemical, metal, electronics, energy and other industries. [1]

In recent years, the ISO14000 series of environmental management standards developed by the International Organization for Standardization (ISO), such as 14001, 14040, etc., have dramatically promoted researches and development in fields relevant to green manufacturing. The ISO14000 series of standards are essentially a set of ideal management standards that contribute to corporate image building and also a "green pass" to enable corporations to enter the international market. They are the crystallization of environmental management experiences in industrialized countries, which take into account the situation of different countries when formulating national standards, trying to make the standards universally applicable. Therefore, the ISO14000 series of standards has promoted the environmental protection of commerce and industry, government organizations, etc., and has exerted a decisive influence on promoting the development of green manufacturing.

China has also focused on green manufacturing in recent years, and many universities and research institutes have done researches in this area. The national "863 Program" and the National Natural Science Foundation have also funded many studies in this field, which have led to significant advancement in the researches on green manufacturing. Among the national "863 Program", CIMSNET, an integrated modern manufacturing system network engaged in information dissemination and resource sharing, taking green manufacturing as one of its key research projects, keeps tuned to and reports the latest research results at home and abroad. *China Mechanical Engineering* magazine issued a special edition on green manufacturing in the 9th issue of 2000. In January 1996, the National Environmental Protection Agency established the Huaxia Environmental Management System Audit Center, which is responsible for the implementation, training and global exchanges of the ISO14000 series of standards, and established a website: China Environmental Management System Quality Certification Centre. The environmental management system standards have attracted the attention of enterprises in China, and many of them have obtained the ISO14000 standard certification.

On November 3, 2004, at the World Engineers' Convention 2004, Xu Kuangdi, then President of the Chinese Academy of Engineering, pointed out that in the 21st century, China needed to take the path of sustainable development and realize the transformation

---

[1] Li Congbo, Green Manufacturing Operation Mode and Its Implementation Methods, Chongqing: Chongqing University, 2009, pp.8-9.

from traditional industrialization to new industrialization. The development of science and technology should not be at the expense of resources, energy, and environment, and engineering technology should follow the path of green manufacturing. [1]

According to economic experts, only 5 percent to 10 percent of all products are green products currently. In ten years, all products will be green in design to ensure their recyclability, disassembly and partial or overall renovation and recycle. In other words, in the next decade, green products will take the lead in the global market. It is no exaggeration to say that the strong green wave of green manufacturing systems has swept the manufacturing companies of countries around the world.

In general, environmental management represented by ISO14000, EMAS, BS7750, etc., has caused corporations to re-examine the environmental pollution they caused, to face their problems and take measures to reduce pollutant emissions in advance, and thus to enhance its environmental benefits to gain a competitive advantage. Whether companies are willing to take environmental protection measures depends on the cost of doing so, the profit they can make, and whether the measure is feasible. More and more domestic and international research results show that the excellent environmental protection capability of enterprises can make them more competitive in the market. For example, with advanced pollution prevention technologies, enterprises can use resources more effectively, and thereby reduce costs, or make more profits by distinguishing from their competitors through green manufacturing. It is these favorable factors that drive enterprises onto a green manufacturing road, and they further promote the overall transformation of China's manufacturing industry.

Among the researches on green manufacturing at home and abroad, the first is to focus on the understanding of it, such as the strategic or macroscopic understanding of the conceptual theory system, technical composition, and policy support involved in green manufacturing. Second, there is research on topical technologies such as green design, green materials, green production processes, green packaging, and green processing. Besides, research on technology support systems of green manufacturing, application support systems, and social support systems has become a research hotspot for green manufacturing.

---

[1] Xu Kuangdi, "China's Engineering Technology Should Promote the Realization of 'Green Manufacturing'", *People's Daily*, Nov. 4, 2004.

1.1.3 Development trend of green manufacturing

Countries in the world today have closely integrated environmental issues with development, emphasizing that without ecosystems protection, there will be no sustainable human development in the future. A considerable number of countries have been committed to environmental protection through the implementation of the "Green Plan". Among them are Japan's "Green Industry Plan" in 1991, Canada's "Green Plan", and the green plans of the US, the UK, and Germany. China has put forward its plan for "Green Development", which together with innovation development, coordinated development, open development, and shared development, has become the scientific development concept and mode guiding China's development during the 13th Five-year Plan period and the even more long-term future.

1.1.3.1 Globalization

The link between green manufacturing and globalization will become increasingly close, reflecting the characteristics and development direction of globalization.

Multinational companies occupy an important position in the current global economic industry. In 1998, the statistics released by the United Nations Conference on Trade and Development showed that in 1997, the number of global multinational corporations was 45,000, plus 250,000 subsidiaries. On average, each company established 5.5 subsidiaries abroad. These companies control 40 percent to 50 percent of the world's gross product, 50 percent to 60 percent of international trade, 60 percent to 70 percent of international technology trade, 80 percent to 90 percent of product research and development, and 90 percent of the foreign direct investment. Among them, the *Fortune* Global 500 companies, the 1 percent multinational companies in the world, account for 90 percent of multinational companies' sales. The Global 500 are highly representative with their unique production and sales methods and close contacts with other companies.

Among the larger multinational companies in the world, manufacturing plays an irreplaceable role in terms of the scale of production, the market for sales, and the profits they earn. In 1994, about 230 companies of the top 500 were engaged in manufacturing, and this scale continued to expand in subsequent years. This expansion can be observed from the ranking of the top 10 companies of the *Fortune* Global 500: In 1994, four of the top 10 companies were engaged in manufacturing. In 1995 and 1996, the number rose to 5. In 1998, it rose to 6. This data number stayed unchanged, and since 1996, the top 2 companies have been manufacturing companies. Similar statistics come from *Business*

Week. It is said that in 1999, among the top 1,000 companies in the world, 9 out of the top 10 were directly engaged in manufacturing or closely related to manufacturing, 7 of them in the United States. [1]

The globalization of green manufacturing is mainly manifested in the industrial transfer, global mergers, global design and manufacturing brought by international trade and international investment. The methods of green manufacturing globalization are: one is to produce green products domestically, and then sell them to other countries; the other is to invest in other countries and establish a base, and then sell the green products to other countries or domestically. From the development of manufacturing in countries around the world, we can see that the processing of spare parts has been globalized. For example, a Boeing 747 has a total of 4.5 million spare parts, which are manufactured in nearly 10 countries, involving more than 1,000 large enterprises and more than 15,000 small enterprises. Moreover, this trend will become more and more prominent, and green manufacturing is also developing towards globalization.

1.1.3.2　Networking

The increasingly fierce competition in the global market will combine information technology and computer technology with manufacturing to form a new and more advanced green manufacturing industry. Only in this way can we respond quickly to the market demand, thereby increasing the efficiency and automation of production, reducing the cost required and better protecting the ecological environment. It can be said that apart from changing the mode and mechanism of production management, scientific and technological innovation and asset restructuring, green manufacturing need to rely on the network platform to enhance its competitiveness, which is called networking. The networking of green manufacturing aims to realize agile manufacturing by connecting enterprises with Internet technology so that they can cooperate for mutual benefit and efficiency. This method breaks the structure of the original resources of R&D, design, production and sales, and enterprises can respond more quickly, with more competitive advantages, cooperate more effectively and share resources, reduce the cost of production and services, and ensure the speed and quality. Networking brings changes and opportunities to green manufacturing enterprises and has achieved a series of results.

A multinational virtual enterprise network project of the American Institute of

---

[1] Ni Yifang, Wu Xiaobo, "The Current Situation and Trend of the Globalization of the World Manufacturing Industry and China's Countermeasures", *China Soft Science*, 2001(10), pp.24-25.

International Manufacturing Enterprises funded by the National Science Foundation of the United States, aims to integrate American manufacturers with Russian manufacturers via the Internet and set an example for enterprises globally. The project published a research report of "Russian-American Virtual Enterprise Network (RA-VEN)". The purpose of the German Produktion 2000 framework program is to establish a global information network of product design and manufacturing. The European Union's Fifth Framework Program funded researches on virtual network enterprises, aiming to provide information sharing for enterprises in EU member states. On this basis, the Sixth Framework Program (2002-2006) intended to draw on the advantages of Internet technology to improve the collaboration mechanisms among the entities within the EU. In a word, green manufacturing needs to work hard to improve the network and establish the "Internet Plus" environment, in order to improve the utilization of manufacturing resources, realize manufacturing resources sharing, improve the response speed of enterprises to the market, and enhance the international competitiveness of the manufacturing industry.

1.1.3.3 Customizing

At first glance, customized production may lead to high production costs or waste of resources due to customer-oriented production. However, with the change of consumption mode in the Internet era, it has dramatically promoted customized consumption, which not only calls for changes in the way of sales but also transformation of production mode. Especially with the maturity of 3D printing technology, enterprises will be able to achieve a rapid restructuring of production techniques, processes, and institutions, as well as an agile response to market demands which will enable them to develop marketable customized products for individual customers. Green manufacturing can also introduce a massive data analysis platform, which can be used to collect and analyze individual customer needs, carry out targeted product development. This trend will inevitably provide opportunities for the development of green manufacturing, and enable customization services to gradually develop to scale and popularization.

Western countries with advanced manufacturing industry have also developed a new way of green manufacturing. In order to use resources more effectively, the United States decided to reduce consumables, waste materials and energy consumption by 15 percent, 90 percent and 75 percent respectively. Germany launched the sustainability initiative Blue Competence, for promoting and communication of sustainable solutions for the Mechanical Engineering Industry, aiming to reduce energy consumption by 30 percent to 40 percent, reduce machine tool's weight by more than half, and completely recycle scrap machine tools. Germany's industry has embarked on a new road by means of the closed cycle and industrial symbiosis, and by means of energy recovery, and storage and new energy technologies. It has realized energy self-sufficiency. Supplemented by the shortened production process, clean technologies such as 3D printing, Germany has innovated its green manufacturing industry with those technological advances. Besides, many new ideas about green manufacturing have been put forward by developed countries in order to take the lead in this industry. For example, waste-free manufacturing created in the United States means that all wastes can be converted into raw materials during the production processes, so there is no waste at the end of the process. Germany's "Industry 4.0" is designed to achieve customized, low pollution and high productivity manufacturing. [1] Only through engineering solutions to a customized and sustainable development can people different needs be satisfied.

1.1.3.4 Informatizing

The informatizing of green manufacturing is to upgrade and innovate the traditional manufacturing industry with information technologies or other high-tech technologies. In the whole process of production, information is gathered or shared so as to allocate resources more reasonably and to enable enterprises to operate more efficiently for more profits and sharper competitive edge. For example, the mechanical products produced by the traditional manufacturing industry can be integrated with the chips and sensors produced by high-tech and information industries so that they can be closely linked with digital communications, automatic control or sensor detection and become mechatronics products, to which technology integration can be done again. In addition, enterprises can use online publicity, online procurement, online marketing and other e-commerce measures to reduce the intermediate links of the industrial chain, so as to reduce costs, and integrate information technology into green manufacturing, and to promote the evolution and upgrading of manufacturing industry. [2]

Information technology and information industry always play a leading role in the global economic development. Informatizing in green manufacturing is to make full use

---

[1] Zhao Jianjun, Yang Bo, "Green Manufacturing: The Future Orientation of Manufacturing Technology Development", *Study Times*, Mar. 31, 2016.

[2] Zhu Sendi, "Globalization, Informatization, Greening—Promoting China's Manufacturing Industry", *Mechanical & Electrical Engineering Technology*, 2004(1), p.9.

of the advantages of information technology, and to promote the sharing of information resources. Information technology in green manufacturing will develop rapidly along the five directions of design digitization, manufacturing equipment digitization, production process digitization, management digitization, and enterprise digitization. In 2013, China's investment in manufacturing informatization amounted to RMB61.95 billion. In 2014, the scale of China's manufacturing informatization investment reached RMB63.31 billion, an increase of 2.2 percent over the same period the previous year. This shows that China has seen the importance of informatization, but the stress on the development of informatization was inadequate and the development was not fast enough. The manufacturing industry is shifting from hardware to software, and services, solutions and so on. It is software that brings functions to hardware, controls hardware, and puts forward requirements for hardware. Therefore, we should abandon the traditional "hardware-based" mode of thinking and develop green manufacturing industry by producing additional value from software and services. The well-known major enterprises over the world, such as GE, Tesla, Google, Siemens, SAP, etc., are all building their new manufacturing platforms. It is possible to unify the entire industry for any manufacturing enterprise, as long as it seizes the commanding heights of information technology.

1.1.3.5 Ecologicalizing

Ecologicalizing itself is the essence, and the most important connotation of green manufacturing. In 2015, the State Council of China issued the *Made in China 2025*, which is the first ten-year action plan designed to transform China from a manufacturing giant into a world manufacturing power. *Made in China 2025*, the guiding principles of which are to have manufacturing be innovation-driven, to emphasize quality over quantity, to achieve green development, to optimize the structure of Chinese industry, and to nurture human talent, focuses on sustainable development in building a manufacturing power and on taking the road of ecological civilization. It also lists "green manufacturing engineering" as one of the five key projects, intending to fully implement green manufacturing, and to build an efficient, clean, low carbon, recycling green manufacturing system. The next goal of the manufacturing industry is greening and intellectual manufacturing. "Green" is the essence of the comprehensive implementation of green manufacturing. We strictly follow the life cycle theory, change the methods previously used in the entire process of design, production, sales, and recycling, and apply the concept of "greening" to all aspects of manufacturing.

In the process of eco-green manufacturing, it is necessary to shape the links of industrial chain and the process of social reproduction by ecological principles, form a "green production system", the whole process of which conforms to the "natural resources efficiency, and ecological environment efficiency", and guide the public to a green lifestyle. It is also necessary to achieve the goal of waste recycling, hazard-free use and quantity reduction according to the flow process of "resources-production/ products-renewable resources-production/products". More importantly, it is necessary to establish an ecological organization system in the future development and form the energy-saving and emission reduction system consisting of enterprises cycle, industrial cycle, and regional cycle.

1.1.3.6 Intelligentizing

Artificial intelligence and intelligent manufacturing technologies will play an important role in green manufacturing researches.[1] Intelligentizing is a control engineering which integrates modern communication and information technology, computer network technology, industrial technology, intelligent control technology, optoelectronic technology, sensor technology, software technology and so on. The purpose is to combine "smart" and "ability" to extend people's faculty. Replacing human control is the most fundamental science and technology in the process of building a digital factory. At present, industrial robots are a typical example of the close integration of information technology and intelligent technology in manufacturing. They have the advantage of replacing humans in repetitive, tedious, persistent work, and can operate in dangerous or harsh environments that are not suitable for human health, as well as complete production as required in quality and quantity. Market demand for robots is growing. According to statistics, China's robot market in 2015 ranked among the world's largest, the 36,000 sets of total demand accounted for 18 percent of the total in global demand, and the total sales of robots in Chinese market in the following years showed a trend of continuous growth, with an increase of 118,000 sets. When the profit of traditional manufacturing industry is constantly squeezed and the demographic dividend is disappearing, today's manufacturing industry has been developing in a new direction, that is, to strive to complete the intelligent transformation of equipment, improve the level of automation in production, reduce the labor intensity, improve the production environment and so on.

---

[1] Liu Fei, Cao Huajun, He Naijun, "The Research Status and Development Trend of Green Manufacturing", *China Mechanical Engineering*, 2000(11), p.109.

In the future, with the decrease in computing cost and the large-scale development of cloud computing, artificial intelligence will be more extensively applied, greatly promoting the development of green manufacturing. Intelligent manufacturing in the future will involve R&D, manufacturing, warehousing logistics, marketing, after-sales service, information consulting and other value chain links, involving the enterprise system architecture such as executive layer, equipment layer, control layer, management layer, enterprise layer, cloud service layer, and network layer, which needs horizontal integration, vertical integration and end-to-end integration. In the process of intellectualization, enterprises in various fields tend to promote the integration of various elements and resources, and enhance the research and development of frontier technologies and the transformation of innovative achievements through capital mergers and acquisitions or strategic cooperation, open cooperation and collaborative innovation. With the increase of computing power and data volume in the future, machine intelligence will advance from perception, memory, and storage to cognition and learning, decision-making and execution, even independent consciousness and innovation. In the era of mobile Internet, the amount of data increases exponentially, which makes it possible to use big data for in-depth learning. With the support of big data, AI applications will also become more extensive. Intelligent green manufacturing is a combination of contemporary science and technology and industrial innovation, which indicates that the national machinery manufacturing industry has reached a certain height and laid a foundation for national industrial development.

1.1.3.7 Integrating

To implement green manufacturing, the problems encountered in the process must be solved in systematized and integrated ways. At present, the integration of green manufacturing includes many aspects: integrated product objectives, product design and material selection in the production process, integrated user needs and commodity applications, integrated green manufacturing, integrated information systems, and integrated green production process. These are the key research topics in green manufacturing.

The integration of green manufacturing is also reflected in the fact that the integrated manufacturing system is indispensable to green manufacturing. The concept of integrated green manufacturing system then arises. The system includes the following six subsystems: green design, green production, quality inspection and quality assurance, material and energy resources, and environmental impact assessment. It is also supported by a digital communication system and database/knowledge base system. The manufacturing system also includes external links. Integrated green manufacturing and the derived technologies and systems will become the focus of future researches.

1.2 What is "green manufacturing"?

1.2.1 Manufacturing, manufacturing system and manufacturing industry

To understand the connotation of green manufacturing, we must first understand the concepts of manufacturing, the manufacturing industry, and manufacturing mode, because they are closely related. Green manufacturing is a modern manufacturing mode, and it cannot be separated from the other manufacturing mode. On this basis, a new manufacturing mode—green manufacturing, has been generated through inheritance and innovation.

1.2.1.1 Manufacturing

Manufacturing activity is the most fundamental activity of human society. Manufacturing is the process of converting raw materials into large-scale tools, industrial products, and consumer products with the help of certain processes and energy by using known skills and combining them with processing procedures (manually or with tools).

Manufacturing can be defined in the broad sense and narrow sense: In the narrow sense, manufacturing usually refers to the process of producing and assembling the raw materials into finished products related to material flow, which is also called "producing" that serves people's daily production and life. In the broad sense, manufacturing involves the entire process of the product life cycle, from market assessment, product design, preparation stage, processing and assembly, quality inspection and warranty, marketing and after-sales to scrap disposal. Generally speaking, manufacturing refers to the manufacturing in its broad sense.

1.2.1.2 Manufacturing system

The modern manufacturing system is a complex, and large-scale system, involving all the production and operation activities of manufacturing enterprises, so different scholars have different understandings of it.

In 1989, British scholar Parnaby defined modern manufacturing system as a manufacturing system is an integrated combination of process and its system, human, organizational structure, information flow, control system and computer, aiming at achieving the economy of product manufacturing and the international competitiveness of product performance.

The definition of manufacturing system announced by the International Institution for Production Engineering Research (CIRP) in 1990 is that manufacturing system is the organic whole of manufacturing production in the manufacturing industry. In the mechanical and electrical engineering industry, the manufacturing system has a integrated function of design, production, transportation and sale.

In 1992, G. Chryssolouris, a professor at the Massachusetts Institute of Technology, defined manufacturing systems as manufacturing system is an organism of people, machines and equipment, as well as materials and information flows.

To sum up, the manufacturing system can be defined as manufacturing system refers to the manufacturing process and the integration of hardware and software involved in the process and the realization of resource conversion to meet social needs as a whole.

Now, we divide the manufacturing system into three parts and define them as follows.

(1) *Structure*

The manufacturing system is an organic whole, which contains all the software and hardware involved in the manufacturing process. The hardware of the manufacturing system mainly includes personnel, tools, raw materials, and energy, etc. The software includes manufacturing theory, technologies, methods, standards, and relevant computer programs.

(2) *Function*

The function of a manufacturing system is to convert raw materials into products or semi-products, which is an input and output system. Six metrics are needed to determine whether the system has advantages: time, quality, cost, service, flexibility, and environment.

(3) *Process*

The manufacturing system includes the entire process of the product lifecycle, including market evaluation, product design, process selection, production assembly, quality inspection, sales service, and scrap disposal. [1]

---

[1] Xue Wei, Jiang Zuhua, *Introduction to Industrial Engineering* (*Second Edition*), Beijing: China Machine Press, 2015, p.284.

1.2.1.3   Manufacturing industry

Manufacturing industry refers to the industry that produces tools, machinery or commodities needed by people through the production process of certain resources and energy (including capital, technology, materials, etc.) according to market demand. Manufacturing industry mainly includes metallurgical manufacturing industry, food processing industry, machinery industry, electronic products, manufacturing industry and so on. According to the National Economic Classification Standard (GB/T4757-2002), manufacturing industry belongs to the secondary industry, but mining, power supply, gas supply, water supply and construction are not included. It is mainly to process and produce raw materials from agriculture and mining industry, and can be divided into 30 sectors, 169 categories and 482 sub-categories.

Manufacturing can be broadly divided into two sections: one is the processing of raw materials or re-manufacturing of finished products, which is often referred to as the processing manufacturing industry; the other is to provide equipment for people's life and national production and construction, which is what we often call the equipment manufacturing industry. The processing manufacturing industry mostly adopts conveyor systems, with fixed production standards and large production capacity. Modern manufacturing is a combination of modern science and technology and manufacturing. Modern manufacturing industry optimizes the original industrial structure. It transforms raw materials by means of using modern high-technology in the process of production. The modernity of the modern manufacturing industry is reflected in the modernity of industry, the modernity of production and the modernity of production organization and management. Any industry that is engaged in industrial production by adopting modern scientific and technological achievements can be called modern manufacturing industry.

Lu Yongxiang, the former president of the Chinese Academy of Sciences, pointed out that the prosperity of the country is closely related to the developed manufacturing industry. The competition between countries is mainly the competition of manufacturing industry, and the hope of the country and the nation lies in the manufacturing industry. A highly developed modern manufacturing industry is the main embodiment of the comprehensive national strength and international competitiveness of a country.

1.2.2 Green manufacturing and its system

1.2.2.1 The conceptual system of green manufacturing

Green manufacturing, also called environmentally conscious manufacturing or manufacturing for the environment, is characteristic of concerns on environmental problems. This manufacturing mode focuses on the concept of comprehensive, coordinated and sustainable development, and indicates that industrial enterprises are aware of their environmental responsibilities, and fulfill their economic responsibilities, environmental responsibilities and social responsibilities.

There are two kinds of green manufacturing. One is the manufacturing of "green" products, especially the equipment that can be used in a renewable energy system and in cleaning. The other is "greening" production, which aims to save energy, reduce consumption and emission by reducing the use of natural resources. The concept of green manufacturing people possess covers the whole product life cycle (PLC). Although green manufacturing means a lot, it mainly involves the following aspects.

(1) Environmental protection

Manufacturing is an everlasting activity. The production will cause pollution and damage to the environment. The habitat of human beings is under the threat of waste and resource shortage. So, product design and manufacturing must be based on the entire PLC and market demand. Products must meet the user requirement and must generate the minimum pollution with maximum use of natural resources. Also, it is necessary to take into consideration the disposal of the products when their life cycle ends: the discharge of the industrial wastewater and dust, and the disposal of harmful elements from spare parts of printed-circuit board and computers.

(2) Resources utilization

If we classify resources by renewability, they can be sorted into two kinds—nonrenewable resources and renewable resources. Oil, coal and other minerals are nonrenewable resources; living things, the soil, and water are renewable resources. In product design, renewable materials must be given priority in material selection, and recycling and reuse should be taken into consideration as well. For example, in mechanical product design, the possibility, convenience and economy of disassembly must be taken consideration from the beginning. In modeling, disassembility should be an important part of computer-aided equipment process design which takes both the processing and assembly structure technology, and the disassembly structure technology.

(3) Clean production

In the production process, it is necessary to reduce its pollution and damage to the environment. Cooling fluid in cutting and grinding process, electrical discharge machining (EDM) process, and working fluid in the electrolytic process, pollute the environment. For this reason, dry cutting and grinding processes were invented, but the chips and dust in dry cutting and grinding processes will cause damage to human health. Thus a recovery device is required. Liquid waste in the heat treatment that can cause serious water pollution and corrosion, and is harmful to human health, and must be treated before discharge. Another example is the noise-pollution in mechanical processing, needs to be controlled under the required level. In order to study product life cycle (PLC) and carry out clean production, the concept of life cycle design emerges, which deals with various factors related to the life cycle. It is a development of concurrent engineering, involving the entire cycle from product concept design to detailed design stage. This entire cycle includes requirements identification, design and development, production, sales, use, processing and recycling.

Green manufacturing is the intersection and integration of many fields and subjects, which mainly includes three aspects: manufacturing, environment and resource.[1] The three aspects overlap and assemble. Green manufacturing has now become a new trend of product manufacturing worldwide, because it conforms to the modern outlook on environment.

In terms of manufacturing, the concept of green manufacturing is a macro concept about the entire PLC from designing to recycling, which is the same as the concept embodied in smart manufacturing and virtual manufacturing. This concept shows the characteristics of the current manufacturing industry: integration of manufacturing and processing.

In terms of the environment, green manufacturing pays attention to the possible environmental and ecological problems, and brings some new concepts, such as green design, green technology, green packaging, clean production and so on. When the service life of a product manufactured by green manufacturing expires, its components can be reused after renovation, thus forming a closed cycle of the product and minimizing the possible damage and pollution to the environment.

In terms of resources, since the world entered industrialization over three hundred

---

[1] Xi Junjie, Chu Suiying, "The Green Manufacturing Technology for Sustainable Development in Manufacturing Industry". *Hoisting and Conveying Machinery*, 2005(9).

years ago, we have consumed a great deal of resources and energy. Instead of exhausting resources, we must find "new" resources for sustainable development. What used to be considered "waste" is now the most important alternative resources. Globally at present, 45 percent of steel production, 62 percent of copper production, 22 percent of aluminum production, 40 percent of lead production, 30 percent of zinc production, and 35 percent of paper products are derived from the recycling of renewable resources. The recycling rate of renewable resources in developed countries and regions such as Western Europe, the United States and Japan has reached about 90 percent. According to the reports of China Resource Recycling Association, US$35 billion to US$40 billion worth of recyclable resources are not recycled annually in China. This equals the annual total value of sales of a medium-sized enterprise in the Global 500.[1] This fully confirms the necessity and urgency for China to develop green manufacturing.

1.2.2.2 Main content of green manufacturing

Green manufacturing is a large sophisticated system, covering the entire product life cycle, and numerous scientific technology support is needed for its implementation. In general, it requires at least the overall technology, special technology and supporting technology. From the perspective of PLC, it can be roughly divided into five stages: green material, green design and manufacturing, green sale and purchase, green use, and re-manufacturing. Therefore, the major contents of green manufacturing are green material, green design, green process, green packaging and green disposal.

(1) Green material

Green material refers to materials that are not harmful to the environment and ecology or human health during the collection of raw materials, the production and use of products, and the recycling and disposal of products. They are generally degradable materials; those products and materials which have been treated to reduce the harm to human beings and the environment are also regarded as green materials. The materials used in green manufacturing are called green materials because they are the most compatible with the environment and ecology. It can use resources most efficiently and reduce environmental pollution during collection, production and recycling. Green materials, therefore, get the name of ecological materials, and some people call them environmentally conscious materials. To implement green manufacturing, the use of green materials is a top priority. The following are factors that should be considered in

---

[1] Liang Xiaoqing, *Regional Development and Local Government Policies*. Beijing: Guangming Daily Press, 2009, pp.160-161.

the selecting of green materials. Priority is given to renewable or recycled materials, reducing the consumption of resources and increasing their resource utilization rate, for sustainable development. Materials selected are supposed to have better compatibility with the environment and produce less pollution. Materials containing toxic and hazardous substances should be avoided. The materials used should be recyclable or easy to dispose.

(2) *Green design*

The performance of the product has actually been confirmed in the design process. Statistics proves that 70 percent - 80 percent of the product properties have been identified at this stage, so we often regard design as the starting point of product life. In the past, human needs were placed in the most prominent position in the design stage, while inadequate attentions were given to avoiding damage to the environment and ecology, and to reducing the consumption and waste of resources. Green design, also known as environmental design or ecological design, refers to the product design that takes into consideration the entire product life cycle including the application function of the product and the impact of the product on the environment and resources. Whether the product can be disassembled, recycled, reused and so on, should all be considered, and taken as a design goal. On that basis, the original design can be optimized to have a favorable impact on the environment and resources on the one hand and to ensure the quality, performance and cost of the product itself on the other hand.

Green design is derived from the traditional design, but it is better than that. The reason why it is better is that it covers the whole process from design to recycling or scrapping with a focus on the core concept of "green". It is sustainable from the beginning of its product life cycle, with consideration to all potential problems and hazards that may occur, and solutions, so as to reduce environmental pollution, lower waste of resources, and to recycle. That is the core of green design, prevention is emphasized with management as support. This is a reform of the traditional design which looks for solutions after pollution has been made. Green design, therefore, lays a firm foundation for green manufacturing.

(3) *Green process*

Green process is closely linked to the clean production as we know. Generally speaking, a green process refers to a clean process, which, on the basis of the traditional process, adopts material science and technology so that the final product is integrated with the environment. The green process aims to reduce energy consumption, environmental pollution and waste to reduce the harm of toxic and harmful chemical products to the environment and human health, to improve the working environment, and to provide effective health protection for production workers.

Green processes can be divided into the following categories: (i) The planning technology of green process: It refers to the pre-planning of the methods adopted in the production process, the instruments and equipment used, the amount and degree of cutting reduction, and the environmental compatibility of the processes adopted to achieve the purpose of reducing energy consumption and protecting the environment. (ii) Process simulation and virtual manufacturing: Process simulation technology is to establish a model of the imitation object and to get the optimal solution through experiment. To apply this technology, many experiments are needed to get the desired results. Through process simulation, we can reduce the waste of resources and environmental pollution during the experiment, and get the results in the most environmentally friendly and convenient way. The same is true for virtual manufacturing, which is to simulate the products and processes intended without consuming energy or affecting the environment. This technology helps us respond to the market quickly, and help us save costs and improve the environment. (iii) Green technology: Reduce material consumption and environmental pollution by using green casting technology, rapid prototyping manufacturing (RPM) technology, chipless processing technology, dry processing technology, green heat treatment technology, and special processing technology.[1]

(4) *Green packaging*

Green packaging is becoming a focus of attention. In the past, at the end of the PLC, most of the non-recyclable are product packaging. The problem is that many packages not only are difficult to recycle, but also have an irreparable damage to the environment. For example, some environmentally harmful chemical materials or plastics, if not treated by artificial means such as incineration, take a long time to degrade and have a negative impact on the environment. Therefore, instead of pursuing luxury and fancy packaging, manufacturers should simplify packaging, which saves resources and reduces environmental pollution. In addition, when selecting packaging materials we must try to avoid substances that are toxic and harmful, or difficult to dispose, and use green and degradable substances, such as paper and other similar materials, changing its size and shape. Also, cutting down the use of packaging materials by changing the size or shape of packages is also an option.

---

[1] Zheng Hualin, Liu Qingyou, "Sustainable Developing Green Manufacturing Technology in Manufacturing Industry and Its Implement", Proceeding of National Advanced Manufacturing Equipment Robotic Technology Forum 2005.

Some of China's products are over-packaged with layers and layers of complicated and luxurious materials, which increases the costs and wastes. On the contrary, developed countries prefer simplicity in packaging. For example, some brands of clothes do not have outer packaging bags, or shoe boxes for shoes. This is how they practice green packaging.

(5) *Green disposal*

The green disposal (recycling) of products is equally important, and it is this phase that makes green manufacturing a closed system. Products that have just ended their lives will enter their next life through recycling. Recycling includes reutilization or reuse. In order to make it feasible to recover products, product structure is given priority today in the design process, through design for disassembly (DFD). Disassembly can effectively make a recovery possible by turning products into parts for further processing. Efficient recycling and reuse of the products can only be achieved by considering the disassembly at the beginning of the design.[1]

In a word, green manufacturing must focus on pollution prevention and reduction by focusing on reducing waste of resources and promoting cycling in the entire process of design, raw material selection, production and social services, in order to achieve comprehensive and coordinated development of the economy, society and environment.

1.2.3 The relation of green manufacturing and other advanced manufacturing patterns

Green manufacturing has a wide range of connotations, thus forming a conceptual system. From the above discussion, we can see the difference between green manufacturing and traditional manufacturing. But it is necessary to briefly explain what differences and connections exist between green manufacturing and other advanced manufacturing patterns to deepen understanding of the essential characteristics of green manufacturing clearly (see Table 1–1).

---

[1] Feng Xianying, *Machine Manufacturing*, Jinan: Shandong Science and Technology Press, 2013, pp.206-207.

Table 1–1   Comparison between green manufacturing and
traditional manufacturing

Item	Mass production	Lean manufacturing	Smart manufacturing	Green manufacturing
PLC (product life cycle)	R&D to disposal	R&D to disposal	R&D to disposal	Disposal to regeneration
Product life concept	Corporate-centered	Market-centered	Market-centered	Market–centered (guiding customers to rational needs)
Connotation of resources	Human resources, finance, and supplies	Human resources, finance, and supplies	Human resources, finance, supplies, and time	Human resources, finance, supplies, waste, and time
Space range	Within the corporate	Close relations with customers and suppliers	A coordinative environment of supply chain	Corporate, society, government
Components of competition	Competition based on low cost	Competition based on the quality	Competition based on the flexibility	Competition based on environmental protection
Core principle	Work division, profit of economy of scale	Elimination of waste	Quick response	Coordinative development, minimum waste and maximum the utilization of resources
Theoretical foundation	Division of labor	Coordination of supply-demand	Integration of resources	Harmony of nature and mankind

Source: Zheng Hualin, Liu Qingyou, Zhang Jinwei, Xiao Xiaohua, Wang Yuepai, "Green Manufacturing Technology for Sustainable Development and Its Implement Strategy", *Machinery*, 2006(6), p.49.

From Table 1–1, we can see the differences and connections between different manufacturing patterns. In order to explore the problem of integration between different manufacturing patterns, we take lean manufacturing as an example. Green manufacturing must be combined with other advanced manufacturing to bring its advantage into full play, and it cannot be completely separated from other manufacturing patterns.

Lean manufacturing was originally summarized according to the mode of manufacturing of Toyota Motor Corporation of Japan. It reforms system structure, personnel organization, operation mode and supply and demand, so that the production system can meet the changing needs of consumers, all the complicated and useless intermediates, finally satisfactory results are obtained in production, sales or consumer satisfaction.

Many enterprises have learned valuable experiences in their previous management process. These experiences help them to reduce expenditures when introducing new management systems, and to improve new management systems as soon as possible.

And companies can benefit from them to fulfill their economic, social and environmental responsibilities.

The comparative analysis of the main features of lean manufacturing and green manufacturing reveals that the two have much in common, as shown in Table 1–2.

Table 1–2 Comparison between lean manufacturing and green manufacturing

Lean manufacturing	Shared features	Green manufacturing
To value staffs' merits and interests	People-oriented	To attach importance to the safety and health of every individual related to the products
Cooperation of groups of versatile people	Teamwork	Experts of different fields responsible for the R&D of products and evaluation of costs and environment
To eliminate waste	To eliminate negative output	To eliminate pollution and consumption
Demands for products in small-batch	Demand-oriented	Demand for green products
Cooperation with other corporates on the supply chain	To emphasize exterior harmony	Environmentally friendly in the factories during the entire PLC
Profit maximization for corporates	Grasping the overall situation	Minimum pollution, maximum utilization of resources and energy in the PLC
The whole outweights the sum of that of its parts	Systemic in the process	Minimum environmental pollution in the PLC

Source: Li Jing, Zhou Zhi, Wang Chang, Wei Dapeng, "Research on the Green Manufacturing Based on the Standard Management System". *Science & Technology and Economy*, 2006(1).

Judging from the shared features above, ideas of lean manufacturing can be integrated into the green manufacturing system. Other advanced manufacturing ideas can also be integrated into green manufacturing so they match up to the mainstream trend of manufacturing development and are possible to develop further; otherwise, they will be replaced by new alternative technologies or processes. In the future, enterprises must pay attention to the environment and develop relevant management systems in order to effectively use resources so that they can make profits and fulfill corresponding social responsibilities, and that their products can be accepted by the public. As the public is becoming increasingly aware of the significance of environmental protection, it becomes more and more difficult for companies that ignore the ecological environment to survive in the future.

Toyota, the birthplace of lean manufacturing, has also transformed to green manufacturing. In the Annual Report of Toyota Motor Corporation 2004, we could see the sign of integration of lean manufacturing and green manufacturing. On the basis of its lean production, Toyota has implemented thorough environmental management in every stage of PLC from development and design, production and logistics scheduling, to recycling and distribution. In 2004, it formulated operation guideline for its environmental management department. Through integration, Toyota's profits were improved, and the environmental benefits obtained. We can conclude that green manufacturing and lean manufacturing is not only a good choice, but also a necessary one.

In addition, there is both connections and distinctions between green manufacturing and re-manufacturing. Green manufacturing cannot be simply interpreted as the re-manufacturing. Re-manufacturing is defined as the rebuilding of a product to specifications of the original product with specific technologies. The performance and quality of the re-manufactured product can match in either aspect with the original manufactured product. In other words, re-manufacturing is making new products out of old ones through redesigning—under the premise of ensuring high efficiency, energy saving and environmental protection. In addition, re-manufacturing has changed the traditional open system into a closed system of manufacturing, scraping and re-manufacturing. But no matter how advantageous it is, re-manufacturing is only a link in green manufacturing, a manufacturing process of one certain kind of product. Green manufacturing is more comprehensive and complicated. Green manufacturing reflects the concept of sustainable development from itself and in PLC. It re-examines the entire process of manufacturing from design and production to using and scrapping. This model must take into account the problems that production may cause problems to the environment. Therefore, we should minimize negative impacts, and make more efficient use of resources, energy, so as to coordinate economic, social, and environmental development. Green manufacturing not only considers the friendliness of recycling to the resources and environment at the manufacturing stage, but also considers the environmental and social benefits in product use, packaging, and transportation.[1]

1.3   Strengthening China's green manufacturing industry: an urgent need

Green manufacturing is a global strategy that helps to optimize and upgrade

---

[1] Zhao Jianjun, Yang Bo, "Green Manufacturing: The Future Orientation of Manufacturing Technology Development", *Study Times*, Mar. 31, 2016.

industries, improve human life and promote economic development. Therefore, it has great significance and value, which will be shown as time goes by. We must either make changes now and get ready to embrace it, or fall behind in corporate and national competition or be surpassed by other countries, eventually losing market share, having an economic downturn and a decline of comprehensive national strength, and even once again becoming a backward country subjected to other more powerful countries.

1.3.1 The necessity for China to develop green manufacturing

When the "green" trend swept the world, China, the largest developing country and a world manufacturing power, urgently needed a perfect green turn in manufacturing. Domestically, resources and environmental constraints are prominent in China. Globally, international pressures on China in the reduction of greenhouse gas emissions in global climate change is increasing, and green barriers to products are becoming serious. And ecological civilization values can be realized by developing green manufacturing. Therefore, it is very necessary and important to develop green manufacturing in China.

1.3.1.1 The limitations of resources and environment

In the past years, the rapid growth of China's economy has been characterized by huge input, high consumption, high pollution, and low output, which inevitably aggravates conflicts between man and nature and eventually destroys our habitat.

China is in the stage of industrialization and rapid urbanization. In the past 40 years since the reform and opening up, China's economy has developed rapidly. It's GDP has experienced a leap-forward development from RMB364.5 billion to RMB68.91 trillion, and the total economic output has risen from tenth to the second in the world, with an average annual growth of about 9.5 percent, and the per capita GNP increasing from US$190 in 1978 to nearly US$8,000 in 2009. The urbanization process in China has also been accelerating. From 1978 to 2015, the total number of Chinese cities has increased from 193 to 661, and the scale of cities has undergone tremendous changes. Megacities have increased from 13 to 54, large cities from 27 to 85, medium-sized cities from 59 to 226, and small cities from 115 to 296. At the end of 2015, the built-up area of cities nationwide was 32,500 km^2, and urban population density was 870 people per square kilometer. By the end of 2016, the national urban population was 577.70 million, and the urbanization level was 43.9 percent, an increase of 0.9 percent over 2015. In 2016, the national fixed assets investment in urban areas was RMB9,347.2 billion, accounting for 85 percent of the total fixed asset investment; the per capita fixed assets investment in urban areas was RMB16,198, 40 times of that at the beginning of the reform and opening up (the year of 1980).[1]

China's rapid development is remarkable, but it has also paid heavy prices: resources are becoming scarcer and pollution is becoming more serious; urban expansion has made "urban maladies" intensified: population expansion, and water and electricity shortage, traffic congestion and environmental degradation. The supply and demand of energy resources are in a very serious condition.

It is generally believed that 50 percent external dependence of oil is an internationally accepted alarm level. If a country's dependence on foreign oil is beyond that limit, it will become greatly difficult for the country to obtain continuous and cheap oil supply from the international market. There will be a risk of a disruption in the supply of oil at any time. At present, China's dependence on foreign oil has exceeded 60 percent. At the same time, China has changed from a coal exporter country to a coal importer country, and the energy supply is becoming more urgent. In terms of energy reserves, China's per capita proved recoverable reserves of oil and natural gas are only 7.7 percent and 4.1 percent of the world.

China's environmental condition is worsening. On the one hand, China is faced with the depletion of resources; on the other hand, the continuous deterioration of the environment is becoming more and more serious. Generally speaking, China's current environmental pollution has seriously affected the whole country, with nationwide atmosphere pollution, water pollution and land pollution. This is completely different from the UK, Japan, and other developed countries where "pollution only occurred in industrial areas and cities and their surrounding areas" in the early industrial period. In China, the severeness of pollution in those heavily polluted areas has already exceeded that in the UK and Japan in the past. For example, the cadmium content in the sediments of the lower reaches of the Xiangjiang River (Hunan Province of China) has exceeded the cadmium content in the "Itai-itai Disease" area in Japan. Moreover, more heavily polluted areas are being "fermented". Seventy percent of the river systems are polluted, 40 percent of which is seriously polluted, and more than 95 percent of the rivers flowing through the cities are severely contaminated. More than 300 million rural residents in China do not have access to clean drinking water, and more than 400 million urban

---

[1] The National Bureau of Statistics of China, "The Reform and Opening Up is Building the Brilliance, A New Era of Economic Development Coming Up—The Significant Changes in Economic and Social Development in China since 1978", *People's Daily*, Nov.16, 2013.

population do not have fresh air to breathe. It is estimated that China's population will reach 1.46 billion in 2020, and the total economic output will quadruple. The burden of pollution control will be quadruple or quintuple.

Resource depletion and environmental pollution have posed a serious challenge for China's new round of development. In this sense, the "green" trend is coming at the right time when China is exploring new modes of manufacturing development. Realizing a green transformation of manufacturing and economic structure has become the key to China breaking through the "bottleneck" of resources and the environment.

1.3.1.2 Growing international pressures

With the sustained and rapid development of the economy, China's greenhouse gas emissions have also grown rapidly. By the end of 2015, China's total greenhouse gas emissions have been second only to the United States, ranking second in the world. In recent years, climate changes have become a hot issue in international public opinion. The Copenhagen Climate Summit at the end of 2009 attracted widespread attention from the world. The international public opinion is extremely unfavorable to China, and there are louder voices demanding China to reduce carbon emissions. When the UN Secretary-General Ban Ki-moon visited China in July 2009, he said that "China holds the key to determining the success of climate negotiations" and stressed that China has an unavoidable obligation in global climate change and greenhouse gas emission reduction.[1] Faced with the complexity of the climate issue, China has always adhered to the principle of "common but differentiated responsibilities" and advocated that developed countries should first solve the problem of large scale of emission in the past and at present, and improve their production methods and give developing technological and financial support to developing countries. Developing countries should, on the other hand, solve their economic problems, and adopt a sustainable development approach to save energy and reduce emissions and protect the environment. This has also given some time, money and technology for China to develop green manufacturing.

China's foreign trade is also in urgent needs to achieve growth transformation of green manufacturing. Export-oriented, and low-value-added processing trade model is an important factor boosting China's sustained and rapid economic growth. As China is at the bottom of the global division of labor and product value chain, the resource and environment are seriously consumed. Trade at the expense of an unpredictable ecological deficit in exchange for a huge trade surplus in China seriously affected

---

[1] He Jun, "What Can China Do in the Era of Low-carbon Economy?" *China Economic Times*, Nov. 27, 2009.

China's international image. The environmental problems caused by the "world factory" have been inviting criticism from the international community and China threat opinion on natural resources. At the same time, developed countries often set up green barriers and exert moral and economic pressure on China's trade, using environment issue as an excuse. Therefore, while safeguarding its legitimate rights and interests, China should change its extensive manufacturing mode to deal with trade problems and enhance its "green" competitiveness in international manufacturing, trade and financial markets.[1]

1.3.2 The profit of the green development of manufacturing industry

The financial crisis in 2008 slowed down the world economy, and the manufacturing industry was stricken hard, with many factories collapsing. The traditional manufacturing model was proved unable to adapt to the requirements of the new era. The global financial crisis and economic recession have also provided an opportunity for green manufacturing to change the bad image of destroying the environment by prioritizing environmental issues. Green manufacturing has become the general trend of the development of the manufacturing industry, and it has become the main driving force and a new engine for revitalizing a nation's economic growth. Countries have launched their own plans of green manufacturing, and on that basis, they have established a series of trade and economic development plans for global economic recovery through the green transition. The value of green manufacturing can at least be seen in four aspects: the enterprise, the manufacturing industry, the national economic level, and the ecological environment.

1.3.2.1 Green manufacturing: the only way for long-term benign development of enterprises

With the rising cost of raw materials and energy, many countries set stricter emission standards for enterprises and stricter environmental management standards for products. Enterprises must find a sustainable development path to achieve self-enhanced development with positive feedback. Many enterprises start from within the organization for environmental footprint reduction, cost saving, and new product development.

For example, DuPont, a 208-year-old world-renowned chemical giant with a

---

[1] Li Xiaoxi, Hu Biliang, *The New Transition of China's Economy*, Beijing: Encyclopedia of China Publishing House, 2011, pp.333-334.

production value of over US$29 billion, had started the reflection on the company's value proposition before Greenpeace exposing environmental issues to the world. They made a strategic choice and shifted DuPont from a petrochemical-based company in the past to global leader in plant-based chemical raw materials and new environmentally friendly products. This change is not only a result of the expectations of DuPont's senior managers and scientists for future development, but also of their understanding that the company's chemical products and organic polymer products at that time would become commodities, the company's profitability would drop significantly over time. This change has greatly improved DuPont's reputation. In 2005, *Business Week* put DuPont the first on the list of Top Green Companies. Ceres Venture Fund, a well-respected environmental monitoring organization, ranked DuPont as the first in the United States and the second in the world in addressing the business challenges of climate change.

DuPont's starting point is to establish a strong internal network to significantly reduce energy costs and toxic emissions, and to play a leading role in the subsequent "Responsible Care" project throughout the chemical industry.

It can be said that only green manufacturing can usher in the new life of the enterprise. The implementation of green manufacturing cannot only enable enterprises to achieve economic benefits, improve the competitiveness in the market; more importantly, it also generates environmental benefits, so that resources are properly allocated, the utilization rate of resources is improved, and the sustainable development of enterprises is truly realized. For traditional manufacturing industries, such as steel, non-ferrous metals, petrochemicals and chemicals, bio-pharmaceuticals, light industry, printing and dyeing, etc., it is necessary to carry out a green transformation. Green technologies such as the integrated system of wastewater recycling, waste gas treatment, energy conservation and consumption reduction, online data collecting and sharing in production processes, and environmentally friendly materials are used in the manufacturing industry. Processing technologies like clean and efficient casting, forging, welding are used to make the whole production process green. We must research and develop green products with characteristics of low energy consumption, low pollution, and recycling. For energy-consuming machines such as generators and internal combustion engines, we must further improve their energy conversion efficiency. And eliminate technologies that cannot keep up with the pace of green transformation and do not meet the concept of sustainable development. Emerging industries are supposed to implement green manufacturing, establishing a green information sharing platform, and promoting the greening of new technologies and new energy.

China's extensive development mode has already caused a waste of resources. With a fixed amount of domestic resources, China's industrialization can succeed only by changing the traditional model, adhering to sustainable development, featuring high efficiency, low consumption, less pollution, and high technology. In the current context, companies must not only make profits, and pursue market influence. They must also assume their social responsibilities and contribute to environmental protection and energy conservation through green manufacturing. At present, many domestic and foreign enterprises have taken the lead in green transformation—reducing production costs, improving profits and protecting the environment and save resources through green design, green materials, green production, and green recycling.

1.3.2.2　Green manufacturing: the strategic choice of sustainable development

Sustainable development has been proposed for a long time which may be achieved in different ways in different countries, but one thing is generally agreed that without sustainable development of manufacturing mankind will certainly not be able to the survive and develop in the long run. According to the new definition of world resource researches, sustainable development is "the establishment of processes and technical systems that produce little waste and pollutants". It does not refer to clean production of certain products, nor is it limited to "end-of-pipe" environmental protection. It is the transformation of the entire production system. To control environmental pollution from the origin is to consider the impact of the entire PLC on the environment during the manufacturing process, maximizing the use of raw materials and energy, reducing the emission of hazardous wastes, selecting green materials, implementing the green design, green technology, green packaging, green use and green disposal. China is currently taking a path of sustainable development, and the green manufacturing road advocated in the manufacturing sector is also a correct path for modern manufacturing.

In recent years, people's awareness of environmental protection has been improved, and they will not only consider whether the products can meet their own needs, but also consider whether the products will adversely affect the environment when making purchases. People hope to buy more "green products". Green products account for a growing proportion in international trade and are increasingly attractive and competitive in the international market. In order to improve green products R&D, countries around the world have established green product certification and green labeling systems. The implementation of the green label system is of great significance to enterprises, manufacturing industries, consumers and countries. Only by complying with people's "green" demands can the manufacturing industry continue to break the "green" barriers in international trade and occupy the international market. The world's major multinational corporations and well-known enterprises hold a very positive attitude towards environmental management standards. Therefore, in order to develop globally, the manufacturing industry must implement the ISO14000—series of standards in environmental management, at every stage of the PLC.[1]

Green manufacturing is a new direction in China's exploration of sustainable development. It reflects China's emphasis on sustainable development. In such an era of economic globalization, the strategy of multi-national enterprise and developed countries often represent a new direction of technological innovation and industrial transformation. Developing countries should seize this opportunity and accept the challenge to lay the foundation for their advantages in the transformation and reshuffle of the manufacturing industry. Currently, when developing countries begin to develop green industry, some developed manufacturing countries such as Japan, the United States and countries in Europe have already been embarked on their journey. This means that we will soon enter a new round of manufacturing revolution and competition. If failing to adjust their strategy in time, the developing countries may fall behind and never catch up. So developing countries must keep a close eye of manufacturing reform in the world's major economies and try to hitch the wagon to a sustainable future.

1.3.2.3   Green manufacturing: one of the most important ways to achieve the strategic goals of sustainable development of the national economy

After the Report of the 15th National Congress of the CPC clearly putting forward the strategy of sustainable development, the Report of the 16th National Congress of the CPC re-emphasized the strategy of sustainable development as one of the three major goals of building a well-off society in an all-around way, pointing out that the ability of sustainable development is constantly strengthened, the ecological environment is improved. Harmony with nature promotes the whole society to embark on the road of civilized development with productive development, prosperous life, and good ecology. The Report of the 17th National Congress of the CPC put more emphasis on comprehensive, coordinated and sustainable development, and for the first time

---

[1] Wu Zhong, Xi Junjie, Xu Ying, "Promoting Green Manufacturing to Realize Sustainable Development of Manufacturing Industry", *Manufacturing Automation*, 2004(12).

included ecological civilization in the report, aiming to basically form the industrial structure, growth mode and consumption mode of saving energy resources and protecting the ecological environment. The concept of ecological civilization should be firmly established in the whole society. The Report of the 18th National Congress of the CPC put forward the idea of building a beautiful country to promote ecological civilization to a higher strategic level and integrate it with all aspects of economic, political, cultural and social construction.[1] We can see from that those strategies stress the same principle: to build an ecological civilization and build China into a country with a good environment. The manufacturing industries must take on their responsibilities. Green manufacturing is one of the important technical ways to achieve these fundamental goals.

According to the *Final Report on Environmentally Friendly Manufacturing* by World Technology Evaluation Center (WTEC), the following equation can be used to measure the total environmental load caused by a country's national economic development.

Environmental load = population*(GDP/population)*(environmental load/GDP)

GDP (gross domestic product) refers to the total market value of all permanent units in a country or region that produce final products and provide services within a certain period. The "population" in the formula is the number of the people; the "GDP/population" is the GDP per capita, reflecting the living standards of the people; and the "environmental load/GDP" reflects the burden of creating unit GDP value on the environment. In the Report of the 15th National Congress of the CPC, the long-term plan for the future is put forward: after China develops into a well-off society, China's economy will experience three important points in time: 2010, 2020 and 2050, and ultimately realize China's modernization. The annual GDP growth rate stays at around 7 percent and will be doubled in 2010. China's population will be kept under 1.3 billion in 2010, 1.4 billion in 2020 and under 1.5 billion in 2050. Therefore, suppose the total amount of environmental load in 2000 unchanged, the decline of environmental load per unit GDP in 2010, 2020 and 2050 can be calculated according to the above formula, as shown in Table 1–3.

---

[1] Yu Guobin, "Historical Achievements, Great Innovation and Fundamental Guarantee of the Socialist System with Chinese Characteristics", *Contemporary World and Socialism*, 2015(1).

Table 1-3   Reduction of environmental load per unit GDP in the next 50 years

Item	In 2000	In 2010	In 2020	In 2050
Population growth multiplier	1	1.077	1.154	1.231
GDP per capita growth multiplier	1	1.827	2.254	23.934
Environmental load per unit GDP Reduction Multiplier	1	0.508	0.258	0.034

Table 1-3 shows that if the impact of economic development on the country's resources and the environment is stable, that is, equivalent to the value in 2000, then by 2050, the environmental load per unit GDP of China will be 1/30 of what it is now. Take automobile manufacturing as an example, by the year of 2010, 2020 and 2050, it is not easy to reduce the consumption of resources, energy, and environmental pollution to 0.508 (about 1/2), 0.258 (about 1/4) and 0.034 (about 1/30) of the current environmental load respectively in the production of a car. Therefore, implementing green manufacturing, reducing manufacturing consumption and environmental pollution is imperative in order to improve the development of the national economy, and to realize the national strategy of sustainable development.[1]

The implementation of green manufacturing will bring about a large number of emerging industries, which are new economic growth areas, and will promote the sustainable development of the economy under the "new normal". For example, a large number of waste products with good recycling value need to be recycled, reused or re-manufactured along with the scraping of automobiles, air conditioners, computers, refrigerators, photocopiers, traditional machine tools and other products, which will lead to the emergence of waste logistics and recycling treatment industry of waste products. The industry of recycling treatment recycles waste products, saves resources and energy, reduces the environment pressure of these products, and adds a new driving force for the sustainable development of the economy as a whole.

1.3.2.4   Green manufacturing: an essential element in achieving global ecological balance

Due to the nature of the material production process, green production is far from enough. the green lifestyle of the public is also important, and the green lifestyle derives not from the public's choice but from the products it uses. With green products, the public can largely reduce domestic wastes and hence have a lesser impact on the environment. On the contrary, with products that are not recyclable, scraping products will cause great harm to the environment and even waste treatment cannot eliminate the

---

[1]   Dang Xin'an, *Practice Engineering Training Course*, Beijing: Chemical Industry Press, 2011, p.293.

adverse impact on the environment. Therefore, in the final analysis, green manufacturing is not only a revolution in the mode of production, but a revolution which also affects people's lifestyle, and sets off a lifestyle revolution.

Environment and ecology are closely bound up to everyone. Improvement of people's awareness of environmental protection is bound to further promote the green demand. Market feedback will also prompt manufacturers to make improvements to meet people's green needs, which will produce more green products. Ecology links human beings together, whether individuals, businesses, groups, or national governments, all inter-depend on one another and need to work together, to deal with their own obligations and responsibilities and the interests of other parties, so as to respond with joint a effort to the future climate and environmental changes. It used to be the practice of traditional manufacturing to intentionally or unintentionally transfer the cost of waste management to society and the public health costs of toxic substances in products and processes to society, but that is becoming history. With the system of extended producer responsibility becoming more and more standardized, this responsibility has now really fallen on the shoulders of manufacturing enterprises.

Manufacturing industry should not take greening as a burden but as a driving force. It should seize the opportunity of green transformation, promoting the energy revolution, accelerating the technological innovation of the industry, so as to achieve a win-win situation of economic development and ecological improvement. The ultimate goal of green manufacturing is undoubtedly not unitary but diversified. It fully weighs the impact and role of technology on the environment and ecology. It considers both economic and social benefits comprehensively in the process of innovation. It no longer seeks profits alone, but at the same time, takes into account ecological friendly, social-friendly and comprehensive development of human beings, and ultimately realize the sustainable development of humanity. Green manufacturing conforms to the basic requirements of the construction of ecological civilization, embodies the value orientation of ecological civilization construction, and it is an important link to achieve global ecological balance.

In the face of the future, we need not only to alleviate the crises but also to find a real solution to the problems. If the manufacturing industry does not take the lead, the ecological crisis will get worse. So instead of waiting for the doom, it is better for the manufacturing industry to act in time and pass on the confidence of change to other industries and the public, and truly replace the previous focus on enterprise interests and heading for green manufacturing.

Made in China 2025, promulgated by the State Council in 2015, is the first ten-year action guideline for the Chinese government to build a powerful manufacturing country. *Made in China 2025* puts forward the guideline of "innovation-driven, quality-first, green development, structural optimization, talent-oriented", adhering to the basic principle of "market-oriented, government-led, long-term development, overall promotion, key breakthroughs, independent development, opening up and cooperation", and adopts the "three-step strategy" to achieve the strategic objectives of manufacturing power. The first step is to rank into the manufacturing power countries by 2025; the second step is to reach the middle level of world manufacturing power countries by 2035; the third step is to enter the forefront of the world manufacturing power countries by 2049, the 100th anniversary of the founding of the People's Republic of China.

In March 2016, the fourth Session of the 12th National People's Congress voted to adopt the "Outline of the 13th Five-year Plan for the National Economic and Social Development of the People's Republic of China". The Outline put forward the strategy of building a strong manufacturing country, pointed out that we should implement the *Made in China 2025* in depth and ensure the superiority of the manufacturing industry. We should deepen the positive impact of information technology on manufacturing industry, promote the development of manufacturing industry towards the goals of high-end, intelligent, green and service, and cultivate new competitive advantages of manufacturing industry.

In November 2016, the State Council issued the "13th Five-year Plan for the Protection of the Ecological Environment" (hereinafter referred to as "the Plan") to strengthen green supply to drive consumption, integrating certification of environmental protection, energy, and water conservation, establishing of a unified green product standards, certification and labeling system.

The Plan also aims to develop ecological agriculture and organic agriculture, to speed up the construction of organic food bases and organic industrial development, and to increase the supply of organic products. By 2020, 100 model green design enterprises, 100 model green parks, and 1,000 model green factories are to be established, and the green manufacturing system will have been established.

The Plan points out that supervision will be carried out in the green manufacturing process, such as design, production, and recycling, that enterprises should be encouraged to carry out green design, green manufacturing, and to use green materials or degradable and recyclable materials in the packaging process. Simple packaging and follow-up treatment and utilization of packaging are encouraged. Green manufacturing and green management should be carried out in factories first to form an industrial chain, of green technology, and to form the green manufacturing industry of China.

From this series of action plans, we can see China's emphasis on the strategy of manufacturing power. The next five years will be a critical period for upgrading China from a manufacturer of quantity to one of quality, and that is the most critical period for the development of green industry. Human beings are faced with the problem of environmental pollution and resource shortage, which requires the major economies of the world to take a path of green sustainable development. Competition between countries depends largely on the utilization of environmental resources, so in order to improve international competitiveness, we should also pay attention to green development. To implement green manufacturing in an all-round way is the strategic task of building a powerful manufacturing country, and is also an important measure to promote the structural reform of the supply side.

Chapter 2
The "New Normal" of Economic Growth and the Dramatic Change in Manufacturing Industry

2.1 A quality–improvement and upgrading stage of the world economy

2.1.1 Structural dilemma of the world economy

At present, there are three main interpretations of the problems in world economic growth. One of the dominant interpretations is that decline in production, consumption and commodity prices has brought the global economy into stagnancy since the outbreak of the global financial crisis in 2008. However, there must be deeper reasons for global economic problems. The second interpretation is that the economy has developed into a new stage in the era of globalization. Therefore, to solve global economic problems, we must first improve the mechanism of co-governance in the context of globalization. The third interpretation, popular in recent years, shows that the global economic problems are caused mainly by structural difficulties in economic growth, and nations must reach a joint effort to promote structural reform. But, we must first have a clear view of structural difficulties. What is the most fundamental structural problem that causes economic difficulties? Why are such problems occurring in today's development stage? Are these problems related to the cyclicality of economic development? Only after we have answers to these questions can we better formulate economic policies for the world's economic development. The author believes that the world economy is trending towards globalization when structural difficulties are the most fundamental causes of global economic problems. The specific structural difficulties can be summarized as follows.

2.1.1.1 Global overcapacity and gross imbalance

With economic development and technological innovation, the world economy has developed rapidly due to the new mode of production and resource allocation, and production efficiency has been greatly improved. Industrialization and the development of the manufacturing industry have led to a rapid increase in economic productivity. At the same time, the optimization and upgrading of the industrial structure have declined the demand for manufacturing, leading to global excessive production capacity. After the breakout of the economic crisis, the demand has further declined, and the economic slowdown policies adopted by various countries have further worsened this situation. In particular, the excessively loose monetary policy in emerging market countries has caused severe misallocation of financial resources. To solve the problem of excessive production capacity and the current global imbalance between supply and demand, it is necessary for each country to conduct cooperative management worldwide. Responses to the crisis made solely by individual countries will deteriorate this problem and the problem will not be resolved.

2.1.1.2 Unmatched supply and demand structure in emerging market economies

The rapid development of the global economy in the past years has been fueled by the developed countries, but the considerable economic growth of developing countries has also made its contribution. However, after the initial rapid growth, developing countries have now entered a period of economic transformation and adjustment. On a world scale, there is a great change in production and consumption. This change is manifested in the improvement of household consumption level, and the constant decrease of Engel coefficient, the development of the service industry, the industry of special feature and high-quality is becoming increasingly popular. However, in emerging market economies, the old supply model has not been improved, resulting in a contradiction between the old supply mode and new consumption structure and there are even serious mismatches in some areas. This problem has greatly restricted economic development.

Therefore, we can draw from the above two points that there are problems of capacity, and of the supply-demand structure. Supply-demand quantity and supply-demand structure work on each other causing an increasingly serious structural problem in the global economy, which needs urgent improvement.

2.1.1.3 Unbalanced global development structure and unequal income

Although the decline in global consumption growth is the result of the economic crisis, the inequality of economic income will be more responsible for it. Thomas

Piketty proposes in *Capital in the Twenty-First Century* that the return on capital of developed economies in Europe and America has always been greater than the economic growth rate. Under this premise, the global economic growth is unbalanced, and the Gini coefficient keeps rising. In other words, the distribution of wealth among members of society is becoming more and more unequal, and the wealth gap is gradually widening. The outbreak of the financial crisis has made this phenomenon even more obvious. The decline of the middle class has changed the distribution of the social classes and the economic structure, and the distribution of global wealth is even more unreasonable. Near the end of 2011, Credit Suisse Research Institute released the Global Wealth Report 2016, which pointed out with statistics that global wealth is actually in the hands of the minority. According to the report, the richest 10 percent of adults own 86 percent of all wealth; on the contrary, the remaining 73 percent of the population only possesses 2.4 percent of the global assets. In the developed countries that are experiencing economic transformation, the wealth gap is expanding. And in emerging economies, the fast-growing economy has also widened the income gap. The global economy has been constrained as a whole by the slow consumption growth of a large number of low-and middle-income population, weakening the impetus of consumption to the economy.

2.1.1.4 A Demographic transition and an aging predicament facing the global economy

Since the beginning of the 21st century, the proportion of the world's aging population has increasingly expanded, and the international community is already an aging society. If the age of 65 years and older is taken as the standard for the elderly, the world's aging proportion in 2012 was 8 percent, and it rose to 8.5 percent in 2015. According to An Aging World: 2015 published by the US Census Bureau, the number of the aging population in the world reached 617 million in 2015, and the number will get a continuous increase, which is expected to reach 1.6 billion by 2050. By then, the aging population will account for more than 21 percent in 94 countries and 39 of them will have an aging population of over 28 percent. There are two reasons for ageing: firstly, the baby boomers after the Second World War are becoming the aging today; secondly, the European and American countries that are the first to enter the aging society have not yet come out of this stage. But at the same time, new developing countries have followed their steps, so the whole world has gradually become an aging society. According to the theory of demographic transition, the population of an aging society will enter a stage of low birth rate and death rate, and this stage will have a great impact on the economy: In the first place, the increase of the aging people means that the labor force will decrease, which will lead to a decline in productivity in the long run. Next, the aging and slow-growing population will result in fewer banks savings, which will affect the development of the investment industry. Finally, the increase in the aging population will cause the decline of overall consumption level. Therefore, the seemingly normal aging trend will have a very adverse long-term impact on the economy in terms of productivity, savings rate and consumption level.

2.1.1.5 The global economic governance structure in hot water

After the financial crisis, people began to think more about the way out for globalization in addition to dealing with problems. Some phenomena, such as the rise of trade protectionism, the impact of Brexit on European integration, and Trump being elected then president of United States made it urgent and necessary to consider the issues of globalization and deglobalization. According to economic theories, market forces and technological innovation in the globalization mechanism play a motivational role in global economic development. However, the trend of trade protectionism, populism and deglobalization after the financial crisis have forced people to reconsider whether there are problems with globalization. The author believes that the problems are not about globalization itself, but about the governance mechanism at the present development stage of globalization. Firstly, there is a problem with governance measures. Most countries focused on monetary stimulus after the crisis, instead of giving priority to solving the fundamental problems such as structural surplus. Secondly, there are unbalanced and unequal structural problems in the governance process. The rights, obligations, and demands of emerging economies are somewhat neglected in globalization, and their positive role in global economic growth and global governance got overlooked as well. This generated greater difficulties in economic growth. Thirdly, the previous governance mechanism is not perfect enough to deal with emerging problems, such as the widening gap between the rich and the poor in the development process, capital flows and regulation, and the coordination of monetary and economic policies among countries. On the one hand, these contradictions have constrained global economic development; on the other hand, they have boosted the prevalence of the mentality of deglobalization.

"Rome was not built in one day." The above economic difficulties are gradually arising in the process of global economic development and finally have a negative impact on the current economic operation. If we want to lead the global economy to find a way out and get out of the predicament, what we need to do is to solve problems facing the current world economy—carrying out reform on the economic structure and governance mechanism.

2.1.2 A new way out for the world economy under the "new normal"

Many things are cyclical, and global economic growth is no exception. In the course of development, the world economy is now in a period of transition from the old to the new, in which the old cycle has not completely finished, and the new cycle has not yet fully formed. This stage is relatively unstable, which may make people skeptical of the process of globalization. The only certainty is that in a long time after the financial crisis in 2008, the global economy has entered a moderation in economic growth that can be called the "New Normal", which has affected the development momentum within the world economy. The world economy needs a transition from this unstable stage to a fresh cycle—the next stable normal state. And it has to complete the adjustment and transformation from factor-driven growth to innovation-driven development, from the traditional international division of labor system to the transformation and adjustment of the global value chain system, as well as the transformation and adjustment from the old governance methods to the new one.

The transformation of the world economy proves that the global economic development has stepped into a new stage. In addition to applying the traditional Smithian growth pattern, we should also use Schumpeter's new model when analysing the problems in world economic development. Smithian growth relies mainly on the division of labor, that is, to promote growth efficiency with the division of labor. The author believes that Smithian growth is very vulnerable to the market division of labor in the economic cycle. Therefore, the practice of breaking the limit is to cross this economic growth cycle, which means to cross from the old cycle to the new cycle. At this stage, we must apply the Schumpeter's model instead of the Smithian growth law. In other words, we must form a new production pattern through the innovation of technology and system. Schumpeter's growth is based on innovative development—using innovation to drive economic growth, so the Smithian growth can also be used in this cycle to achieve stable development. However, if the division of labor is restricted by the market, we can turn to Schumpeter's model to develop a new cycle. Therefore, both in Smithian growth and Schumpeter's growth, it is extremely important to rely on innovation to cross from the old stage to a new stage during the transition phase of this transformation. What should be particularly noted is that on the one hand, it is necessary to form new production modes and consumption functions through technological innovation; on the other hand, we must improve global economic governance, and establish and improve new rules through institutional innovation.

Today's world economy has stepped into a "New Normal", and economic reform is embarked on the path of green development. Especially in the face of global warming, resource exhaustion and growing environmental degradation, the trend of green reform in global industry is becoming increasingly bright, which is exhibited in the following four aspects.

2.1.2.1　From a linear economy to a circular economy

In the era of the "New Normal", we should make full use of the advantages of the slowdown of global economic growth to promote the transition from a linear economy to a circular economy, and improve the efficiency of resource utilization. The linear economic development model— "resources-products-waste" model—has always been the dominant mode of economic development since the beginning of the industrial era. It has made outstanding contributions to accelerate the industrialization and modernization of Western countries. However, limited resources and sharply increasing wastes caused severe environmental problems, which make this economic development model unsustainable. From the 1960s to the 1970s, Western countries began to look for a new model to replace linear economy development, and the circular economy model came into being.

The circular economy is a holistic industrial transformation, which recycles waste under the extensive development mode through technological innovation and industrial restructuring. It pursues ecological development instead of profit maximization. The development of the circular economy is an inevitable requirement for the healthy and sustainable development of human civilization in such a resource-shortage era. Many Western developed countries have developed rapidly from a linear economy to a circular economy, but China's transformation is still in its infancy. To achieve economic transformation, we need to have a complete change in development concept, industrial structure and science and technology. In an age of resource shortage, the development of the circular economy is the only way out, and it will certainly bring mankind into a new era of ecological civilization.

2.1.2.2　From a high-carbon economy to a low-carbon economy

Promoting an ecological civilization is an important part of the "New Normal". It's crucial to realize the green circular economy and promote the transition from a high-carbon economy to low-carbon economy. The main driving force for industrialization in developed countries comes from fossil energy, which will also be used to meet the main energy demand of developing countries at the present stage and for a long period of time. The burning of fossil fuels emits a large amount of greenhouse gases, aggravating global warming. Since the 1990s, Western countries began to seek a way out to reduce carbon dioxide emissions. From the United Nations Framework Convention on Climate Change (1992) to the Kyoto Protocol and then the concept of "low-carbon economy", Western society finally explored a road from high-carbon economy to a low-carbon economy. And the development of renewable energies (solar energy, wind energy, and biomass energy, etc.) and clean energies (hydro and nuclear energy) have become a major development model. The transition from a high-carbon economy to a low-carbon economy is related to the survival of human beings, the future of evolution, and the construction of a green and harmonious society. As a profound industrial and social revolution, this transformation still has a long way to go.

2.1.2.3　From the real economy to the e-economy

Innovation is one of the core contents of the "New Normal". At present, all countries in the world have promoted the transformation from the entity economy to the e-economy, which is the outstanding performance of innovation. All countries, especially developed countries, have taken the e-economy as the main driving force for development since the international financial crisis. New technologies and formats such as mobile Internet, big data, cloud computing, and the Internet of Things have begun to change our production, living and interpersonal communication. The e-economy has become the most subversive industrial form in the world. And the economic form is changing from the real economy to the "Internet Plus". Take China's domestic situation as an example, in 2015, the concept of "Internet Plus" is proposed in the "two sessions" ie., the National People's Congress (NPC) and the Chinese People's Political Consultative Conference (CPPCC) in the Report on the Work of the Government. Based on the stage of China's industrialization, "Internet Plus" has a revolutionary impact and driving force on the traditional industry, transforming all traditional industries with connectivity mechanism, and stimulating the traditional industries to adjust productive factors and business models, thereby, promoting China's economic and social transformation and upgrading. After the approval of Chinese Premier Li Keqiang, the "Guideline for Promoting 'Internet Plus' Action Plan" issued by the State Council on July 4, 2015 pointed out that by 2018, the integration of Internet and varied economic and social fields will be further deepened and the new economic form of "Internet Plus" will be formed by 2025. This represents that China's economic development is on the road of the new era of "Internet Plus", which promotes the transformation of the real economy to the "Internet Plus" economy. [1] In April 2016, President Xi Jinping hosted a symposium on cyber security and informatization, in which he stressed that China has entered the "New Normal" of economic development. The "New Normal" requires new drivers of growth, and the Internet has enormous potential for that. We must make rigorous efforts to integrate the Internet more deeply into the real economy, and to improve resource allocation and increase total factor productivity using information flows to facilitate the flow of technology, capital, talent, and materials, so as to contribute to innovative development, to transform the economic growth model, and to restructure the economy. [2]

2.1.2.4 From traditional manufacturing to green manufacturing

Under the "New Normal", promoting the transformation of the traditional manufacturing to green manufacturing is an important way to solve the environment and resource problems caused by the economy's "normal" development. Manufacturing is the foundation of the country, the impetus of rejuvenating the country, the foundation of strengthening the country, and the mainstay of economic development. Since the industrial revolution, the development of the world powers has shown that the development level of the manufacturing industry determines the strength of the country to a large extent. Green manufacturing is re-manufacturing, and it is an industry that carries out reparation, transformation and recycle of the waste products with advanced technology. First of all, green manufacturing is of low cost, and product life is extended by re-manufacturing technologies, and the cost is 50 percent less than that of the traditional manufacturing. In addition, green manufacturing can save 60 percent of energy, 70 percent of materials, and reduce air and water pollution by 80 percent. [3] Re-manufacturing has become a new format in the world's manufacturing industry with the above advantages. Many Western countries have established the concept of "using re-manufactured products to protect the environment", guiding and accelerating the

---

[1] "Guidance on Actively Promoting 'Internet Plus' Action Plan by the State Council", http://www.xinhuanet.com, Jul.4, 2015.

[2] Xi's remarks at a symposium on cyber security, informatization, http://www.people.com.cn, Apr. 26, 2016.

[3] Ye Guojie, Chen Chengfeng, Wu Weijie, "Green manufacturing in Enterprises", *New Technology & New Process*, 2007(10), pp.5-8.

transformation of traditional manufacturing to green manufacturing. The transformation from traditional manufacturing to green manufacturing is mainly reflected in four aspects: first, the driving force of manufacturing shifts from factors like cost and investment to technological innovation. Second, the competition among enterprises is no longer limited to cost advantages but also to environmental and social benefits. Third, traditional extensive manufacturing mode transforms into green manufacturing. Fourth, service-oriented manufacturing begins to replace production-oriented manufacturing.

At present, China's manufacturing industry has not yet to take a leading position in the world, and there is still much room for improvement in terms of the ability of band building, technology content, industrial structure, resource utilization rate, etc. China is the world's largest manufacturing country, accounting for the global proportion from 4 percent in 1995 to 20.8 percent in 2013, maintaining its position as the world's largest country for four consecutive years. But despite the large size, China's manufacturing industry is not strong enough, which is manifested in its per capita size of manufacturing, less than 1/3 of that of the United States, Germany, and Japan. With manufacturing industry developing towards globalization, informatization, and servitization, we are now in the midst of transforming from the traditional model and structure to the new technological revolution. It's crucial for China to grasp this opportunity and manage this transformation of manufacturing industry for its economic development. Currently, China attaches great importance to the development of re-manufacturing The *Made in China 2025* launched by the State Council in 2015 developed a blueprint for the transformation of China's manufacturing industry from traditional manufacturing to green manufacturing in the next decade, setting the principle of "innovation-driven, quality-first, green development, structural optimization, and talent-oriented" as the guideline.

2.2 The role of green manufacturing in world economy transformation

2.2.1 Green transformation of manufacturing industry and world economic environment

The past experiences have told us that it is impossible for a country to become a world power without a strong manufacturing industry. Manufacturing played a key role in industrialization. However, in the mid-20th century and the 1970s, there were two industrial transfers—developed countries represented by the United States shifted labor and capital-intensive industries to foreign countries in order to cultivate new industries and enhance competitiveness, slashing the share of manufacturing in the economic structure, which even brought about the birth of the industry hollowing theory. However, the financial crisis let the United States realize that the economy will be difficult without manufacturing industry. Therefore, the US government officially launched the "Advanced Manufacturing Partnership" in 2011 and proposed the slogan of "invents it here and manufactures it here". These measures helped the manufacturing regain its dominant position and let developed countries enter the reindustrialization age, supporting manufacturing again by intelligent manufacturing and reindustrialization. Germany's Industry 4.0, the US's "National Strategic Plan for Advanced Manufacturing", Japan's "Science-technology Industry Union", and the UK's "Industry 2050 Strategy" are the typical examples of such measures. China's "Industry 4.0" —*Made in China 2025* launched by the State Council on May 8, 2015, strives to build China into a strong manufacturing country within 10 years.

2.2.1.1 The significance of manufacturing industry

One of the world's top 100 thinkers, Vaclav Smil, wrote in *The Rise and Retreat of American Manufacturing* that no advanced economy can prosper without a strong, innovative and manufacturing sector and the job it creates. [1] The development experiences of countries around the world tell us that manufacturing is a key component of any modern economy, and its importance is far from being reflected in its contribution to GDP. Moreover, the manufacturing industry is composed of many interrelated and interdependent elements, so the fate of the manufacturing industry naturally depends on many factors, which together affect the overall face of political, economic, legal, educational and social aspects of a country. To give an example, most of the developed countries have experienced an economic downturn after the economic crisis, but Germany is not one of them, and it even had a higher economic growth rate. Germany relied on manufacturing exports to achieve such growth. German manufacturing exports contribute two thirds of its economic growth, ranking as the second largest exporting country in the world. The labor cost of manufacturing is high, and most developed countries prefer to outsource manufacturing. However, this does not inhibit the development of Germany's manufacturing industry. This is due to

---

[1] Vaclav, Smil, *The Rise and Retreat of American Manufacturing*, translated by Li Fenghai and Liu Yinlong, Beijing: China Machine Press, 2014.

Germany's long-term commitment to corporate characteristics, facilitating corporate innovation and tapping into high-tech, superior, and cutting-edge markets. Germany's policy in 2005 directly led to the collapse of the Schröder government, but the German government still insists that the government, enterprises and employees are tightly bound together, and the government promotes people's employment and ensures that they have jobs through measures such as salary reduction, government subsidies and a guarantee for employment. Although this approach does not conform to the laws of the market, in the long run, it reduces the expenses of enterprises; on the other hand, it stabilizes the employment rate. According to the 2009 annual report of the OECD member countries, after the implementation of this policy, Germany has saved about 500,000 jobs in an economic recession.

According to relevant researches by scholars in China, there is a positive correlation between economic development and the development level of the manufacturing industry. Since the reform and opening up, the regional imbalance has gradually emerged with the rapid development of China's economy and society. Many scholars like Lin Yifu (1998), Hu Angang (1995), Zhang Qi (2001) have conducted a comparative analysis on this and have reached a consensus: Regional development in China is unbalanced, and this gap has widened since 1990. Lin Yifu (1998) investigated and compared the differences in per capita GDP in the central, eastern, and western regions. He found that the differences in these regions took the first place, and the difference became increasingly obvious. Wei Houkai (2001, 2002) studied the development of China's manufacturing industry, concluding differences that exist in manufacturing level between provinces, autonomous regions and municipalities in China, and the differences between the western region and south-eastern coastal regions are continuously expanding after the reform and opening up. From the above research findings, we can find that economic differences between regions are related to the manufacturing differences. Ling Dongmei verified the relevance and consistency of them. On the other hand, structural optimization and economic transformation in urban development have also had an impact on the manufacturing industry. The trend that the service industry has gradually become the mainstay, which has been unstoppable. However, after the financial crisis, it's an indisputable fact that many countries have supported manufacturing again. So in the future urban development, how are we supposed to respond to the situation in China that in most cities economy still relies mainly on the secondary industry? What proportion should manufacturing take in the economy? Should the manufacturing industry be moved out of the city centre, or should there be a reservation selectively? These questions need to be further considered.

In the development of the world's metropolis, the manufacturing industry is no longer account for as large proportion as before, but this does not necessarily follow that the manufacturing industry has withdrawn from the historical stage. On the contrary, in New York and London, for example, manufacturing is still developing and has driven the twin engines of the manufacturing and service industry in the US and UK. Although the proportion of manufacturing has declined, it maintains a stable status and has contributed to the national economy. Singapore, as an international metropolis, has ensured the stable status of manufacturing during the transformation from the economy of entrepot trade to the current economy of finance, manufacturing and foreign trade.

2.2.1.2 The significance of manufacturing industry in the world's metropolises

The governments' willingness to develop and support the manufacturing industry indicates that the manufacturing industry conforms to today's sustainable development. In the world's metropolis, governments especially attach great importance to the development of manufacturing. The specific reasons can be summarized as follows.

First, manufacturing can create huge economic benefits and wealth, which is of great appeal to any government and country. According to the World Bank's World Development Report 2009, the world's industry value added accounted for 28 percent of total GDP in 2007, with manufacturing value added accounting for 18 percent of total GDP. The World Trade Organization's International Trade Statistics 2009 pointed out that, in 2008, the proportion of world trade in services was less than 20 percent of the total trade. In the economic crisis, the volume of world goods trade still maintained a growth rate of 1.5 percent, achieving US$15.33 trillion, of which the trade volume created by the manufacturing industry reached 68.22 percent, which is the most important source of world trade. And a promising manufacturing industry is an indispensable and important development factor for every city.

Second, the manufacturing industry has laid the foundation for service industry transformation for cities. Although the service industry is occupying an increasingly dominant position, the manufacturing industry is still an indispensable pillar industry in social and economic development. All scientific discoveries and technological inventions need to be transformed into productive forces through specific manufacturing industry, thereby contributing to the economy. According to the Input-Output Table of 2005 issued by the United Nations Development Programme, every unit increase in the manufacturing of coking coal, refined petroleum products and nuclear fuel with the minimum impact on the service industry, will generate 0.4362 demand for the service industry in their final use. Only by relying on manufacturing can cities make a better transition towards service industries. New York, Chicago and Los Angeles were the centers of light industry, heavy industry, and electrical machinery manufacturing industry before they became today's international metropolises. This is enough to show that the manufacturing industry is a carrier of their transformation.

Third, the manufacturing industry has created a large number of employment opportunities. Focusing only on the employment of highly-educated and highly qualified talents with ignorance of other classes in urban development will be unfavourable to social stability and development. In New York, 30 percent citizens without high school diploma are employed in the industrial sector, accounting for 58 percent of the total employed population; while more than 65 percent of the employed population have a high school education in non-industrial sectors and only 42 percent of it is in the industrial sector. The industrial sector plays an important role in providing employment for the population who is less skilled in English. In the industrial sector, 18.5 percent of its employment population is less skilled in English, but only 8 percent of them is in the non-industrial sectors. The unemployment rate in London, which is higher than the average unemployment rate in the UK, is rapidly increasing with the rapid decline in manufacturing, and has gone beyond the warning line for many times, reaching 9.1 percent. [1]

Last, the twin engines of the manufacturing industry and service industry can guarantee that the city's economy can transform smoothly and stably during the economic cycles. Chicago of the United States has experienced a situation of almost comprehensive shrink of the manufacturing industry from 1950 to 1990. The population has dropped from 3.6 million to 2.8 million and manufacturing industries have moved away. However, Chicago citizens strove to the recovery, driving development with the twin engines of the manufacturing industry and service industry. In addition to maintaining the growth momentum of the service industry, they also focused on the development of diversified manufacturing, including high-tech manufacturing industry, food processing, publishing and printing, etc. Currently, Chicago's GDP has led all cities in the United States. In addition, its communications equipment industry, heavy machinery industry, light industry, electrical equipment industry, medical equipment

---

[1] Jiang Manqi, Xi Qiangmin, "The Status, Role and Vitality of the Manufacturing Sector in the Development of the World Metropolis", *Nankai Journal* (*Philosophy, Literature and Social Science Edition*), 2012(2), pp.124-132.

industry, metal manufacturing industry, plastics industry, food processing industry, production technology industry rank first in the United States, forming an economic structure of the coexistence of modern service industry and manufacturing. On the contrary, in the financial crisis of 2008, GDP growth in London metropolitan area is -4.4 percent, employment growth is -2.2 percent, resident income growth is -2.8 percent, and overseas immigrants fell by nearly 60 percent within two years.

2.2.2 Manufacturing: the engine of economic growth

2.2.2.1 Green manufacturing: an inherent requirement for changing the economic development mode

Currently, countries in the world have reached a consensus that the manufacturing-oriented entity economy can guarantee the sound and steady growth of the national economy on the basis of material acquisition and processing and manufacturing. The development of the entity economy is also the main manifestation of national competitiveness. After the financial crisis, most countries have turned back to manufacturing development. But faced with increasingly severe environmental problems and resource shortage, what they need to do is to take a path of sustainable development. The concept of "green economy" was born then. China also takes green economy as the national development strategy. We are willing to work with other countries to make contributions to emission reduction and energy conservation and environmental protection through innovation in technologies and systems. For all countries, it's worth thinking whether the manufacturing industry as a pillar industry can meet the requirements of "green development" and how to meet the requirements of "green development" in such a context.

As a key point in the global economic competition, the manufacturing industry has been highly valued by all countries. Manufacturing has become a pillar industry for the creation of wealth globally. However, at the same time, it is also a major source of environmental pollution, and if improperly handled, it is bound to be a hazard to the environment. First of all, the manufacturing process is a complex input and output system, in which the input resources are transformed into products and wastes, thus causing environmental pollution. Traditional manufacturing creates benefits for humans at the expense of energy and resource consumption and environmental damage. In the mid-20th century, the countries involved in the Second World War tried to restore their economy, and expand the scale of the industry. However, due to the lack of environmental awareness at that time, global environmental degradation caused by industrial pollution has become a serious problem since the 1970s. Today, each country pays more attention to the protection of ecology and resources faced with such a deteriorating environment. In 1972, at the United Nations Conference on the Human Environment in Stockholm which focused on the relationship between environmental protection and economic development, the concept of "sustainable development" was formally proposed and discussed. Whereafter, different countries and organizations carried out a series of elaboration and researches on this concept and recognized its importance. The manufacturing industry is faced with the significant challenge of emission and pollution reduction for sustainable development. Green manufacturing, a sustainable production model that meets environmental protection requirements of energy saving and pollution reduction, is gradually emerging. Aiming to overcome the drawbacks of traditional manufacturing, green manufacturing looks at product life cycle from various angles, starting with green design, ensuring green production in the process and following up on subsequent assembly, packaging, recycle, etc. In the whole process of manufacturing products, we must ensure that there is fewer resources consumption and environmental pollution and enterprises must take their environmental and social responsibilities while pursuing economic interests. There is no doubt that the "green wave" is setting off in the world, and traditional manufacturing is developing towards greenization. We must vigorously promote green technology, adhering to adopting green raw materials, green design, green production, and green packaging, and build an information sharing platform supported by national policies and laws. Any enterprise which is not "green" will fail in market competition due to resistance in society and legal restriction. Green manufacturing, a dynamic concept, instead of an absolute one, is in an ever-developing process. The concept of "big manufacturing", which is globally recognized, includes almost all manufacturing industries that produce industrial products, such as machinery industry, chemical industry, metallurgical industry, etc. Therefore, green manufacturing will penetrate into every aspect of every industry.

2.2.2.2   Green manufacturing: the practice of green development in China

Firstly, green manufacturing is the mainstream of the world's manufacturing industry. Green manufacturing is the embodiment of sustainable development strategy in the manufacturing industry, aiming to improve human productivity through new science and technology advancement, and to ensure environmental benefits and promote the sustainable development of the international community. From 1999 to

2001, the US government took green manufacturing as its target of competition and reform and took corresponding measures. The National Science Foundation assisted the World Technology Evaluation Center to establish a special committee for environment-friendly manufacturing technology evaluation, which conducted an in-depth study and analysis of the latest development of enterprises, schools and governments in developed countries and regions such as Europe and Japan in green manufacturing, technological improvement and policy settings. After comparative study with its current situation, they concluded that America is no longer dominant and needs to change. In China, "National Outline on Medium- and Long-term Science and Technology Program (2006-2020)" clearly defines green manufacturing as one of the three major ideas for the manufacturing development. The outline proposes that China should vigorously promote green manufacturing and supervise the whole product life cycle from design and production to sales, recycle and reuse, integrating the idea of green manufacturing into the whole process of this cycle and paying attention to energy conservation, environmental protection, low energy consumption and high efficiency, so as to make China's manufacturing industry rank among the best in the world.

Secondly, green manufacturing can drive the development of China's circular economy. The 16th National Congress of the CPC proposed to list sustainable development as the basic goal of building a well-off society in an all-round way— "The capability of sustainable development will be steadily enhanced. The ecological environment will be improved. The efficiency of using resources will be increased significantly. We will enhance harmony between man and nature to push the whole society onto a path to civilized development featuring the growth of production, an affluent life and a sound ecosystem." In March 2006, the 11th Five-year Plan for National Economic and Social Development of the People's Republic of China (hereinafter referred to as the 11th Five-year Plan), building a resource-saving and environment-friendly society is listed in one of the important tasks during the 11th Five-year Plan period. Building a resource-conserving and environment-friendly society means that we must reduce unnecessary resource consumption and waste and environment pollution, while we also ensure that human beings can obtain sufficient economic and social benefits at all aspects of social construction during the whole process of economic development. In 2006, the State Council clearly pointed out in the work focus that the circular economy is regarded as an important way to build a resource-saving and environment-friendly society and achieve sustainable development; it is necessary to develop a circular economy, implementing pilot initiatives of circular economy in key industries, industrial parks, cities and rural areas; improve preferential tax policy for comprehensive utilization of resources and recycling of renewable resources to promote comprehensive utilization of waste and recycling of used resources. In this cycle of resource production—product manufacturing—product consumption—product waste—resource reproduction, the priority to make the whole system an enclosed circulatory structure is the final regeneration link, without which the whole system will no longer exist. In this case, resource reproduction has become a very important part of the manufacturing industry structure. The major task of green manufacturing is to achieve greenization from design and production to sales, utilization and regeneration in the whole product life cycle, that is, low resource consumption, low environmental pollution, high utilization efficiency, and less harm to human health. Therefore, green manufacturing is a key supporting technology to the construction of a resource-saving and environment-friendly society and to a circular economy, which is proposed by the 11th Five-year Plan.

Thirdly, green manufacturing is an effective way for China to achieve the goal of energy conservation and emission reduction. China's economic growth is at the expense of excessive environment destruction and energy consumption. According to the data of 1999, China's carbon dioxide emissions 3,077.7 tons per million US dollars of GDP, which is 11.8 times that of Japan in the same period, and 1.4 times of India, ranking third to last in all 60 countries (or regions). This shows that China is less competitive in the environment. According to IMD World Competitiveness Ranking, China's GDP grew by 7.3 percent in 2001, but the net GDP growth rate after removing energy consumption was 5.79 percent. In 2000, its GDP grew by 8.0 percent, and the net GDP growth rate after removing energy consumption was 7.16 percent. By comparing the data of these two years, China's energy consumption is growing rapidly, and China's economy maintains an increasing dependence on energy.

The 11th Five-year Plan proposed a binding indicator that reduces the energy consumption per unit of GDP by about 20 percent and the total discharge of major pollutant by 10 percent during this period. The "Decision of the State Council on Strengthening Energy Conservation" issued by Xinhua News on August 31, 2006 clearly stipulates that by the end of the 11th Five-year Plan, the energy consumption per 10,000 yuan of GDP drops to 0.98 tons of standard coal, the average annual energy saving rate 4.4 percent, and the energy consumption per unit of key products has reached or approached the advanced international level at the beginning of the 21st century. In 2006, the implementation of the unit GDP energy consumption gazettes system required each province to accomplish its target of energy-saving and cost-reducing, and the government will negotiate with key enterprises and sign a letter of responsibility. The central and local governments and enterprises had to attach importance to energy conservation and emission reduction and took it as their routine work, making China once obsessed with energy conservation and emission reduction. For enterprises, the implementation of green manufacturing and the adoption of green technologies and techniques is one of the main methods to achieve the target of energy saving and cost reduction.

Fourthly, promoting green manufacturing is the need to break through international trade barriers. With China's accession to the World Trade Organization, the integration of the world economy, and the decrease of traditional non-tariff barriers, green trade barriers have become the main toll-gate of international trade. Green trade barriers include green tariff, green technical standards, green environmental standards, green market access systems, consumers' awareness of green consumption, etc. The integration of environmental protection measures into international trade rules and objectives is the development trend of environmental protection but at the same time, causes the green trade barriers. As the largest developing country in the world, China has paid a heavy price in the face of the green barriers established by developed countries. According to United Nations' statistics, China's annual export adversely affected by green barriers amounts to US$7.4 billion. Many experts have proposed measures to break through green trade barriers, such as introducing ISO14000 and China Environmental Labelling Products Certification, participating in negotiations of environmental provisions of international environmental conventions and international multilateral agreements, and strengthening research and formulation of environmental economic policies. Meanwhile, experts agree that improving science and technology and productivity is one of the basic means to break through green trade barriers. The popularization and application of green manufacture technologies will contribute to technological innovation and improve the environmental awareness of China's export products, and will help break through the green trade barriers, thereby promoting export trade and stimulating the development of related industries.

Fifthly, green manufacturing is the requirement of the global trend of green product consumption. Many companies are willing to take the effort to develop green products because they realize that this will become their competitive advantage lies in future enterprises. For example, Eastman Kodak Company has developed a new type of camera called "Fun Saver", 87 percent of which can be recycled. The "Electronics and

Environment" annual seminar, sponsored by famous electrical companies such as MCC, has become one of the most influential academic conferences of IEEE; Haier Group developed a washing machine that washes without washing powder in 2003. Since August 2006, Greenpeace has launched a list of green electronic products. According to the statistics of its 10th issue of 2008, most companies are gradually reducing the toxic substances of their products and improving their recycle. The green direction of government policy and people's growing awareness of sustainability have gradually changed people's consumption concepts, and green products have gradually become the first choice of consumers. Enterprises are beginning their pursuit of innovations in green manufacturing, re-establishing their competitive edge through green design and green production, and by reducing environmental pollution and resource consumption. In such a context, the government, the public and enterprises should all take green manufacturing as a significant direction of development in the next step.

2.2.3 Green manufacturing: the vane of economic change

Internationally, researches on green manufacturing can be traced back to the 1980s. In 1996, the American Society of Manufacturing Engineers published a blue book on green manufacturing. In 1998, it published an online theme report on the trend of green manufacturing on the Internet. Recently, developed countries and regions such as the US and Europe have poured significant capital, manpower and resources to the study of green manufacturing in both developed and developing countries, and green manufacturing has become a global concern. All countries and regions are moving in the new direction of green manufacturing. Research centres and research institutions specializing in green manufacturing have been established around the world, such as Consortium on Green Design and Manufacturing of University of California, Berkeley, Environmentally Benign Manufacturing of Massachusetts Institute of Technology, Sustainable Design and Manufacturing of Georgia Institute of Technology, Sustainable Futures Institute of Michigan Technological University, the Green Design Institute of Carnegie Mellon University, Yale University's School of Forestry & Environmental Studies' Centre for Industrial Ecology, Green Manufacturing Research Association of Michigan State University, Environmentally Conscious Design and Manufacturing Laboratory of University of Windsor, Canada, the Institute for Manufacturing at the University of Cambridge, the Centre for Sustainable Design in the UK, the Life Cycle Engineering Department at the University of Stuttgart, Germany, and the Centre for Design Practice Research of the Royal Melbourne Institute of Technology University,

Australia, etc. In China, there are many research institutes for green manufacturing and related issues in recent years, including Manufacturing Engineering Research Institute of Chongqing University, Zhizhuo Green Manufacturing R&D Centre of Tsinghua University, National Defense Key Laboratory for Remanufacturing Technology of China Academy of Armored Forced Engineering, Green Design and Manufacturing Engineering Institute of Hefei University of Technology, Institute of Biomedical Manufacturing of Shanghai Jiaotong University, and Research Centre for Sustainable Manufacturing of Shandong University, etc. As China's economic development enters the "New Normal", the turning point of China's industrial economy from high-speed growth to medium-high-speed growth has arrived. During this period, we should take full advantage of the "New Normal" and upgrade the quality and efficiency of manufacturing. Researches on green manufacturing in China and other countries has achieved rich theoretical fruits.

2.2.3.1 The theoretical basis for green manufacturing

The theoretical basis mainly includes theoretical models and methods. *The Green Manufacturing Blue Book* points out that the implementation of green manufacturing must undergo a long period of sustainable development, and its implementation process has several important characteristics. First, the leadership of the enterprise should support the development of green manufacturing. The top management of a company plays a major decision role in determining the direction and strategy of development, so the successful implementation of green manufacturing mainly depends on their decision. Second, there must be a strong implementation team, because the high-tech science and technology and professional policy are far from enough. They can play a guiding role in technology and in decision-making, but every worker, salesman and service staff take part in the real implementation process. Therefore, everyone must make efforts for the successful implementation of green manufacturing. In this case, every member of the team should stay consistent and focused, so that the team can work to the full extent under the guidance of clear team goals. We must let team members focus on solving specific problems, and provide them with the necessary help and training. The problem-solving procedure should go from discussion to implementation. Every member must adopt the consistent quantitative standards like how much waste should be discharged in the production process, and what recycling rate should be achieved in the recycling process. Third, a green manufacturing project must be selected after careful studies and investigation. In fact, every green manufacturing is a long-term process with multiple efforts, which explains that this is not based on any individual or any company. In this long-term process, all parties can accumulate experience and draw lessons, which is also conducive to the next step of development. Fourth, the establishment of corporate culture. Corporate culture can have a significant influence on the conception of every employee and the overall development trend of the enterprise. Therefore, the establishment of the conception of green manufacturing and relevant rewards and punishments system can effectively promote the development of green manufacturing.

According to a report by the Massachusetts Institute of Technology in the survey of more than 50 companies in the United States, Europe, and Japan, research and application of green manufacturing in these companies still have various deficiencies, and they need to make more efforts on environmental protection and resources saving. The report compares the green manufacturing status of the United States with other countries, pointing out that the level of development in the United States is not as good as in other countries. The report also proposes that green manufacturing lacks a common evaluation criteria, and due to the different characteristics of each manufacturing industry, it is difficult to make a unified industry plans.

Professor Bras of the Georgia Institute of Technology divides green manufacturing engineering into several stages: end treatment and environmental engineering, pollution prevention, environmentally conscious design and manufacturing, industrial ecology, and sustainable development. He points out that many factors drive the implementation of green design, including relevant laws and regulations, customers' green demand, green mark certification and ISO14000 certification, etc. He proposed that enterprises promote green manufacturing from two directions: the first direction is to innovate the original technologies and techniques, and the second direction is to establish a special organization to ensure the implementation of green manufacturing. Based on the analysis and researches of green-manufacturing theoretical models and methods, companies can better understand the meaning of green manufacturing and play a practical role in the later implementation of green manufacturing.

2.2.3.2 Practical foundation of green manufacturing

With the concept of green manufacturing continuing to develop, and with its related theories keeping improving, currently it appears critically important to put the theories of green manufacturing into practice. At present, either developed countries or developing countries all are vigorously marching along the respective road of the green manufacturing which emerges as a roughly similar path basically guided by policies, regulations and laws functioning as the road signs, such as the series standards of ISO (Environmental Management System) established in developed countries, EU's regulations of RoHS (Restriction of Hazardous Substance) and WEEE (Waste Electrical and Electronic Equipment), Germany's Blue Angel green product accreditation program, and the US's environmental certification of products like Energy Star. As a result of the severe shortage of water, soil and resources worldwide, China has highly valued green manufacturing as a major strategy to deal with the lack of resources and energy. Now under the global trend of green ideas, countries, governments, enterprises and many consumers focus on green themes. For example, governments have deployed green development strategies, enterprises have initiated green manufacturing plans, and consumers have developed green awareness, which has contributed a lot to the development of green manufacturing by forming the very set of top-down green ideas. The phenomenon shows that green ideas hold the key to green manufacturing. Products from green manufacturing will have no or little pollution for the ecological environment in terms of production process, production materials and the whole process of product consumption. They can be recycled, re-manufactured or reused even after being discarded. It can be seen that green products produced by green manufacturing are more suitable for people in today's society. With science and technology developing, and with the national policy green-oriented, green products will ultimately become the most popular leading products in the markets. Recent years have seen closer exchanges and cooperation between National Technical University of Ukraine and Zhejiang University of Technology, and numerous studies have been conducted. Many great achievements have been scored by taking advantage of laser processing technology which is of high efficiency, high quality and low consumption in green manufacturing. Through independent research and development, three series of laser-specific powder materials resistant to cavitation, high temperature, erosion and corrosion have been developed. In addition, they have also come up with the composite strengthening technique like supersonic laser deposition, electromagnetic synergy laser processing, laser combination additive manufacturing. Nowadays, scores of industrial ecological parks in the world are being planned or under construction, most of which are located in the US, Austria, Sweden, Holland, French, the UK and Japan, etc. Many overseas companies have applied green manufacturing to production.

SIEMENS AG (Germany) has been making efforts to improve material and machining process, producing lead-free and chlorine-free products, design environment-oriented products based on low cost, recycle and reuse scrapped electrical products, formulate formal environmental regulations required by the customers although there are no specific policies for implementing ISO14001, and conduct product life cycle assessment.

Toyota Corporation (Japan) has established green procurement specifications for its 450 suppliers, given top priority to painting process in processing, set a complete set of waste standards in order to continuously enhance the disposal of waste and garbage, and reduce waste in the production process.

Ford Motor Company (America) strives to reduce energy consumption in the production phase and manufacture cars by choosing lightweight material. Besides, a panel has been set up to study the life process of a car from design and production to sales and recycling, estimate the environmental pollution and energy consumption caused by production following the principles of green design, and include recycling in the thinking scope of the enterprise.

Hitachi Limited (Japan) has been working on lead-free soldering. It also has defined the recycling mode of the products, enabling the designers to take the recycling-related issues into account from the initial phase of the life process. Furthermore, a complete information sharing platform has been developed, too.

The practice field of green manufacturing in China has laid a good foundation for development. Since the reform and opening up, China's manufacturing industry has made astounding advances. Especially since 2010, China's manufacturing industry has ranked first in the world, and has entered the ranks of the world's manufacturing powers. In May 2015, China's State Council put forward *Made in China 2025* strategy to fasten its step in building a manufacturing power. Green manufacturing is inseparable from scientific and technological advances, and the rapid development of science and technology is impossible without the strong support from the government, including the in-depth exploration made by universities and research institutions. Up to now, China has been working on numerous key green projects. For example, China Academy of Machinery Science and Technology has completed such key projects of the 9th Five-year plan as the selection of clean technologies and the establishment of the database. After conducting comprehensive investigations on machinery industry which used to be a highly polluting industry, including the needs of green technology and the development trend of the green design in several industries, the research institute has eventually developed a technology system that highly integrates machinery industry with green design concept. At the same time, vehicle disassembly and recycling technology are being studied. At present, China is carrying out research on

"Environmental Green Technology Evaluation System" funded by the National Natural Science Foundation. The study of the whole system focuses on how to conduct green technology evaluation. The green technology evaluation system first established a green concept, then applied ETV (Environmental Technology Verification) evaluation technology to the examination of green design and green manufacturing, and in the end, a green ETV evaluation system was formed for machinery industry. Colleges and universities in China began to attach great importance to green innovation. For instance, Tsinghua University has created green projects. It has even built a bridge of friendship with American advanced manufacturing laboratories for long-term cooperation and research. And major breakthroughs have been made in the systematic study of green design theory and method. Shanghai Jiaotong University has long formed a partnership with Ford Motor Company (America) to cooperatively make a breakthrough in the recycling project of abandoned automobiles. It has also co-worked with China Materials Recycling East China Branch of the Ministry of Foreign Trade to compose a feasibility report on "probing into a one-stop management mode involving Chinese automobile sales, maintenance, second-hand car trading and recycling". Although faced with challenges and difficulties, other universities in China are all vigorously dedicated to the research of green manufacturing technology, including Central China University of Science and Engineering, Zhejiang University, and Beihang University, etc. On the whole, under the strategic deployment of the Chinese government, universities and research institutes have been involved actively in the construction of green development, and have formed professional teams of green manufacturing, which plays a pivotal role in the development of green manufacturing in China and even in the world.

2.3 The transformation of China's manufacturing industry from tradition to green

2.3.1 The transformation with Chinese characteristics from traditional manufacturing to green manufacturing

2.3.1.1 Transformation direction of China's manufacturing industry

In recent years, China's manufacturing industry has been growing at such a fast pace that it has gradually occupied a dominant position in the world and become a major manufacturing country. However, as a result of the dramatic change of the global ecological environment, the overall lack of resources and energy, and the ever-changing manufacturing pattern in the markets of the new era, manufacturing industry in China will have to focus on the overall situation, analyze the developing law of the manufacturing industry from all aspects, accurately grab the opportunities, and conform to the trend of the times. Nowadays, the traditional manufacturing industry must be transformed into green manufacturing, which is the general trend of the world. The driving force of this transformation lies in the development of green technology as well as the linkage among such links as green design, green production, and green consumption. China is facing numerous challenges and risks, but under such circumstances lie great potential opportunities of tapping into the leading green manufacturing industry. China embarks on its green transformation from the following aspects.

(1) *Economic creativity has been significantly promoted*

China's manufacturing industry has gradually taken the world's leading position since 2006 with its economic creativity significantly enhanced. In 2009, the added value of China's manufacturing industry reached RMB11,011.85 billion, surpassing the United States in one stroke and ranking first around the globe. In 2012, the added value of China's manufacturing industry was 1.26 times higher than that of the United States, remaining the first place in the world. From 2004 to 2011, the added value of China's manufacturing industry rose from RMB5,174.85 billion to RMB15,059.72 billion, with an average annual increase of 16.5 percent. And the proportion of manufacturing added value to industrial added value stabilized at 80 percent or so, and 32 percent[1] of the share of GDP. All records have amply demonstrated that China's manufacturing industry plays a vital role in the process of China's rapid economic development.

(2) *The scientific and technological innovative ability has been remarkably improved*

China's manufacturing industry could have never led the world without the Chinese government's investment in manufacturing-related scientific and technological innovations. In recent years, China has increased its investment in scientific research and technological innovations. The investment ratio in 2012 is roughly three times of that in 2003. From 2003 to 2012, the R&D investment and input personnel of the manufacturing industry have an average annual increase of 3.76 percent and 14.59 percent respectively. It is precisely because the state has an important strategic plan for

---

[1] Liu Jun, Cheng Zhonghua, Li Lianshui, "Development of China's Manufacturing Industry: Current Situation, Dilemma and Trend", *Yuejiang Academic Journal*, 2015(4), p.17.

the role of scientific and technological progress in the manufacturing industry and increases the investment ratio that the innovation ability of the manufacturing industry in China has been greatly enhanced. The number of patents granted by China according to international patent standards in 2003 is 106,060, and reached 788,280 in 2012, with an average annual increase of 24.97 percent. And the number of tripartite patents granted by China rose sharply from 1,458.7 in 2003 to 18,573.3 in 2012, with an average annual increase of 32.66 percent. [1] Thanks to the high-speed advancement of science and technology, and the substantial improvement of innovation ability, China has occupied a place among numerous innovative powers.

(3) *Energy saving capability has been enhanced*

The value added to China's manufacturing industry enjoys a rapid rise. However, the consumption of energy also soars at high speed. Energy consumption is chiefly reflected in the use of coal. And coal consumption has been going up all the way. Moreover, the consumption of electricity has also multiplied. The dependence on and excessive use of such non-renewable resources have promoted the development of the manufacturing industry but also given rise to resource depletion and environmental pollution. However, in recent years, the situation has been gradually improving. Judging from the data analyses of the past decade, while the energy consumption of China's manufacturing industry keeps increasing, the energy consumption per unit output value is continuously decreasing, which indicates that China has attached greater importance to the greening of manufacturing, improving utilization efficiency by reducing reliance on energy and cutting down on energy consumption.

(4) *The ability to protect the environment keeps improving*

The fast development of manufacturing industry has also brought about an increase in waste pollution discharge. Taking air pollution as an example, sulfur dioxide is the most polluting gas which has the greatest impact on the atmosphere in the manufacturing industry. Although the emissions of sulfur dioxide tend to increase with the rapid growth of the manufacturing added value, it can be seen from the decreasing trend of sulfur dioxide or other pollutant emissions per unit output value that China has been devoted to the transformation of the traditional manufacturing industry to green manufacturing industry, continuously reducing the pollution caused by the manufacturing industry to the environment.

---

[1] Liu Jun, Cheng Zhonghua, Li Lianshui, "Development of China's Manufacturing Industry: Current Situation, Dilemma and Trend", *Yuejiang Academic Journal*, 2015(4), p.20.

2.3.1.2   Distinctive Chinese characteristics reflected in the transformation of China's manufacturing industry

Made in China 2025 satisfies China's urgent need to adapt to international competition. We can say with pride that China owns the largest scale of manufacturing industry in the world. Among 500 main industrial varieties, 220 of China's products rank first in the world. However, the large scale never equates with a superpower. Chinese Premier Li Keqiang points out in an article published in *Qiushi*[1] that China has a lot to learn in its push for higher-leveled manufacturing—not only should we makeup lessons in remodeling and optimizing the traditional practice, but also in green manufacturing and intelligent updating, accelerating the application of intelligent technology and equipment such as 3D printing, high-end CNC machine tools, and industrial robots, etc. Moreover, the key to the implementation of Made in China lies in the development of intelligent manufacturing and the transformation of the manufacturing industry led by science and technology. In conclusion, the manufacturing industry is not only an important driving force to promote Chinese economic growth and social development, but also a trump card to ensure China a certain share in the global market. The following parts illustrate the way China shifts its traditional manufacturing industry into Green practice with distinctive Chinese characteristics.

(1) *Changing from factor-driven strategy to innovation-driven strategy*

Since the 18th National Congress of the CPC, the Party has proposed building a moderately prosperous society in an all-round way. The National 12th Five-year Plan for the Development of Science and Technology takes innovation-driven development as the fundamental task and emphasizes that the road of independent innovation with Chinese characteristics and the implementation of innovation-driven development strategy are important means for building a moderately prosperous society in an all-round way. China has long been the number one super manufacturing power in the world. However, the technological content is low, and innovation ability is insufficient. Especially with the advancement of science and technology, the instability of the global economy may contribute easily to the changes in the pattern of the manufacturing industry. Therefore, China no longer has a large number of the low-cost labor force as it used to，and the situation of high resource consumption and serious environmental damage has never been improved qualitatively. It can be seen that China's manufacturing industry, large but not strong, needs to adapt to the times, transforming the traditional

---

[1] Qiushi Journal is an official publication of the Central Committee of the Communist Party of China. —*Tr.*

factor-driven pattern and gradually turning to innovation-driven one. The future development of the manufacturing industry will depend largely on the progress of science and technology, so we must come up with a new path of technological innovation with Chinese characteristics in a short time.

(2) *Changing from extensive manufacturing to sustainable manufacturing*

The current production mode of China's manufacturing industry presents an extensive way—energy consumption and environmental pollution upsurge with increased production. Although the unit energy consumption and pollution amount have been decreasing gradually, there are no substantial changes, which has had a severe negative impact on our living environment and the quality of life. To fulfill the restrictive indicators of the 13th Five-year Plan, the manufacturing industry is required to transform the traditional production mode from extensive manufacturing with high energy consumption and high pollution emissions to a brand-new green production mode of high energy efficiency and low pollution emissions. It is sustainable manufacturing that meets this requirement of integrating advanced green technology, green design concept and green process into the manufacturing industry, which puts the whole manufacturing industry chain in the optimum structure of low energy consumption, low pollution, as well as high quality and high efficiency, thereby making our manufacturing industry really bigger and stronger.

(3) *Changing from low-end manufacturing to high-end manufacturing*

In the context of the information age, we are witnessing a new generation of the industrial revolution—a digital revolution which makes a difference to the entire value chain. The development of high-tech manufacturing industries like information technology, the Internet of things, intelligent technology, and biomaterials will inevitably reshape the conventional industry, forming an industry mode adapting to new technologies. At the moment, China has implemented the development plan of *Made in China 2025* launching high-end manufacturing industry. The manufacturing industry in China must seize the opportunities of science and technology so as to make vigorous efforts to reverse the situation through the high-end technological commanding point of strategic manufacturing industry.

(4) *Green manufacturing and standard leading*

In September, 2016, the Ministry of Industry and Information Technology and the National Standards Committee jointly issued the "Guidelines for the Construction of the Green Manufacturing Standard System" (hereinafter referred to as the Guidelines), which has defined the green manufacturing standard system including seven parts: comprehensive foundations, green products, green factories, green enterprises, green parks, green supply chain, green evaluation and service. The Guidelines also clarifies the key areas of green manufacturing in various industries, and the list of recommendations on key standards, pointing out the direction for the continuous development and improvement of green manufacturing standard system.

2.3.2   The Chinese mode: from traditional manufacturing to green manufacturing

2.3.2.1   Pioneer cities like Hangzhou and Lianyungang implemented the incentive policies of technology research and development

As the trend of green manufacturing sweeps the world, China would no longer wait for chances to come but work to realize green and sustainable manufacturing with low carbon emission by accelerating the manufacturing industry revolution under the guidance of scientific and technological advance. To achieve green manufacturing, products should be designed, produced and packed in green ways with low energy consumption. Besides, problems emerging within the life circle of products and the way of recycling after the end of use should also be taken into full consideration. *Made in China 2025* has put stress on the green transformation of the traditional manufacturing industry, especially the basic manufacturing industry—to shape a green manufacturing industrial process system with low energy consumption, low pollution as well as recycling and re-manufacturing by more R&D investment and innovation of green science and technology.

Hangzhou, the capital city of Zhejiang Province in the southeast of China, as a pioneer, having invested plenty of human resources and material resources in the research and development of green science and technology, pursues a road of green manufacturing in its unique way. In the "Guiding Opinions on Boosting Intelligent Manufacturing in Hangzhou to Promote Industrial Transformation and Development", it points out that the traditional industry of high energy consumption and high pollution is no longer suitable for the current development of the manufacturing industry. That means that it is essential to make a great contribution to green technology which is of effectiveness in energy consumption and low pollution emissions to accelerate the green transformation. Now Jiangsu Province specializes in environmental protection techniques, such as intelligent sorting of waste, intelligent dust removal, air pollution prevention and sewage treatment. However, the research and development of technology must closely rely on their R&D centers and other research institutions and fully mobilize all forces to actively participate in the research and development of green technology. Lianyungang, a city of Jiangsu Province in southeast China, have been pushing for its green transformation from a traditional mode with its distinctive characteristics. It united military enterprises with civil corporations to advance civilian technology by giving full play to the technological advantages of military enterprise and promoted the comprehensive development of military-civilian integrated industries.

2.3.2.2 Pioneer cities like Wuxi, Chengdu and Tianjin implemented the incentive policies of technological transformation

Since most corporations in China encounter a bottleneck of Green technology innovation research and development due to the lack of independent innovation ability, therefore, the incentive policies of technological transformation serving as a measurable stimulus bring out the green transformation of manufacturing in original enterprises. The technological transformation of green manufacturing mainly aims at replacing the tradition high energy consumption, high-polluted, high-carbon, non-recycling mode with low energy consumption, clean, low-carbon, recyclable re-manufacturing.

In 2015, Wuxi, a city of Jiangsu Province, conducted in-depth investigation and research on the five major local industries including central air conditioning, industrial kilns, residual heat and pressure, green lighting and electrical machinery. It mainly aims to figure out the potential of these five industries in green transformation, and finally established a key contract with these energy management projects to cut down cost by reducing energy consumption and ultimately promote enterprises to realize green manufacturing.

The government of Chengdu (the capital city of Sichuan Province in the southwest of China) has registered remarkable achievements in its regional green transformation of manufacturing industry by providing financial support to accelerate green technical transformation in enterprises. Moreover, the government launched Chengdu Industry "1313" Development Strategy[1] and prominently listed pioneer fronts worth of propelling

---

[1] Chengdu Industry "1313" Development Strategy aims to establish one modern industrial system clear hierarchy, prominent advantages and high ecological efficiency, and classify three development levels so as to optimize manufacturing structure and promote development in purpose. And thirteen key industries feature prominently on the priority list including Electronic Information, Rail Transit, Automobile, Petrochemical, Aero-space, Biomedicine, New Energy, New Materials, Energy Conservation and Environmental Protection, Metallurgy, Food, Building Materials and Light Industry. —*Tr.*

in the future including electronic information, rail transit, automotive and other industries. Meanwhile, other areas like aerospace, biological pharmaceuticals, new energy, new materials, energy conservation and environmental protection industries also enjoy its accelerating development under the financial support from the government and form a sense of Green Manufacturing—bringing about a manufacturing with high efficiency and low pollution emissions by speeding up the improvement of traditional manufacturing technology.

Through the pilot and demonstration of key enterprises and key areas, Tianjin (a municipality in the north of China) is gradually promoting technological transformation. First of all, Tianjin has carried out the green technological transformation in the basic manufacturing industry—established benchmarking enterprises for green manufacturing by investing industries in developing green ideas, including foundry, forging, welding and heat treatment industries. In addition, it started to popularize green technology vigorously, and gradually formed a chain-like, then a network-like manufacturing system green of low-energy consumption, low-pollution. The government also actively develop the re-manufacturing industry, focusing on automotive parts, construction machinery, machine tools, large-scale industrial equipment, electrical machinery, and other products and key components, and set up a number of re-manufacturing demonstration projects and demonstration bases to promote the large-scale development of the re-manufacturing industry.

2.3.2.3   Pioneer provinces like Jiangsu Province and Yunnan Province implemented the incentive policies of construction of green manufacturing system

In the light of *Made in China 2025*, constructing a green manufacturing system of "4+2" model plays a critical role in promoting green manufacturing in an all-round way. The figure "4" refers to producing green products, establishing green factories, constructing green industrial parks and building green supply chain; the figure "2" stands for expanding green enterprises in scale and number and reinforcing law enforcement and supervision on those enterprises. Jiangsu Province and Yunnan Province do well in these aspects and set other provinces good examples.

To promote the construction of green manufacturing system, Jiangsu Province started with key industries to step up the implementation of green technology which ultimately forms demonstration projects. In this regard, re-manufacturing, set as a good example, encourages other industries to recycle and reuse waste products, which will not only cut down the cost but also deplete the waste of energy and resources.

Moreover, the government of Jiangsu Province imposes a green tax, a preferential tax on green manufacturing corporations, to encourage more enterprises to conduct a green transformation. Besides, the prices of various resources started to be divided as another means of incentives.

Chapter 3
The Core and Basic Elements of Green Manufacturing System

3.1 Design ideas: the core of the green manufacturing

3.1.1 Green ideas in product design

The increasingly fierce and sharp conflicts between man and nature emerging draw humankind's reflection on their own behavior. Fortunately, a new idea, serving as a new guideline, conceived by design field has triggered a great revolution on manufacturing. Foreign scholars having a long head make a strong case for that unless we appropriately deal with the ecological reality the humankind's civilization will continue to thrive. After that, the green design comes to the concern of people's lives. That means the human beings begin to embark on research and development of technology to advance green designing to deal with the destruction of the natural environment caused by human production. And the new mode of manufacturing reshaped by green design will not shift the basic social structure but do realize increasing production while reducing energy consumption and pollution emissions. To that extent, green ecological technology has gradually become a major research field in major countries, mostly focusing on energy saving and pollution reduction. However, green products and green technology we have been striving for since the 1990s are gradually be eliminated by the modern market which is consistently complex and volatile simply, because they no longer meet the needs of economic development. Since we are aware that the traditional manufacturing mode and its so-called green products are too ideal to advance with times, we determine to make a difference and adapt to the development of the global market. What we need is a comprehensive and dynamic green manufacturing mode designed to closely interrelate various factors, like social development, cultural differences, and environmental change, etc., which effectively help human to conciliate conflicts between man, society, and nature. In order to achieve the goal, people change the traditional ecological technology and the way we think ethically, socially, economically and politically. After analyzing global ecological problems, technical and ethical issues with a philosophical perspective, we strive to integrate human, society and nature as a whole, and form a three-dimensional composite ecological structure system. In this manufacturing process, designers are required to be far-sighted to bring out green designs especially by overcoming complexity and volatility of the current market.

3.1.2 The basic ideas of green design

Green design has never stopped but improved with the times instead and has been growing and changing all the time. People remain disparate over the theoretical exploration and practical application of the green design in each period, however, the content of green design has constantly been enriching, but its fundamental purpose has never changed—aimed at achieving the harmony and unity of human, society, and nature. Its basic ideas are as follows: first, the traditional design mainly aims at economic benefits, while the green design puts the benefit of the ecological environment in the first place, emphasizing the ecological benefits as the core. So the attention in the redesign should finally focus on the ecological benefits, and make full use of the advanced technology to realize the green design; second, when it comes to redesign, all factors in the whole product chain, mainly including how to cut down energy consumption, reduce discharge of waste and save resources, are required to be given full consideration so as to make up the defect of being incapable of realizing energy saving and emission reduction in traditional design; third, the green design also requires full consideration of the interaction not only between human beings, society, and nature but also between human survival and nature development. The 3R principle, once a leading green manufacturing idea, focuses on reduction, reuse, and recycling. The 3R principle requires that green production and high energy efficiency should be taken into consideration at the beginning of production. Besides, parts of products can be recycled and re-manufactured after out of work. As for the rest parts that cannot be reused and cannot bring economic value will adopt harmless methods to dispose. Since the 3R principle already had conformed to the basic requirements of green manufacturing at that time, it was totally accepted and absorbed in green manufacturing.

Green design under the guidance of 3R principle first emphasizes the energy consumption and pollution of waste in the production process which should be dealt with as the primary problem in the design process. Secondly, the green design puts stress on that the whole ecological design is based on advanced science and technology. Therefore, it is necessary to find new energy, materials and scientific production mode by taking advantage of the innovation of science and technology. Finally, pushing for green science and technology is not the ultimate goal of the 3R principle. It remains committed to using science and high-tech technology to solve ecological problems, and ultimately achieve green production and improve the living environment of humanity. Therefore, in the design stage, we should consider all the objectives to be achieved throughout the products' life cycle, including function optimization, quality assurance, more ecological benefits, and reasonable economic benefits. Besides, we even need to take factors like green waste treatment, recycling and re-manufacturing into careful consideration.

The connotation of green design has been constantly enriched and developed so far. Nowadays, it has completely shifted the traditional design concept irrespective of ecological environment matters. Now it pays more attention to the harmonious development of human and nature, human survival, and sustainable development. To grasp the new relationship, factors as follows need to be integrated, advanced and improved: functional attributes, material and technical attributes, economic attributes, artistic attributes, environmental attributes, and ethical attributes. These attributes have developed new connotations on our previous principles and concepts. And a set of three-dimensional structure system with distinct levels has been formed among the attributes, all of which serve the sound development of ecology. Therefore, green design not only represents the integration of ecology and designing but also is regarded as a practical form which can save energy efficiently and recycle. The most important thing is that it represents the consideration of human beings on the environment and social responsibility from the perspective of globalization.

3.2 Basic elements of green manufacturing system

3.2.1 Green design in products

The core of manufacturing is a product, as the core of products lies in design. Product design exists to plan and manage the design process of every part involved in the life circle of products, including product attributes, the production process of various indicators and after-sales issues at the very beginning of the massive production process, which plays a vital role in manufacturing. The various factors should be taken into full and careful consideration while designing. Even small design negligence in the design process will be at a huge cost to make up for the design defects in the production process. On the contrary, if every factor can be fully considered in the design process, the superiority of the product will stand out in the competitive market. Therefore, every enterprise pays great attention to product design and believes that a creative pursuit of perfect and delicate product design will be conducive to capture the market share as a decisive strategy.

However, at present, most product designs only focuses on the level of function and performance, but neglect to integrate the comprehensive characteristics, such as technological, economic and environmental matters emerging in the whole product life cycle. Therefore, green ideas prevail in products throughout the whole life circle unless we incorporate green ideas into products from the design stage. And the main content of the design framework represents as follows.

3.2.1.1 Environment-oriented product design

(1) *Environment-oriented product scheme design*

Product scheme design mainly integrates the selection and design of the product in every part, including principles, methods, overall layout, product types, and other aspects. In the case of ensuring basic conditions such as product function and quality, the environment- oriented product scheme design exists to select or design an optimized product scheme to maximize resource utilization rate and minimize environmental pollution during its manufacturing process. The environmental impact of the product and its manufacturing process are primarily determined by the difference of the product scheme and the quality of the product scheme design. For example, Freon refrigerators and non-fluorine refrigerators will cause different environmental pollution, especially during use.

(2) *Environment-oriented product structure design*

In order to reduce the consumption and waste of resources and the destruction of the environment, environment- oriented product structure design aims to improve and adopt a more reasonable and optimized structure consistently. There are many ways and measures in this regard, such as simplifying the product structure by adopting multifunctional and comprehensive parts which also includes simple connection methods so as to reduce the number of parts of the overall device; optimizing the layout of components in order to constantly change and adapt the relationship among components and the size of the relevant dimensions, so that the overall product which results in the size, volume and weight of the components is relatively reduced; improving the stress state of the components so as to reduce the resource loss caused by the failure of the components.

(3) *Environment-oriented product material selection*

Improper product materials may cause great environmental pollution. Therefore, the selection of environment-oriented product materials requires to cover every part involved in the whole materials' life circle, including material preparation, processing, use, and scrap disposal. For instance, disposable paper cups boast them environmentally friendly simply because they seem to be easier to be recycled compared with polystyrene cups. And we all generally prefer the paper cups and consider the material of their greener. Although the paper cup product itself is proved to be green, the paper production process has a great impact on resources and the environment. So before we draw a conclusion that disposable paper cups and polystyrene cups which works green to the environment, we still need a more careful and comprehensive analysis. Unfortunately, due to the complexity, we still haven't summed up a reliable analysis to assist in selecting materials which are more eco-friendly. To sum up, it is necessary to consider the relevant factors from all aspects and multi-angles in order to select the best product materials.

3.2.1.2 Design and upgrading of environment-oriented manufacturing environment

Manufacturing environment refers to factories, workshops, and manufacturing units in the manufacturing process. Factors like composition and layout of equipment and facilities in the manufacturing environment, in fact, potentially put an impact on energy consumption, working environment and eco-environment. And we have many cases to prove the point. A high energy consumption machine not only triggers energy waste but also takes a toll on the environment. Besides, the unreasonable layout of equipment or production line may hinder the optimization of production as a result of a waste of resources. Furthermore, the adverse environment in the workshop directly affects production as well as employees' mental and physical health, which may include both trigger accidents. Consequently, the environment-oriented manufacturing environmental design or upgrading exists to create a sound manufacturing environment in accordance with the requirements of production. However, to achieve the goal from this aspect entails us to consider both technologically and managerially.

3.2.1.3 Environment-oriented process design

Environment-oriented process design also refers to green process planning. Process planning is an optimized selection and plan design of manufacturing methods and process. It includes two aspects: optimization of process plan and optimization of process parameters. The optimization of process plan aims to pick the best plan among all available process plans, while the optimization of process parameter promises to select the most optimized process parameters based on process requirements and standards to improve the production process, such as optimization of cutting parameters in cutting engineering. Extensive research and practice have demonstrated that decision on different process designs will ultimately cause the distinctive affection on energy and resources consumption, as well as environment either. In conclusion, green process design, upgraded planning for the better production process and production line, aims to optimize the manufacturing process into an energy-saving and green way while also embracing products' economic and social benefits. Therefore, to achieve a more environmentally friendly goal during design plan optimizing, it entails considering the following factors. First, focus on energy consumption especially consumption of raw materials and auxiliary materials. Second, pay more attention to pollution emissions in the ecologic environment and vocational safety in the working environment. Upgraded and developed from the traditional process planning, the process planning for green manufacturing inherits merits from the traditional practice instead of totally repudiate it，aimed at, as an auxiliary means, making the manufacturing process greener.

3.2.1.4 Environment-oriented product packaging design

Environment-oriented product packaging design aims to optimize product packaging from the perspective of environmental protection to minimize resources consumption and waste. There are many approaches and measures in this regard we could do to achieve the goal. For instance, adopting a recyclable packaging or packaging materials which can be used repeatedly; minimizing the environmental pollution caused by packaging waste by adopting recyclable and renewable materials; reducing the waste of packaging materials as many as possible through improving the packaging scheme and structure.

3.2.1.5 Environment-oriented product recovery design

As a systematic engineering issue, environment-oriented product recovery entails taking the efficiency of recycling into consideration since the beginning of the product design. That will mean it is essential to pay more attention to the disassembly and reuse of parts and components, the recyclability of product materials, the degradability, and disposability of raw materials and replace incineration disposal or landfill disposal as much as possible.

3.2.2   Green manufacturing process

China's manufacturing industry has long been in the top position in the world. However, A major feature of China's manufacturing industry is large but not strong. Although China enjoys the rapid development of manufacturing industry, it is also suffering from severe scarcity of resources and energy and ecological environment deterioration. And these problems especially emerge more prominent and urgent in the basic manufacturing industry, mainly due to the close relationship between the basic manufacturing industry and other various industries, which has a great impact on the ecological environment. Hence it is required that the selection of raw materials and the design of manufacturing equipment must be eco-friendly. Following the current world trend of environmental protection, Chinese government should give top strategic priority to the greening of manufacturing industry.

Since the long-term development of the domestic machinery manufacturing industry has not considered the impact on the environment, it has caused enormous pollution and waste to the ecological environment, resources and energy while enjoying its rapid development. Therefore, the green transformation of traditional manufacturing holds the key to shift the current situation of high-energy-consuming and high-polluting. That means new manufacturing mode will integrate green ideas from each stage by fully considering the whole life circle of products to minimize waste and pollution caused by manufacturing and raising products recycling rate after the end of use.

3.2.2.1   Machinery manufacturing mode

Nowadays, China's manufacturing remains divided into two parts namely traditional manufacturing mode and green manufacturing mode.

(1) *Traditional manufacturing mode*

In the machinery manufacturing industry, the open-loop production system is adopted as a traditional manufacturing mode which, in fact, abusively takes advantages of natural resources under an extensive management mode. And its production life circle is shown in Figure 3-1.

Research indicates that traditional manufacturing mode is a producing way which unreasonably and abusively extracts resources we need from nature without considering natural endurance and ignoring environmental protection, in consequence, bringing out large quantities of waste and emissions of polluting gases and liquids, which has been severer more than ever. Besides, the traditional manufacturing mode requires plenty of simple labor which means a large number of labors are needed. One of the main factors that traditional manufacturing mode takes a toll on the ecological environment is that it neglects pollution caused during the use stage of products, like noise, waste gas, and wastewater. Furthermore, it never pays attention to products recycling. That means a product will be directly eliminated merely because one of its parts doesn't work anymore, which results in a huge waste of resources.

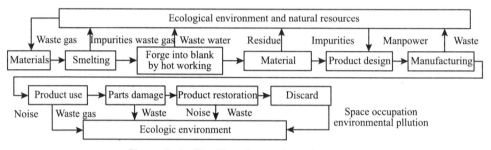

Figure 3-1　Traditional manufacturing mode

(2) *The green manufacturing mode*

As an optimized production mode, the green manufacturing mode manages to control the whole process since the beginning. It promises to bring out product-process of low energy consumption, low pollution and high efficiency and manufacturing mode under the guidance of environmental protection and waste recycling (see Figure 3-2). In conclusion, to realize green manufacturing mode depends on the development of green technology and complete production process which entails paying more attention to the selection of raw materials, clean producing and recycling. That will mean the green manufacturing mode is designed to fix all the unreasonable parts in the manufacturing process.

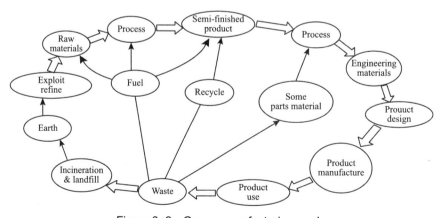

Figure 3-2　Green manufacturing mode

3.2.2.2   The main part of the green manufacturing mode

(1) *Selection of materials and green materials*

We used to pay less attention to what we had done, which posed a negative impact on nature like contaminating and energy wasting when producing for a long time. Notably, the selection of green raw materials has never been valued resulted in taking a toll on the environment and consumers' physical condition due to the selection of some high-polluted materials. That is how we can tell that the selection of materials plays a critical role in the basic parts of the whole process chain and realizing green manufacturing.

Faced with these problems, we generally use green materials which not only meet the functional needs of products but also do no harm to the ecological environment due to its pollution-free and recyclable nature, so as to reduce the pressure on the environment and alleviate environmental degradation, and enhance people's awareness of environmental protection, at the same time, Figure 3–3 shows the aspects that should be considered when selecting industrial materials.

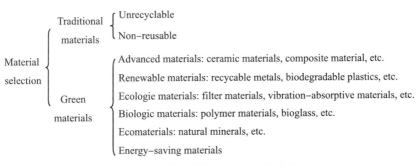

Figure 3–3   Selection of materials

(2) *Product design and green design model*

Traditional design ideas only focus on factors of gaining market profits like how to raising production efficiency and improve production function while ignoring factors related to environmental protection, such as energy consumption, pollution and material recycling. On the contrary, considering more about the continuation of human civilization, the green design model exists to takes more responsibilities of environmental protection while assuring products quality and function. What's the most important in green design model is to focus on the product life cycle, and achieve the goal from aspects like the choice of green materials, clean production, low energy consumption, low pollution, and recyclability. In other words, factors as follow, at least, should be taken into consideration of green design model.

(i) Product simplification. In the process of product design, we should pay attention to practicability and cut off unnecessary decoration as much as possible. This not only saves time and resources of materials, but also reduces the pollution to the ecological environment, and even helps to simplify the management over production.

(ii) Processing. Green technology and methods and low-polluted raw materials should be adopted in processing to minimize the impact on the ecological environment, cut off resources waste, and overcome tough problems of unrecoverable parts lists on the prominent place in the processing stage.

(iii) Disassembly of products. Product designers allow for the recyclability in the first place, promising to bring out products with structures easy to recover. Arguably, the disassembly of products holds the key to recyclability in this regard. That means the nature of disassembly helps to reduce unnecessary waste by replacing damaged parts once there are problems with products instead of eliminating the whole products. Consequently, we are sure that the nature of disassembly also plays a critical role in green manufacturing.

(iv) Recycling. Every decision made by product designers takes full account of material selection and recovery benefits to ensure that products can be recycled, processed and re-manufactured after ends its life cycle, and even forming new products. That is how we cut down considerable energy waste and pollution emissions. The recycling of general waste products can be divided into several levels, as shown in Figure 3–4.

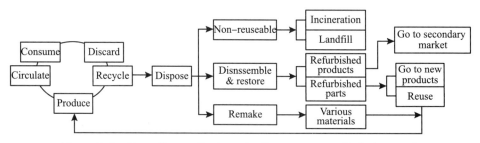

Figure 3–4   Recycling methods under the green manufacturing mode

(v) Easy to transport. Under the condition of guaranteeing its function integrity and even without increasing cost, products should also consider the safety issues in the delivery to the market, mainly because of the inevitable improper transportation, which can directly lead to damage and scrap.

(3) *Manufacturing process and green manufacturing model*

China's manufacturing industry for now, still cannot make good use of advanced green science and technology, resulting in the traditional rough production at the cost of resources consumption. And the manufacturing industry has not been fully automated so far, which leads to a large number of resources and energy consumption and products of non-standardized quality. And higher reject rate will also trigger many environmental pollution problems.

In the 21st century and even in the future, humanity will inevitably encounter ecological environment problems. Conservation of ecology will become the world's theme. Manufacturing industry should actively adapt to the characteristics of the times and take low energy consumption, low carbon and low pollution as the basic task of green manufacturing. China will remain committed to the green manufacturing down the road and stay focus on the green ideas—lowering energy consumption, carbon, and pollution in production, while extending product life cycle as far as possible and reduce pollution during the product use. Details are shown in Figure 3–5.

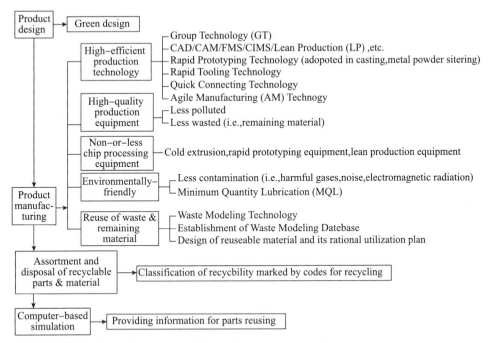

Figure 3–5   Contents and hierarchical structure of green manufacturing

(4) *Management and green management mode*

Green management plays a critical role in the construction of ecological civilization in China, directly affecting the harmonious and unified development of economy and environment. Not only has the Chinese government established the legal system concerning the protection of the ecological environment but also remained committed to constantly enriching its content and developing its connotation. The establishment of the legal system holds the key to precaution and prevent, which legally control the enterprise's waste discharge. Existing ISO14000 series of environmental management system standards are also aimed at improving the level of green management to raise economic efficiency and reduce environmental pollution.

At present, enterprises have also launched a series of environmental protection measures according to their realities. As shown in Figure 3–6, Plan-Do-Check-Action is one of the environmental management modes. It is to be continued to improve according to the implementation results of environmental protection measures in enterprises.

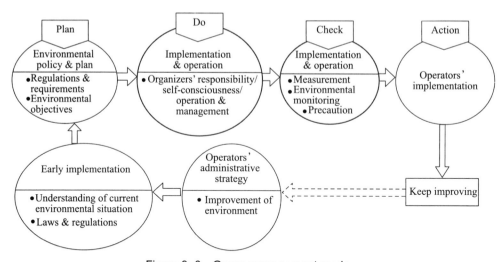

Figure 3–6　Green management mode

The global shortage of resources and energy has emerged as a prominent problem. China, however, suffers worse hardship of insufficient resources and serious ecological damage. The transformation of manufacturing from traditional production practice to green production one will serve as an important measure to ameliorate the grim situation. Therefore, we must seize opportunities and apply advanced science and technology to production to promote the green transformation of production mode and ecological civilization construction.

3.2.3 Green supply chain

3.2.3.1 The connotation of green supply chain

Since the 1990s, the green supply chain has become the concern of governments and scholars all over the world and has attracted the attention of all walks of people. However, the green supply chain remains an emerging product with the connotation of initial development. Bearing disparity of culture, society and other factors, different green supply focuses on different parts. Nourished by green ideas, green supply chain exists to reconcile the conflicts between the ecological environment and economic development and bring out an available management mode by systematizing production circle. Compared with traditional supply chain, the green supply chain, based on and developed from the traditional one, stands out for its more scientific management, more advanced technology, making full use of the various stages of production to achieve coordinated economic and environmental development, and thus ultimately achieve the main purpose of the win-win outcome of both economic and environmental benefits. Not only does the supply chain cover the environmental management of products in a different period of life circle, but also pay attention to the enterprises' entity in the green industry and products recycling after the end of use, even including consumers' selections, products use and other aspects. It manages to promote the vigorous development of green manufacturing through gaining green competitiveness and pursues the integration of all links in the supply chain, that is, to realize energy conservation and emission reduction, and to achieve great economic benefits. Therefore, we believe that green supply chain is designed to embed the green ideas into every part of the products life cycle, including design, material selection, production, sales, consumers, and recycling. It will comprehensively consider the ecological environment and economic benefits during each period. Ultimately it aims to achieve the coordinated and optimized benefits in ecological, social and economic fronts by adopting a modern management mode connecting enterprises, departments, and consumers as a whole.

3.2.3.2 The main contents of green supply chain

Green supply chain basically includes every part of traditional one, but upgrade traditional contents into green ones, mainly like green procurement, green manufacturing, green sales, green consumption, green recycling, and green logistics.

(1) *Green procurement*

The primary task of green production is to select and purchase materials for manufacturing, which should be ecologically friendly. That is to say, materials in the production process must ensure not only the integrity of product functions but also bear the nature of low pollution and recyclability.

(2) *Green manufacturing*

A general strategic plan, namely a green design, figures prominently in the whole process of green manufacturing, extensively guiding every part in green production including energy-saving, disassembly, recyclability and other aspects of products. Besides, it also entails managing the process of green manufacturing and its technology. Therefore, to bring out green manufacturing, it requires to reduce the emission of pollutants as much as possible, including contaminated liquids, gases, solids, and even noise.

(3) *Green sales*

Green sales bridge the gap between enterprises and customers. Green products not only remind consumers of awareness of environmental protection while meeting their needs but also entail enterprises to improve green products' quality and function to gain more economic profits.

(4) *Green consumption*

Customers are encouraged to establish an awareness of green that means green products are preferably selected by consumers and properly treated after the end of use in case of damaging the environment.

(5) *Green recycling*

It realizes recycling and remanufacturing after the end of use to prolong the rest value.

(6) *Green logistics*

Logistics industry has become a universal and huge industry in China. However, as an emerging industry, there are many problems, especially in environmental protection. Therefore, green logistics requires making full use of resources in the logistics process, forming an efficient logistics structure and reducing environmental pollution.

3.2.3.3 Analysis of the current situation of green supply chain

The international trend has shown that many foreign enterprises have embarked on research and implementation of green supply chain at present. In fact, the green supply chain management model has been wildly used in the auto industry. General Motors, for instance, is considered to be a successful role model in this regard. Over time, China has shown the exclusive solicitude for the economic benefit resulting in limited awareness and understanding of green supply chain. Thus green ideas haven't been entrenched in the nation, from the government to enterprises and consumers, as a consequence of sluggish development in the green supply chain compared with the rest of the world. Recently, "non-green" problems are prominently getting the way of the development of the supply chain in China. Some major food businesses including KFC (Kentucky Fried Chicken) were reported to have added Sudan I[1] in food in 2005. Moreover, in 2008, Sanlu Group Co., Ltd. was accused of contaminating infant formula milk with exceeded content of melamine directly resulting in malformation of infants. All sensational cases have posed dramatic effects on society and directly aroused consumers' concerns about green products and the rethinking of the supply chain. It's reported that in July 2005, seriously-excessive aluminum was detected in the puffed food produced by Shanghai Huayuan Food Co., Ltd. due to the negligence in material selection in the green supply chain. Similar problems remain in the textile industry in China—most corporations in this industry haven't applied for ecological textile certification simply because they generally ignore the environmentally-friendly nature of materials when they select raw materials. All these examples have demonstrated that China is still lack of awareness of eco-environmental protection. Hence the whole nation should be cultivated with green ideas of far-reaching meaning. As China has joined the WTO, more severe challenges of being standardized and qualified are emerging with more chances to conduct transactions with developed countries, while western critics have questioned the quality of green products made in China. Recent years have seen that some far-sighted manufacturers in China have embarked on setting up a management model of the green supply chain based on their realities, aiming to break the barriers of green products export. Generally speaking, China is still weak in awareness of environmental protection，and cannot accurately grasp the development of a green supply chain. However, it has put forwards the Construction of Ecological Civilization and pushed for the construction. It's believed that the construction will cultivate the nation with ideas of

---

[1] Sudan I (also known as CI Solvent Yellow 14 and Solvent Orange R), is an organic compound, typically classified as an azo dye. It is an intensely orange-red solid that is added to the coloring of waxes, oils, petrol, solvents, and polishes. Sudan I has also been adopted for colouring various foodstuffs, especially curry powder and chili powder, although the use of Sudan I in foods is now banned in many countries, because Sudan I , Sudan III and Sudan IV have been classified as category 3 carcinogens (not classifiable as to its carcinogenicity to humans) by the International Agency for Research on Cancer. Sudan I is still used in some orange-coloured smoke formulations and as a colouring for cotton refuse used in chemistry experiments. —*Tr.*

green and sustainability and strengthen environmental legislation and law enforcement. Since enterprises are aware of the importance of environmental protection in the development while people pay closer attention to the ecological benefits than ever, with the development of society, the green supply chain is destined to replace the traditional one.

3.3 Integrated development of green design and traditional manufacturing

3.3.1 Transition of the design concepts in manufacturing process

Casting, forging, heat treatment, surface treatment, and cutting are composed of basic manufacturing processes which constitute the core technology of the industries like automobile, petrochemical equipment, electric power equipment, shipbuilding, steel equipment, textile equipment, machine manufacturing, and others. These basic manufacturing processes are wildly applied in the equipment manufacturing industry. According to some statistics, plastic deformation gives shape to 75 percent of steel products in the world, while welding forms 45 percent of the metal structures. The parts made of steel, aluminum alloy, iron, and other materials account for more than 65 percent of the weight of a car, but before they become parts of the car, they have undergone casting, plastic deformation, welding, and other processes.

As China lagged behind the West in terms of processing technology and equipment level, such drawbacks as high energy consumption and the consequent environmental pollution were unavoidable. According to some statistics, the energy consumption of the four most basic manufacturing processes—casting, forging, heat treatment, and welding—accounts for 70 percent to 85 percent of the total consumption in the machinery industry.

European countries and the United States attached great importance to the development of basic manufacturing processing technology and included the processing technology of casting, forging, welding, and heat treatment on the top ten technologies of future concern. At the beginning of the 21st century, the United States made a plan for the development of casting, forging, heat treatment, welding, and other processes, and constantly revised and improved it. They set definite goals in the years by 2020.

China is a major country in terms of manufacturing technology and equipment. The processing scale of casting, forging, welding, and heat treatment ranks first in the world. In 2014, China's casting output amounted to 42.6 million tons, forging and stamping output exceeded 20 million tons, and heat treatment products exceeded 15 million tons. *Technology Roadmaps for Chinese Mechanical Engineering* published in 2011, clearly sets out the development goals of basic manufacturing technology: by 2020, indexes of energy consumption, material utilization rate, per capita productivity, processing precision, automation, noxious gases, and waste emissions must reach the level of developed countries in the early 21st century, and by 2030, these indexes must reach the level of developed countries in the 2020s. [1]

While China's energy-saving technology and equipment in basic manufacturing has improved significantly in these years, there is still a big gap compared with the world's advanced level; this gap is embodied in the following aspects: undesirable product quality and reliability, low production efficiency, substandard manufacturing technology, inadequate use of advanced technology such as automation and digital and intelligent equipment, and the level of energy consumption, material utilization, pollutant emissions are far behind international level.

3.3.1.1 Casting status quo

China has a total casting output of more than 40 million tons, equal to the sum production of the United States, Japan, and Germany, thus ranking as the world's largest producer of castings and serving as the world's foundry production base. China's iron castings account for 75 percent of the total castings, steel castings account for 13 percent, and non-ferrous alloys account for 7 percent.

Casting begins with remelting and is, therefore, one of the energy-intensive manufacturing processes. Its energy consumption accounts for 25 percent to 30 percent of the total in machinery industry, whereas its energy efficiency is only 17 percent. In recent years, various foundries have taken measures to modernize manufacturing processes. For example, they have upgraded smelting units, replacing cupolette furnaces and main frequency furnaces with intermediate frequency induction furnaces, to reduce energy consumption and emission reduction; they have incorporated advanced technologies in production, such as lost foam casting, V-process, and patternless casting, to increase processing yield, and as a result, unusable products have dropped by 160 percent. Companies and foundries that have tried to modernize their casting processes include Weichai Holding Group Co., Ltd.(Weichai Group), Guangxi Yuchai Machinery

---

[1] China Mechanical Engineering Society, *Technology Roadmaps of Chinese Mechanical Engineering*, Beijing: Science and Technology of China Press, 2011.

Group Co., Ltd.(Yuchai Group), YTO Group Corporation's engine foundry. Their energy consumption per ton of castings in 2010 was reduced to 294-375 tons of standard coal, approaching nearer to the average level of 276.3 tons of standard coal of the casting industry in Germany.

The foundry industry not only emits smoke and dust but also discharges a large amount of waste sand and other residues. Owing to the raising of environmental awareness and the application of environment-friendly technology, the industry has succeeded in reducing emissions in recent years. Now, melting and refining furnaces, sand processors and abrators have been furnished with dust removal devices. As a result, harmful emissions to the atmosphere have been significantly reduced; the cold-setting resin sand system has been installed with a regeneration unit, and consequently, the recycle rate of used sand maintains above 90 percent; the clay sand recycler applies the technique of "thermal combustion plus mechanical lapping", and the result is that over 85 percent of used sand can be recycled. [1]

While the foundry industry has made some achievements in energy conservation and emission reduction, the large number of foundry enterprises in China, their small average size, and the backward technology and equipment all contribute to comprehensive utilization of resources 1 to 2 degrees lower than the international standard, defective rate 5 percent to 10 percent higher, and the processing allowance 1 to 3 degrees higher. The average energy consumption of each ton of castings is 60 percent higher than that of developed countries. Furthermore, the production of a ton of qualified castings also produces an average of 0.2 to 0.3 tons of waste residues, 0.4 to 0.7 tons of waste sand, and 2.3 tons of carbon dioxide and nitrogen oxides. China's total amount of pollutants discharged from each ton of castings is 3 to 5 times that of industrially developed countries. [2]

3.3.1.2 Forging status quo

In 2014, China produced 12.3066 million tons of forgings, an increase of 11.76 percent year-on-year, ranking first in the world in terms of scale. In spite of such a large scale, the conflict between industrial development, environment, and energy has become increasingly prominent. [3] Backward equipment and severe pollution have

---

[1] Shan Dezhong, Yang Jing, "Energy-Saving and Emission Reduction and Equipment in the Field of Thermo-mechanical Processing", *Foundry Technology*, 2009(5), p.583.

[2] Zhang Yi, "Bohong Group Strives to be the Global Leader in Casting and Forging Industry", *Sichuan Daily*, May 16, 2013.

[3] Research Report on China Forging Market and Development Trend (2015-2020).

curbed the rapid development of the forging industry in China. Burners discharge a large number of particulate matters into the air. The forging process consumes plenty of lubricants, which eventually contaminate water and soil. To be environment-friendly, the forging industry must follow the road of energy conservation and emission reduction.

In recent years, China's forging industry has made great efforts to conserve energy and reduce emission. It has developed a waste heat quenching technique, which has produced 20 percent of the forging pieces; it has utilized simulation software CAD/CAM, thus reducing trimmings. The application of new materials and surface coatings help prolong mold life span; mechanization and automation help improve efficiency; better process management helps enhance the quality of the product; furnace upgrading and water recycling lead to resources conservation; the application of hydraulic hammers, variable frequency double-disk friction presses and screw presses contribute to energy conservation. Also, the industry has stopped using graphite lubricants, and a better environment has been seen in the forgeries.

Although China's forging industry has made great efforts to conserve energy and make better use of resources, we have much to do to catch up with industrially developed countries, for we lag behind developed countries 15 to 20 years in terms of an overall assessment of processing level, equipment manufacturing, basic theoretical research, and production management. Our energy consumption per ton is 0.83 tons of standard coal, whereas it is only 0.52 in Japan. The steel consumption per unit of output is 1.3 to 1.5 times that of developed countries, the utilization rate of forging materials is 1.5 times, and the emission of harmful substances is about 3 to 4 times.

3.3.1.3 Welding status quo

In 2014, China's annual steel output exceeded 1.126 billion tons, and nearly 50 percent of it went through welding before various components or products came into being. Major engineering projects and high-end equipment manufacturing stimulated the use of arc welding, laser-hybrid welding, and friction stir welding. New materials and structures also contributed to the development of such linking technologies as brazing and bonding.

It is true that our manufacturing industry has undergone a considerable transformation, but high energy consumption, inadequate material utilization, harmful effect on the environment, and substandard equipment—all these problems loom formidable. Detailed delineations are as follows.

(1) *China's welding industry features low efficiency and energy intensity*

For example, the mechanization and automation level in China's shipbuilding welding is about 65 percent that of Japan and South Korea, the labor productivity is about 2 percent, and the annual shipbuilding capacity per capita is about 10 percent to 15 percent. A majority of shipbuilding enterprises in China still depend largely on manual electric arc welding and submerged arc welding. The electricity consumption of welding accounts for more than half of the total electricity in shipbuilding. Besides, material saving management is also undesirable.

(2) *Welding consumables produce a considerable amount of contaminants*

China makes half of the world's welding consumables. When these materials are applied, they go through melting, evaporation, combustion, or other processes, giving off a large amount of dust and harmful gases. Meanwhile, some of them contain toxic elements such as lead and halogen. In other words, our production and living environments are subject to their adverse effects. Although more environment-friendly materials such as low-dust welding consumables and lead-free solders have been in use in recent years, their quality is not comparable to those applied in developed countries. At present, the market shares of high-dust welding materials in China is as high as 50 percent, while in Japan it is only 15 percent. Indeed, we are in urgent need of welding materials of high boiling point and low dust. Besides, although the use of Sn-Pb solder is globally restricted by Restriction of Hazardous Substances (RoHS) and China's "Management Methods for Controlling Pollution by Electronic Information Products", due to its toxic and harmful properties, it remains in the market.

(3) *Welding equipment and technology wait to be upgraded*

Generally speaking, 50 percent of the welding process is carried out automatically. Welder robots that can be used for the production of major equipment, and special welding devices, are mostly imported from overseas, for those tools produced in China are not desirable in terms of automation, stability, and reliability.

3.3.1.4 Heat treatment status quo

Heat treatment is essential for the service life of mechanical components. 70 percent to 80 percent of mechanical parts, 60 percent to 70 percent of machine tool parts, and 100 percent of tools need heat treatment. In China, there are more than 10,000 heat treatment processing plants, about 200,000 heat treatment furnaces, and approximately 15 million kilowatts of installed capacity. Nearly 30 million tons of various parts are heat treated every year.

In recent years, China has made significant progress in heat treatment processes and equipment. Half of the energy-saving transformation has been completed, and 60 percent of heat treatment can be performed in a low or non-oxidizing environment. Tempering is increasingly used instead of normalizing preheating, and the part processed by tempering has been doubled within the past five years. Dozens of practical equipment technologies have reached the advanced international level. For example, the double-deck roller- hearth continuous annealing spheroidizing furnace has been brought forth for bearing's precision controlled heat treatment; one of its advantages is energy-saving, for the energy consumption of heat treatment has been reduced below 200 kWh/ton; precision high temperature controlled multi-purpose chamber furnace has been developed for gear's precision controlled heat treatment; it can save more than 30 percent energy than carburizing heat treatment; IGBT induction heating equipment is gradually replacing the conventional tube induction heating equipment; the air cooler for quenching medium and the compound heat exchanger with heat pipe, save both energy and water.

However, there is still a big gap between China's heat treatment technology and developed countries'. The average unit energy consumption of China's heat treatment enterprises is about 500 kWh, far behind the international level of 200 kWh to 300 kWh. At present, the total amount of thermal aging work in China's machinery processing industry is 320 million tons. If thermal aging treatment is applied to all these materials, it will consume 26.45 million tons of standard coal per year. Salt preheating treatment causes serious pollution and brings hazard and risk, but it is still wildly used in China. In contrast, this treatment technology is practically no longer in use in industrial countries. In Europe and the United States, the overall labor productivity of the heat treatment is about RMB650,000 per person, whereas, in China, it is about RMB110,000 per person, only 1/6 of the world's advanced level.

For the basic manufacturing processes to be energy and material saving, China has been doing extensive researches into new types of energy-saving technologies such as green casting, precision forging, harmless welding, lightweight composite material forming, and new modes of laser processing; it has also attached importance to the modernization of equipment of welding, high-temperature casting, and automated assembly. As a result, China has succeeded in bringing forth a number of energy-saving technologies and new types of equipment, and gradually transformed process design concepts. Examples of such technologies include drill pipe friction welding and deformation heat treatment process, digital precision casting without a pattern. New technologies of energy saving and emission reduction for car stamping have been developed and applied. Researches have also been carried out on lost foam casting technology of 300 horsepower tow transmission box and gearbox, and on application and demonstration of environment-friendly welding materials, green welding technology, as well as integrated energy conservation and emission reduction technology in the foundry industry. Besides, high-pressure roller mill technology featuring high-efficiency and energy-saving, digital automatic dyeing packaged technology and equipment for cheese, and large-scale blast furnace of energy recovery generation unit have been developed and applied.

Therefore, our goals are the green manufacturing processes that effectively utilize resources, save energy and protect the environment. As green technologies can resolve resources limitedness and environmental problems, they shall lead the machinery industry to the road of sustainable development.

3.3.2 Green design concept in conventional manufacturing processes

The design concept of green manufacturing in the basic manufacturing processes features precision control, cleanness and efficiency, intelligent processes, and recycling.

3.3.2.1 Precision digitization

Along with the development of information technology, especially modeling, simulation, and automation, there has emerged digital technology which is aimed at precision control of structure and performance. This technology has driven the basic manufacturing processes from "experience-based" operation to "precision control" operation, and it is conducive to energy-and-material saving. Specific advantages of digital control are as follows. First, digital, information, and intelligent concepts are integrated into the manufacturing processes to realize intelligent decision making, adaptive process control, intelligent control of error compensation, fault self-diagnosis, and intelligent maintenance. In this way, the forming and processing accuracy, production efficiency, and material utilization rate have been improved. Second, precision forming technology produces metal parts with exact geometric shape and size, in other words, no additional processing is required before they are used. As material flow is properly controlled, the material fibers are not broken and are distributed as required. Also, as the formed parts need no or less further processing before they are put to use, their fiber morphology is left undisturbed to the greatest extent, and as a result, they possess desired mechanical strength, have a longer service life, consume less energy, and produce less material wastage.

3.3.2.2 Cleanness and efficiency

Since natural resources are limited, and the environment is under enormous pressure, the basic manufacturing processes characteristic of high consumption of raw materials, low energy efficiency and severe pollutants discharges have been replaced by energy-saving and environment-friendly technologies. In other words, manufacturing processes have become more sophisticated, and the result is that raw materials have been saved and energy conservation and emission reduction achieved. At the same time, some advanced forming technologies, such as composite forming, have been applied to realize the short-flow forming of machine parts. These technologies make full use of the materials and heat energy left over from earlier stages, or they integrate several processes to re-engineer the entire manufacturing workflow. In this way, the energy efficiency and productivity of the equipment have significantly been improved.

3.3.2.3 Intelligent process

Traditional processes have undergone constant optimization. When working principles remain unchanged, the basic manufacturing processes (casting, forging and heat treatment) have had their process parameters or integrated system optimized. The integrated system consists of process equipment, auxiliary technology, structural materials and process materials, and inspection and control. Through this transformation, those basic processes have achieved high efficiency, low energy consumption, less/no pollution, automation, and intelligence. What is especially remarkable is that intelligent manufacturing units have come into being.

3.3.2.4 Recycling

While ensuring that product designs are not affected, the basic manufacturing processes not only pursue low energy and material consumption and low pollutants emissions but also aim at waste-free manufacturing. Waste-free manufacturing means that no waste comes out of the manufacturing process, or the resultant waste can be used as a raw material in other processes and no further waste is produced. The technologies of re-manufacturing and recycling will help form a closed service life cycle of resources and energy, thus reducing solid waste, and improving the utilization rate of resources and energy.

3.3.3 Transition from the traditional manufacturing process to green design

3.3.3.1 Setting up demonstration projects

It is urgent that some leading enterprises in the industries of casting, forging, welding, and heat treatment should set up demonstration projects in some particular sites. The key manufacturing processes of these demonstration projects must undergo green transformation; the mass production process for electromechanical products must be subjected to green transformation—energy conservation and emission reduction. The purpose of these projects is to accumulate experience and then introduce the experience to the whole industry of manufacturing.

3.3.3.2 Making workshops green and digital

It is a matter of necessity that workshops of foundry, stamping, welding, heat treatment and cutting be transformed to be digital, green, and thus efficient. Green manufacturing will lead to the emergence of many new industries, such as the industries of green motorcars, green home appliances, and software making.

3.3.3.3 Establishing a specialized basic manufacturing process center

The application of intelligent digital equipment means the elevation of the automation level of the manufacturing process. So it is of vital importance to establish, in places where equipment production is concentrated, a basic manufacturing processes center that features efficiency and energy-saving. The key to achieving green manufacturing is integrated information and technical methods. On the one hand, it is necessary to establish a product information model (PIM) and a product data management (PDM) system. On the other hand, it is worthwhile to integrate the multidisciplinary knowledge involved in the product development process, as well as various technologies and methods, so as to provide a supportive, integrated engineering environment for green manufacturing.

3.3.3.4 Establishing an energy efficiency management and assessment center

The industry has to set up a management and assessment center, using professional methods and tools to supervise those workshops of casting, forging, heat treatment, welding, and machining. In this way, a paradigm for evaluating and optimizing the energy efficiency of the machinery line can be set up and then used commercially.

Chapter 4
The Internal Motivation of Green Transformation

4.1 The rise of green values

4.1.1 Green values: comprehensive embodiment of the humanistic spirit

Karl Marx once suggested that "An animal forms only by the standard and the need of the species to which it belongs, whilst man knows how to produce by the standard of every species, and knows how to apply everywhere the inherent standard to the object. Man therefore also forms objects by the laws of beauty." [1] Green manufacturing's exploration of science and the creation of technological products is itself a process of pursuing beauty. As the inventor and user of technological products, a man should standardize the application of technology, making it beautiful, thus realizing man's dream of living in a poetic environment.

4.1.1.1 The humanistic pursuit of R&D personnel

The pursuit of humanistic beauty by R&D personnel is the prerequisite for their pursuit of humanistic technical beauty. R&D personnel's research philosophy, sense of value, artistic taste—all these qualities are sometimes more important than professional knowledge. [2] These qualities will be surely embodied in their green manufacturing researches.

(1) *People-oriented research philosophy*

In terms of origin, man is the masterpiece created by nature in its long-term evolution. The emergence of man is a miracle in the universe. [3] In the long history of development, human beings have created a splendid material culture with their arduous

---

[1] Karl Marx, *Economic and Philosophic Manuscripts of 1844*, Moscow: Progress Publishers, 1959, p.31.

[2] Ren Dingcheng, *A Science and Humanities Reader for College Students*, Beijing: Peking University Press, 2004, p.9.

[3] Li Ruifeng, "Human-friendly Technology and Harmonious Development of Society", *Science, Technology and Dialectics*, 2005(10), p.75.

labor. By giving full play to their subjective initiative, human beings have displayed their capacity when they are trying to transform the material world. No interest is related to only one individual, but common interests that are related to human beings as a whole. This means respect of each other and understanding of each other. In the era of green manufacturing, we should bear in mind the philosophy of people-orientedness, which is synonymous with humanism, aiming to satisfy the material and cultural needs of all members of society. As a matter of fact, this philosophy is the essence and core of the scientific development outlook, the ultimate goal of socialist production and driving force for technological innovation in the era of green manufacturing.

Technology is a "double-edged sword". While it brings benefits—rich material products, it also brings problems, some of which even threaten the long-term development of human society. Researchers are the leading force in the development of science and technology, and their values and conduct play an important role in the direction of sci-tech development. In the era of green manufacturing, researchers should follow the scientific concept of putting people in the first place. In other words, before a technology is applied to production, they must consider whether it is in human's long-term interest and whether it is conducive to intergenerational and international equity. They must anticipate the consequences of its application: if the technology is likely to run contrary to human interests, environmental conservation, and ecological balance, its application has to be suspended until rectification is made, or abandoned if rectification is impossible. Such scientific researches will largely satisfy people's needs and benefit people's life. It is scientific, developmental, vigorous, humanized and full of human touch.

In this green manufacturing era, the idea of people-orientedness or people-friendliness implies that technology is just a means to reach the end of healthy and sustainable development of economy and society. People-friendly technology must be agreeable to nature, society, and people themselves. In other words, it is a technology featuring humanistic beauty. It concerns its impact on people, aiming to make itself better serve people by respecting their rights and interests.

(2) *Truth-seeking attitude*

The goal of scientific research is to discover the laws of the unknown world, to explore the truth, and to promote the development of society. Whether a researcher has a seeking truth attitude will inevitably determine the credibility of his/her research results. Discovering the unknown and exploring the truth are unchanged subjects for scientific research. Being truthful and practical is the basic principle that scientific research needs to observe in green manufacturing, and it is the manifestation of scientific and technological workers' personality beauty.

Personality is the sum-up of one's value, dignity, and moral accomplishment. People's value appeals are diverse, and one of them is the pursuit of noble character. This pursuit can enrich their psychological world, improve their ethics and help shape the beauty of one's personality. [1] Personality beauty involves one's charm and cultural attainment. There are two forms of beauty, namely, internal beauty and external beauty: the former is fundamental, exerting a profound influence on people's conduct and behavior. Besides personality beauty, one has humanistic beauty in his/her character; they both help assert one's worth and dignity and realize one's all-round development.

(3) *Endowing technical products with humanistic beauty*

Technology and art were first collectively referred to as craftsmanship. With the improvement of productivity and the advent of the division of labor, technology has gained independent status, just related to production, while art approached the field of fine arts. However, with the continuous growth of social products and the rapid advancement of technology and art, these two divisions of labor are inclined to converge in this era of green manufacturing.

Since the art that people pursue is the art of technology, technology should be the technology of art. Because artworks have elements of modern technology, they look more fashionable and appealing; in the same way, if the design of a technical product bears artistic factors, it will look more pleasant and original. The convergence of technology and art is the call of the times.

The artistic cultivation of sci-tech workers refers to their understanding and application of art-related knowledge, and their ability to integrate technology and art. It embodies their technical level, artistic attainment, and other qualities. Product designers with some artistic taste can introduce artistic ingredients into his/her works, endowing the products with novelty, uniqueness, and artistry. Besides, consumers will appreciate the practicality and aesthetics of the products.

The most significant trait of artistic works is beauty. Technicians with artistic attainment can combine product design with artistic creativity. Therefore, the artistic beauty of green technology also rests on whether the design is creative and whether it can give people a new sense of artistic beauty.

---

[1] Cai Ping, "From the Thinking of Confucianism and Taoism to See the Beauty of Personality", *Journal of Shihezi University* (*Philosophy and Social Sciences*), 2002(6), p.21.

From the perspective of users, they expect the technical products to look differently from those of the same type and give them fresh new experience when these products are serving them. If the users are satisfied with their appearance and their service, then we should say these products have lived up to the originality of the designers.

4.1.1.2 Humanistic pursuit in green product design

Technical design is the initial stage of technology R&D. Designers take the lead in the advancement of technology. For technical achievements to be in line with people's interest, technical designers in this green manufacturing era should endow their works with humanistic beauty, or rather, the ultimate concern for people should be taken as the most important norm for technical designs. For this purpose, the following rules have to be observed.

(1) *Not wasting of resources for the sake of our living environment*

The famous philosopher Xunzi (313-238BC) in the late Warring States Period of ancient China once remarked: If you strengthen the fundamental works and moderate expenditures, then Heaven cannot make you poor. China is rich in natural resources on its vast territory, but after forty years' economic construction since the implementation of reform and opening up in 1978 without considering environmental costs, a considerable part of those resources have been consumed. If we continued to exploit and utilize them without restraint, the present shortage of resources would deteriorate, and the global ecology would have to sustain a growing burden.

The resources on earth that human beings live on are not inexhaustible but limited and precious. At present, non-renewable resources are draining at an accelerating rate and are in danger of depletion. Hopefully, some sci-tech means can help achieve effective utilization and conservation of resources. This is a major program related to our ecological environment and is also a key issue for the harmony between the progress of civilization and peace of nature.

Making full use of green materials is the primary step of technological economization. Green materials are those that can be renewed and recycled, and those that bring little pollution and are environmentally compatible. Toxic and radioactive materials should be avoided. For example, the beautiful bamboo flooring made of renewable bamboo trees embodies the spirit of green production.

(2) *Programming neat procedures*

To program a neat production procedure, the programmer has to have rich design experience and be steeped in relevant theories and skills. He/she has to be able to filter out unnecessary operations so that the production process is neat, efficient, and practice of economy.

In scientific research, scientists pursue logic lucidity and scientific beauty when they derive formulas and generalize theorems, while in technological research, technicians pursue integration of scientific beauty and humanistic technical beauty when they design neat procedures. Then, the operators will find neat procedures convenient and practical.

4.1.1.3 Humanistic pursuit in the production process

(1) *Creating a pleasant production environment*

Production environment refers to the working ambience of workers and is an essential factor in assessing production conditions. Its congeniality with workers and production tools plays a vital role in improving labor productivity and relieving workers' sense of burden.

In industrial society, the relationship between workers and production tools is such that workers use machines for mass mechanical production in plants and workshops. Labor productivity stays at a certain level in a particular historical period because it is restricted by social and historical conditions, but it fluctuates in the same period due to the impact of the working environment. An optimized environment consistent with technical aesthetics can greatly improve labor productivity and add to products' competitive edges in both quality and quantity. Many factors make up the production environment, including color, lighting, sound, equipment's positioning, ventilation, temperature, humidity, and the ambience outside the workshop—all of these influence workers' psychology for production.

The designer of a production workshop should combine electric lighting, natural light, and the visual psychology of color. The purpose is to save energy and provide a pleasant and cozy environment for the workers. In terms of auditory sensation, there should be as little production noise as it can be in the workshop, for it can upset the workers and cause them easy to fatigue. Appropriate positioning of equipment enables workers to avoid unnecessary detours from one piece of equipment to another, and help reduce the occurrence of accidents and occupational diseases. Good ventilation, proper temperature, and humidity will increase people's working enthusiasm and pleasure. In brief, an agreeable working environment will enable people to feel at ease and thus concentrate on what they do. When the production tools and other elements in the environment set the worker in a good mood, she/he is apt to be at their best, ready to tap their potential. This is not only related to production, but also to the individual's enhanced sense of self-making.[1]

The pleasant production environment is an indicator of humanized production, hence an indicator of people's pursuit of humanistic beauty of technology. The proper management of the relationship between people, machines, and environment should inform the concept of people-orientedness so that people are at their best while working. This concept means a concern for the welfare of the workers. In a congenial environment, workers tend to be physiologically and psychologically ready for the job; they tend to work energetically and thus efficiently. Eventually, they will develop an enhanced love of their line of occupation and their life itself.

(2) *Creating a fresh human-machine relationship*

Since the industrial revolution, machinery and equipment have been used extensively in the manufacturing industry, replacing traditional manual labor. Though the advancement of technology has greatly improved labor productivity, new machines are constantly pushing some workers out of the factory floors; the other workers who cannot be replaced by machines are confined in a narrow space due to the sophisticated division of modern machinery production. This confinement results in that the workers have no chance to confront the product as a whole, let alone experience the process of production as a continuum. Under this circumstance, workers are just adjuncts of machines; they are not dynamic or creative. It seems that it is the machine rather than the worker that has made the product.[2]

When workers repeat the same movements in following the manufacturing process, they are reduced to part of the equipment, having no thoughts or ideas of their own. In other words, their initiative and creativity are suppressed by the machine. To our terror, scientific development does not free man from nature's power or liberate him physically and mentally; on the contrary, it veers in the opposite direction, posing an alien force against man—this is the alienation of science.[3]

More than that, with the advancement and development of science and technology, human beings have encroached ruthlessly into nature and plundered natural resources in an unbridled manner. Consequently, nature is left with so many scars that its self-recovery mechanism struggles hard to recover or bring it back to its vibrant state, but

---

[1] Lan Xing, "The Practical Significance of Scientific and Technical Aesthetics: Advocating a Pleasant 'Environmental' Design", *Shandong Social Sciences*, 2003(1), p.108.

[2] Luo Yunyun, *Aesthetic Application*, Beijing: Social Science Academic Press, 2002, p.152.

[3] Xu Hengchun, *Aesthetics for Science and Technology*, Xi'an: Shaanxi People's Education Press, 1997, p.29.

failure seems inevitable. The ecological imbalance will inevitably lead to ecological crisis. Many products are made at the expense of the environment or our ecosystem. Thus environmental pollution, soil erosion, deforestation, greenhouse effect, ozone depletion, and reduced biodiversity have threatened the survival of humanity.

Conventional technical manufacturing highlights the value-in-use of the product but does not care whether it is beautiful or not. In the manufacturing process, workers blindly pursue economic interests and neglect ecological factors, which is the primary cause of severe industrial pollution. It follows that there should be an inclusive norm for the quality of the technical product: it must be pragmatic, good-looking and environment- friendly at the same time.[1]

The new human-machine relationship in the era of green manufacturing requires that technical research be pragmatic, and that the products—the results of technical research—be pleasant-looking and ecology-friendly. The combination of pragmatics, aesthetics, and ecology in technical innovation is an embodiment of humanism in science and technology. Actually, the combination of technical beauty with ecological concern is a prerequisite for the harmonious relationship between man and nature, and a prerequisite for the sustainable development of human society.

(3) *Implementing clean production*

Clean production concerns another key technology that brings sustainable development from theory to practice. It is also a new concept that requires that all aspects of production take environmental protection into consideration. The preliminary stage of the clean output is to ensure that energy and feedstock be as clean as possible and contain as few pollutants as possible. This means controlling pollution at the source and improving energy efficiency. For the production process, there is the cleanness norm: resources and energy should be conserved, and the raw materials that cause severe pollution and do harm to equipment must be minimized in quantity. Then there are stipulations for the quality of the product. A product has a life cycle, which begins with the selection of raw materials and ends with the disposal of the used product, with product making and use in between. The negative impact of each stage of this cycle on the society and natural environment should be addressed.

The conventional end-of-pipe treatment practice has proved to be no solution, for its pollution control mode is expensive and yet ineffective. Then there has emerged

---

[1] Chen Qingshuo, Qian Xiaoqing, Wang Ping, "The Intrinsic Linkage of Technical Ecology and Aesthetics", *Science and Technology Management Research*, 1996(6), p.37.

clean production technology, which can strike a balance between economic benefits and ecological conservation. This production mode will further liberate productivity, and promote sustainable development of industry and agriculture. [1]

Green manufacturing and clean production, the former concerning product design while the latter production process, incorporate eco-humanism in technical innovation. This is an indication that manufacturers no longer blindly pursue economic interests, but consider products' ecological impact and man's long-term interests. These two technologies aim at reducing resources waste and environmental pollution from the outset of production.

Clean production and green manufacturing protect both the ecosystem and the long- term interests of humanity. In line with eco-humanism, they enhance productivity without doing harm to people's living environment. As they attach importance to the beauty of nature and our environment, they are technologies informed by eco-humanistic beauty.

4.1.2 Man's renewed understanding of nature's values

4.1.2.1 Human beings in the context of green manufacturing

The trend of green manufacturing proposes that we do away with the ideology of anthropocentrism to regard man as a creature equal to the other creatures on the earth. This entails the fundamental transformation of values; the new values embodied in green manufacturing prevent ecological crises to happen. But we should take a rational attitude toward anthropocentrism. First, as a proposition on values, anthropocentrism does not contradict with other basic propositions of the society. What's more, we should also acknowledge that anthropocentrism is valid to some extent. Abolition of this ideology would be against common sense. Nature is an all-embracing system, in which man is an important part, coexisting with others. Human development is simultaneously driven forward and restricted by nature. Anthropecology often divides complex ecosystems into three distinctive but closely related sectors: society, economy, and nature, which testify the interdependence between man and nature. So there is no "anthropocentrism" or "non-anthropocentrism" in the strict sense of the word. The renewal of people's ecological outlook has a profound impact on the natural environment and human development. In the history of civilization, man's attitude

---

[1] Shang Hua, Wang Wenjun, "Effect of Clean Production on the Sustainable Development", *Journal of Weinan Teachers College*, 2005(7), p.31.

toward nature underwent two major transformations. The first is from man's self-consciousness of existence to anthropocentrism. In this period, the industrial revolution yielded tremendous success, and technology optimism prevailed. The other side of the coin was excessive resources consumption, environmental pollution, and ecological unbalance—all of these have adversely affected the survival and development of human beings. The second transformation is from anthropocentrism to the outlook of sustainable development. Due to human beings' overproduction, natural resources are becoming increasingly scarce, and the ecological system has been seriously damaged. Human beings have come to realize the importance of sustainable development and put forward the coordinated development strategy of economy, society, resources, and environment. This strategy will help to form a model of coexistence between man and nature, thus turning over a new leaf in human history.

4.1.2.2 The fusion of man's and nature's values

Historically, man's pursuit of self-worth ran contrary to the wholesomeness of nature. At present, to establish ecological ethics, it is necessary to fuse man's self-worth with ecological values. This fusion cannot be accomplished without man's rational cognitive and pragmatic activities. Human beings are capable of abstract logical thinking. Thus they are not short of a sense of equality between themselves and nature. In the current context of green manufacturing, ecological ethics means breaking the shackles of anthropocentrism and extending the love among people to the whole nature. Man's self-worth or intrinsic value was created in his continuous practice, thus a product of social activities, while nature's value is spontaneous, resistant to any change by people's subjectivity. Ontology asserts that natural ecology, as an objective existence, has its value and has no essential difference in value from living beings. Nature has value, but it is the man's responsibility to protect this value. Man discerns and reflects on the relationship between himself and nature, and believes that it is his obligation to stand guard over nature. Man's sense of responsibility is a child of his logical reasoning and ethical norms. And ethical norms are the key to his value. Man's ability of value judgment eventually leads to the unveiling of nature's value.

4.1.2.3 Values' integration and uplifting in the context of green manufacturing

Reading into man's intrinsic value and nature's value for a full understanding is the key to transcending anthropocentrism and non-anthropocentrism. Value relationship is a function of the object itself in relation to the existence and development of the subject, and is an interesting relationship between the subject and the object, a kind of "fursichsein". By reading into the values, we come to something fundamental: values represent man's dominant position on the earth. Therefore, we must approach the ecological value properly. If we should regard ecological value as something detached from human beings, then we would get it wrong. To transcend the anthropocentrism and non-anthropocentrism, and to achieve the fusion of intrinsic human value and natural value, we should realize that man needs to play an essential role in the process of understanding and transforming nature and to objectify his essence to nature. Only in this way can man properly understands his essence. Just as Marx remarked, "In creating a world of objects by his personal activity, in his work upon inorganic nature, man proves himself a conscious species-being."[1] Practice is a bridge between man and nature. Through practice, man has attained the goal of utilizing the service of natural resources in their production and personal life. Besides, in the process of transforming nature, man's essence is objectified to nature and is manifested by nature. For example, such scourges as a shortage of resources and environmental pollution are the aftermaths of man's over-exploitation of natural resources, destruction of ecological system and neglect of sustainable development. Thus nature is the very basis on which man survives and develops himself, and it helps him discover his essence in the process of his understanding and transforming nature. If we approach nature humanistically, then nature will let us see man's essence: the pursuit of truth, goodness, and beauty. To return man's incessant pursuit, nature endows him with abundant resources and energy. On the contrary, if a man approaches nature inhumanely by relentless plundering, then nature will retaliate against a man with an ecological crisis or environmental deterioration. Global warming, resources depletion, desertification, and smog, etc., these are negative indicators of man's essence. In other words, our approach to nature will be returned to us by nature; in either direction, man's essence is manifested, positively or negatively. Therefore, awe for nature's value is equivalent to an affirmation of man's value; or rather, respect for nature means respect for the man himself. Since nature can testify and reveal man's essence, man, for his part, is obliged to offer humanistic concern for nature.

To sum up, a full understanding of the relationship between man and nature leads to the propositions of green manufacturing and green consumption. These propositions are conducive to the strategy of sustainable development of human civilization, especially sustainable development in industry.

---

[1] Karl Marx, *Economic and Philosophic Manuscripts of 1844*, Moscow: Progress Publishers, 1959, p.31.

Along the path of sustainable development, a balance should be struck between man's value and nature's value, or between wholesome ecology and people's material demands. Only in this way, can a win-win scene be staged on this planet.

4.1.3   Revolution of values: green values

4.1.3.1   The issue of values is fundamental to the solution of ecological crises

As spiritual appeals, values are the guiding force for the pursuit of human material interests, and they influence and even determine how people pursue material interests. On the surface, values seem to have nothing to do with the current ecological crisis, but in essence, values influence human material production and daily life. The ecological crisis has a great deal to do with the wrong values. Therefore, the ecological crisis is not just a consequence of the government's wrongdoing or policy failure.

While we are trying to understand the ecological crisis from the perspective of values, we are reminded of the "anthropocentrism"—a dominant value ever since the Industrial Revolution. This idea emphasizes that man is the master of the universe and thus in a position to exploit everything on the planet for his interest. With this idea in mind, man has been transforming and utilizing nature at his will. However, improvement of social productivity and progress of human civilization should not be achieved at the cost of the ecological environment. The ever-growing desire of human beings has led to their exploitation of nature, but they were so ruthless that massive natural resources have been wasted and huge pollution has followed up as a consequence. What they were doing not only challenged the law of nature but also threatened to wipe out themselves from the earth. Though human civilization has attained such a high level, humans are still worried how to survive and subsist, for energy resources are running out, and water, soil and even atmosphere have been polluted to such an extent that they fall short of human needs.

Ecological crisis precipitates human beings into an unprecedented predicament. If nothing was done about it, human beings would disappear someday from the earth. Therefore, human beings have begun to reflect on their relentless behaviors since the Industrial Revolution. Now they have become aware that only by coexistence with nature can they continue to survive. So the path of ecological civilization has been taken—the ideal and only path. At the end of the 20th century, the Chinese government already noticed the crisis of natural resources and environment and began its commitment to natural resources conservation and environmental protection. It issued a series of laws and regulations to prevent environmental damage and pollution. For instance, factories or plants which were heavy polluters were ordered to reform themselves or shut down. However, these efforts did not yield desirable results.

Since the implementation of the reform and opening up policy in 1978, China has made rapid economic progress, and all of its goals have been reached except ecological ones. The reason for the unfulfillment of ecological targets lies in the values behind "anthropocentrism". These values led to the thinking patterns and behaviors that aimed at achieving the goal of economic growth but went against conserving natural resources and environment. Only by changing those values and related thinking and behavioral patterns, or rather, only by coordinating economic growth and ecological conservation, can we get ourselves out of the present environmental crisis, bringing the ecology back to its safe and sound condition.

To develop a cycling economy, or construct an ecological civilization, which is designed to pursue progress and protect the environment simultaneously, we must change our values, from "anthropocentrism" to green values, for the latter emphasize harmony and coexistence between man and nature.

In history, man has positioned himself opposite to nature. Now there come green values. We uphold green values for several reasons. First, green values change the notion that man is the conqueror of nature, providing a mode of thinking and behavior for the harmonious development of man and nature. Second, green values assert that everything in the ecosystem has its value, thus extending the ethnic community to include the entire ecosystem on the earth. Third, green values constitute a core ecological ethics at the time of the global ecological crisis. Thereupon, green values are a driving force for ecological civilization construction and sustainable development.

4.1.3.2 Green values have triple strengths in the dynamic system of economic development

(1) *Green values are the most stable, sustainable and potentially energetic motive force*

There are many kinds of motive forces to achieve the green economy, but most of them are external motive forces, while green values are endogenous motive forces, which have great advantages regarding sustainability and stability. If the green economy is developed under the government's policies and instructions, it will probably be treated passively and unseriously. In the process of developing a recycling economy, adjustments need to be made quickly keep up with changes in the market. However, policy restrictions will weaken the flexibility for adjustments and thus miss opportunities. The role of green values is crucial. If it roots the green concept in the minds of the people, recycling human beings will be more proactive, more rational and more selfless in the process of developing a recycling economy. It can be seen that green values are a tremendous potentially energetic motive force.

(2) *Green values can cultivate the action-takers spirit of self-restraining*

The recycling economy cannot be achieved overnight or under the compulsion of national policies or government's calls. If we aim to get rid of the nature-destruction production ways in industrial civilization and thus achieve ecological civilization, we should not only actively respond to the national calls for ecological civilization but also spiritually establish and consciously fulfill the conduct code of green values, which embodies Chinese nation's spirit of self-restraining. On the road of developing a recycling economy, green values must be rooted in people's minds. They have invisible restraining power on people and can effectively promote the development of ecological civilization.

(3) *Green values can inspire action-takers' creativity*

In the human ecological civilization, the recycling economy is an unprecedented undertaking. We will face difficulties that we have never met before. If human beings cannot fully understand the green values and change the passive behavior as well as the traditional thinking patterns and working approaches, we would not be able to solve the problems in developing recycling economy. The deep understanding of green values can effectively enhance the creativity and subjective initiative of human beings, and make people act by the laws of natural ecology with the aim of achieving the harmony between human being and the nature in the production activities and daily behaviors. The creativity of the action takers, inspired by green values can solve various problems encountered in the process of developing a recycling economy.

4.2 The transformation of production, life, and ways of thinking

4.2.1 Sustainable development of modern manufacturing

4.2.1.1 The emergence of sustainable development issues

Through the long-term practice of the Industrial Revolution, humankind has opened a new chapter in the information age. Looking back at the history of the industrial revolution, from the invention of the steam engine to the first automobile production line built by Ford Motor Company, the manufacturing industry has advanced by leaps and bounds. However, we must learn that in the process of industrialization, especially in the development of manufacturing, many non-renewable resources have been consumed and serious environmental pollution has been generated, which have destroyed the homeland where we live, resulting in the inability of the natural ecosystem.

The data shows that the 21 types of electromechanical products used in various industries of the national economy are high-pollution and high-energy consumption products. The electricity consumed by these electromechanical products accounts for 60 percent to 80 percent of the total electricity consumption in the country, and the coal consumed accounts for 50 percent of the total coal consumption in the country, and the gasoline consumed accounts for 55 percent to 60 percent of the total gasoline consumption in the country, and the diesel consumed accounts for more than 40 percent of the total diesel production in our country. Due to the characteristics of high pollution and high energy consumption, these products have caused a severe ecological crisis in the course of development. China's automobile manufacturing industry has achieved rapid advance after long-term development and reform. However, compared with developed countries, China's automobile manufacturing industry lacks innovation capability, and its independent competitiveness is fairly low. It also faces problems such as lacking resources and energy and causing environmental pollution. Therefore, in the process of manufacturing progress, we must form the idea of green development, save resources and energy, update manufacturing technology and achieve sustainable development. Since the 1960s, human beings have been alerted that many resources on the earth are limited and non-renewable, so they began to pay attention to the ecological environment and natural resources. Since the 1980s, the idea of sustainable development has sprouted on a global scale. In 1987, the United Nations World Commission on Environment and Development for the first time defined the concept of sustainable development that is to meet the needs of contemporaries without compromising future generations to meet their needs. In the modern information age, sustainable development has a new meaning: on the one hand, it needs to remain to make progress to meet people's material and cultural needs; on the other hand, it must save resources, energy and protect the environment, and even improve the current harsh ecological environment in the course of development. The idea of sustainable development has become strategic thinking, which requires social progress and economic advance to be driven by innovation rather than high consumption and high pollution. For example, the sustainable manufacturing industry proposes the idea that measures to protect the environment and save resources and energy need to be integrated into the early stage of product research and scheming. In the design and application stage of the product, we need to focus on environmental protection and energy conservation, choose high-quality raw materials and fine manufacturing processes. After the end of the product lifecycle, the product should be recyclable and reusable.

4.2.1.2　Sustainable development points out the direction of manufacturing

The future advance of products and markets also points out the path of the sustainable development of the manufacturing industry. Future products include tangible products and intangible ones, which will pay more attention to the diversification and stratification of products and the provision of adequate services. In the future society, diversified and layered products will be more favored and replace the traditionally standard modelized products. Future products are becoming more technical and green, and global markets are more closely linked to each other and become a globalized market. We can reconfigure resources through information technology, which is also an important measure to achieve sustainable development. The sustainable development model is gradually moving towards intelligentization. By encouraging enterprises to improve their independent innovation capabilities, we can make traditional manufacturing products smarter and more environmentally friendly. Only when future products are recyclable, featuring no pollution and low consumption, the sustainable development of the future society can be formed. Only by vigorously promoting green manufacturing models and technologies can we achieve sustainable development in the manufacturing industry.

4.2.1.3　Green manufacturing: the green revolution in manufacturing

The traditional manufacturing industry is not only the pillar industry but also the high pollution and high consumption industry of our national economy. To achieve sustainable development of manufacturing industry, it is necessary to boost production technology, rationally utilize resources and energy and reduce pollutant emissions. The essential mode of sustainable development is to realize the green manufacturing, not only paying attention to the monetary profits of enterprises, but also comprehensively coordinating the relationship between production, environmental protection, energy saving, and green development. Green manufacturing is a modern manufacturing model that takes into account environmental and resource efficiency. It aims to make the environmental impact of the product throughout the product lifecycle from design, manufacture, packaging, transportation, and use to end-of-life disposal virtually zero, with as little resource and energy as possible and coordinate the economic profit of enterprises and the sustainable development of the society. Green manufacturing reflects the concept of sustainable development. Green manufacturing products are more competitive and can enhance the capability of increasing exports and earning foreign currencies.

(1) *Views on environment protection*

Green manufacturing requires the entire product cycle, from market research, product planning, product design, product manufacturing, product sales, product use, and product recycling and complies with the concept of environmental protection and saving the resources.

(2) *Design concept*

For the design of the product, we must change the original pursuit of the cost and profit and pay attention to the environment and resources. Green design is to consider the factors such as product performance, quality, and cost and development cycle to the maximum extent of the product. All the content and factors involved will be selected and optimized to minimize potential environmental damage caused by the whole process of the product. In the process of product design, we must abandon the "one-time use" concept and learn that products can be recycled and reused.

(3) *Management concept*

Many enterprises, especially manufacturing enterprises, now hold high the banner of "green manufacturing". Their products are indeed low- pollution and low-emission products, which meet the requirements of the law. But the pollution in the production process is often ignored. Promoting green manufacturing can improve the situation of high pollution and high waste, which cut the manufacturing cost and reduce the damage to the environment and truly enhance the utilization of resources. For workers, green manufacturing will also create a decent working environment.

(4) *Green manufacturing is promising, promoting the advance of other economic sectors*

The implementation of green manufacturing requires strict control and supervision in every production step, but it will also trigger a series of technical problems, such as how to recycle and dispose of the used products. If an enterprise can take the idea of sustainable development as its guiding ideology, upgrade production technology, and carry out green manufacturing, it will take more market shares and obtain substantial economic profits.

4.2.2 The sprouting of green consumption

Under the influence of capitalism and the Industrial Revolution, Western society realized the transition from agricultural society to industrial society and the industrial lifestyle of "pursuing convenience and advocating consumption" was also accompanied.[1]

This kind of life and consumption model stimulates consumption and has certain positive implications. However, this lifestyle featuring advocating consumption and convenient consumes a lot of resources and energy, pollutes the ecological environment, causes an ecological crisis and highlights the negative impact of industrial civilization. In 1987, British scholars John Elkington and Julia Hailes defined "green consumption" in their book *The Green Consumer*, which also pointed out that to realize green consumption, it is necessary to stay away from the following products: (1) goods that harm human health; (2) commodities that consume excessive resources and energy; (3) goods that are over-packaged; (4) goods extracted from rare species; (5) goods that harm the interests of developing countries. At the United Nations Conference on Environment and Development, held in Rio de Janeiro in 1992, *Agenda 21* was formulated, clearly stating that all countries need to make their efforts to promote sustainable consumption. Since then, the concept of green consumption has spread around the world and caused a huge storm. The consumption pattern in the industrial civilization period advocated consumption and convenience, which has resulted in excessive consumption of resources, energy, and environmental pollution. So only green consumption can fundamentally alleviate the ecological crisis. Practicing green consumption, comprehensively coordinating the relationship between consumption, environmental protection, and energy conservation and achieving the integration of development and sustainability is also in line with the essence of green consumption.

Green consumption mainly has the following meanings: firstly, people are encouraged to choose green manufacturing goods. Secondly, people need to pay attention to reducing pollution emissions and rationally disposing of waste in the process of consumption. Finally, people's consumption perceptions need to be changed, and they should pay attention to energy conservation and environmental protection. The concept of green consumption has changed people's traditional consumption perceptions that advocate personal consumption and convenience, which coordinately combines personal consumption and ecological protection and abandons traditional

---

[1] Shigeru, Iwasa, *Environmental Thoughts and Marxism*, translated by Han Lixin, et.al., Beijing: Central Compilation & Translation Press, 1997.

excessive consumption behaviors. Besides, if people adhere to the way of green consumption, it will encourage manufacturing enterprises to adopt the green production to produce green products, thus to abandon pollution, protect the ecology in the upstream and promote the harmonious coexistence of people, nature, and society.

The idea of ecological in the consumption process is the standard for evaluating green consumption. The ecological consumption means that we must meet the needs of contemporaries in the process of consumption without hurting the needs of future generations and maintain the natural balance. Green consumption not only requires the rational use of resources and energy but also involves the reduction of pollutant emissions as much as possible. People pay attention to the ecological consumption when practicing green consumption, that is to say, they carry out fair, equitable and sustainable consumption. We cannot undermine the rational consumption of others because of our consumption, nor can we jeopardize future generations' consumption. Besides, green consumption is also constantly improving in its developing process. The zero growth theory in Western economics advocates zero economic growth and zero population growth, with a pessimistic attitude toward economic growth. However, if economic growth and population growth stopped, the entire society would lose vitality, and both the economy and society would be stagnated and are likely to have social crises. Most countries now recognize the negative effects of zero growth and avoid their economy and population toward zero growth. Green consumption draws on the negative impact of zero growth. On the one hand, it emphasizes that in the process of consumption we must follow the laws of nature, protect the ecological environment and conduct consumption rationally. On the other hand, we have to elevate people's material and cultural living standards through technological innovation to avoid zero growth.

4.2.3 The change of thinking mode of man-machine relationship

4.2.3.1 Conversion of man-machine relationship

(1) *The progress of the human-machine relationship in the manufacturing industry*

In the natural economic period with low productivity, the craftsmen mainly bear the heavy responsibility of producing products. The craftsmen who had high production skills and techniques used production tools to produce all kinds of exquisite products to meet people's needs. The man-machine relationship at that time was mainly characterized by the relationship between craftsmen and production tools. The craftsman's skills and experience were combined with simple production tools, that is to say, humans and machines are in a low-level harmonious relationship. To improve labor productivity, craftsmen had created more advanced production tools, which was in line with the philosophy of ergonomics. In ancient China, Confucianism represented by Confucius and Mencius was orthodox. Craftsmen's social status was low and had no opportunities to learn scientific knowledge. They could only rely on their experience accumulated in the long-term production practice. China's manufacturing industry has been lagging behind other countries for many reasons, one of which was the low social status of craftsmen. The first industrial revolution initiated by the United Kingdom was a huge revolution in human history. Human beings had entered the steam era, and the machine production (mainly referring to the steam power) had largely replaced human manual labor. Human beings have gradually been freed from heavy physical labor and gained substantive status. Social productivity had been continuously improved along with human beings and machines in a relatively harmonious relationship.

The emergence of various manufacturing machines had satisfied people's ambitions in pursuit of higher production efficiency and machines had become the core of manufacturing in a certain sense. With the second industrial revolution coming, human beings entered the electrical era. The automatic production lines had also been applied to the manufacturing industry, and the production efficiency of the machine had been further improved. However, with the further improvement of production efficiency, there existed inevitable contradictions between man and machine. It means that people had become a component of the production line, ultimately serving machine production, which we call human beings' alienation by science and technology.

The research on human-machine relationship caters for a practical need. In the 1880s, Frederick Winslow Taylor, the father of scientific management, conducted research on human-machine relations and produced the following results. First, people need to adapt to the application of the machine by improving their theoretical knowledge and machine operation skills, which is also the main way to deal with the human- machine relationship. Second, through improved production tools, people can operate a machine more comfortably and safely. The health care industry in the UK had conducted a special investigation on this issue by inviting experts and scholars to study the fatigue of the human body. It mainly studied the posture, working time, workshop temperature, humidity, sunshine conditions of workers on the production line. It aimed to improve the production environment and production norms to ease the fatigue of workers, thus improving production efficiency. Many scientists in other developed countries had also conducted in-depth research on human-machine relationships and applied their theory to production practices, promoting the formation of good human-machine relationships. After the outbreak of the Second World War in 1939, many countries were ravaged by war, and the relationship between supply and demand for products was very intense. Therefore, the manufacturing industry had begun to develop large machines with higher production efficiency. The machines with extremely high production efficiency are beyond the physical limits of human beings. The production process of the machines did not perfectly match the physical and psychological conditions of human beings, resulting in frequent safety incidents. Machine relations have highlighted discord, and experts and scholars had to review human-machine relationships. After studying these safety incidents, we have learned that people have become the decisive factor impacting the manufacturing industry. We also have reviewed the human-machine relationship. In the process of the machine design and production, relevant elements have also been embedded to ensure the comfort and safety of the person who operates the machine, which means that the design of the machine is catering for the human beings.

The modern scientific and technological revolution that began in the first half of the 20th century had made great progress in high-end advanced technologies such as computer technology, modern design theory, and technology as well as modern management. The latest achievements of the scientific and technological revolution are combined with advanced manufacturing technologies, which have helped advanced manufacturing technology achieve leap-forward advance. The manufacturing technology infrastructure has been improved step by step, and human beings have been given priority. The physical and mental health of human beings has been emphasized in the production process, featuring the relatively harmonious relationship between man and machine.

(2) *The relationship between man-machine in the background of advanced manufacturing technology*

Advanced manufacturing technology refers to the combination of technology, equipment, and systems generated by various technologies such as mechanical engineering technology, electronic technology, automation technology, and information technology. The advanced manufacturing technology makes production efficiency higher, and it is gradually developing towards automation, control, intelligentization, integration, and flexibility. The advance of automation has primarily realized the separation of people and machines, allowing machines to be engaged in production alone. Human beings can be separated from direct production procedures, and human subjectivity is further enhanced. The progress of artificial intelligence technology makes the machine highly intelligent, which can replace human beings to complete high-intensity, high-difficulty, and high-risk work. Therefore, people can be freed from heavy mechanical labor and have more time to carry out higher levels of creative labor. In the integrated production, each part of the manufacturing enterprise is closely connected, and the division of labor in production is gradually becoming unclear, and the manufacturing process is a general process of collecting, analyzing, inputting, and applying data. From this point of view, the product is an external manifestation of data. People can participate in all aspects from product planning to after-sales and can fully develop their potentials. The flexible technology in the manufacturing industry is mainly manifested in two dimensions. On the one hand, it refers to the flexible reaction of production capacity, and that is, the machine equipment can carry out small batch production. On the other hand, it refers to the agility and precise response of the supply chain. The flexible production technology allows for both efficiency and flexibility to be achieved, making both machine and human flexibility enhanced. The advance of networked production makes it possible to allocate social resources and human resources rationally. The production process is becoming more macroscopic and comprehensive, breaking through the one-sidedness of traditional production.

Once the irreconcilable contradiction between humans and technology, it will definitely affect the sustainable development of technology. Flexible manufacture system (FMS) and computer integrated manufacturing systems (CIMS) monitoring and manufacturing systems fully illustrate this point. The manufacturing industry in the United States had suffered severe setbacks. After reflection and summarization, they found that the excessive promotion of automation and the neglect of human factors were the deep-seated reasons for manufacturing difficulties. Research conducted by the American Advanced Manufacturing Technology Company shows that 70 percent of the resistance to CIMS comes from people-related factors. After automation enters a relatively mature stage of development, it needs to exert human initiative and creativity at a higher level.[1] Computer integrated manufacturing (CIM) is a philosophy for optimizing manufacturing and production management. With the development of automation and integration industry, manufacturing will inevitably have a disharmonious relationship with nature. In the face of this special situation, we can only respond quickly by relying on our wisdom and own knowledge. The creativity and

---

[1] Tang Daisheng, A Probe into Sustainable Consumption, Chengdu: Southwestern University of Finance and Economics, 2002.

imagination of human beings is the key to solving unexpected problems. In the progress of modern manufacturing, although the role of human beings seems to be getting smaller, it actually has obtained bigger, from the original machine control to the comprehensive high-end management. In 1990, James P. Womack, the professor of Massachusetts Institute of Technology, pointed out in *The Machine That Changed the World* the reason why Japan was experiencing the rapid development in the manufacturing industry. As a country with few resources, Japan gave full play to people's subjective initiative, believed in the idea of people-oriented, moderately adopted automated mechanical production and carried out macro-level scientific control of the entire manufacturing industry. The US government learned from Japan's advanced experience and put forward the manufacturing development planning with characterizing people-oriented and moderately automated.

4.2.3.2 Changing the way of thinking and implementing green manufacturing

The key to changing the traditional way of thinking is to change the paradigm of thinking. It is an internal, stable, repetitive, and exemplary paradigm of thinking based on the world outlook, cognitive system, beliefs, etc. The change of thinking mode is not to propose a new theory or idea under the framework of the traditional paradigm, but to comprehensively consider various factors, concrete analysis of specific problems, and achieve the transformation of the thinking paradigm. In the background of green manufacturing, the thinking of sustainable development must be implemented in all sectors of society.

(1) *Promoting the transition from singular thinking to holistic thinking*

The singular thinking mode is a single, narrow way of thinking, ignoring the integrity and system of things. Moreover, it often just sees one aspect of things and ignores other aspects. When dealing with problems, its means is single, and it is even more likely to go to extremes. It often fails to do a specific analysis of specific problems in ordinary business and cannot deal with problems from the perspective of the macro system. The overall thinking refers to grasping the overall trend and direction of things from a comprehensive and a long-term perspective and thinking and dealing with problems objectively and dialectically. For a long time, we also have such isolated and one-sided thinking in our work. All work aims at GDP, and all indicators only focus on GDP. Taking the GDP as a priority, some government officials proactively engage in vanity projects which seem to be grandeur and political gain outside but harm the people and the society inside. They may result in increases in GDP but also lead to environmental pollution and ecological deterioration, which eventually damages the survival of future generations and causes great disasters. Only by establishing holistic thinking can we promote the construction and development of the Five-sphere Integrated Plan[1] in the whole society and can we drive the overall progress of the country at a higher level. In this process, personal development is also guaranteed. We must establish a comprehensive social management system to enable cooperation among the government, enterprises, and citizens starting from a macro perspective. Any one-sided, isolated, metaphysical thinking mode is not advisable, and these modes of thinking cannot guarantee the implementation of sustainable thinking.

(2) *Promoting the transition from static thinking to dynamic thinking*

The environment in which we live is an ever-changing organic system, and we should use a dynamic and developing perspective to solve problems. Dynamic thinking is a kind of thinking activity that continuously adjusts and optimizes the degree, direction, and content of thinking based on the changes of external objective conditions to achieve the purpose of thinking. Dynamic thinking requires us to abandon the utilitarian thinking of fishing by draining the pond and establish long-term thinking of green and harmony. Utilitarian thinking cuts off the organic transformation between qualitative and quantitative changes. It only pays attention to immediate gains and neglects the natural laws, even wastes massive resources and energies, and destroys the ecological environment, which ultimately has a negative impact on the long-term development of humankind. The long-term thinking is more in line with the transformation law of qualitative and quantitative changes, follows the natural rules, and adheres to the concept of sustainable development in which people and nature live in harmony. Adherence to long-term thinking requires the following points. First, the relationship between quality and speed must be balanced. On the one hand, we need to see that quality and speed are interrelated, that is, without necessary speed, benefits will not be produced; on the other hand, we must pay more attention to the quality and efficiency of development, and we must abandon the old-fashioned path of pollution first and treatment later . We must grasp the unity of quality and speed, dialectically considering the relationship between speed and quality with long-term thinking and continuous thinking. At the same time, we should also pay attention to optimizing resources allocation, protecting the environment, and adjusting the industrial structure. Second, it is necessary to look at the relationship between protecting the ecology and promoting

---

[1] The overall plan for promoting all-round economic, political, cultural, social, and ecological progress. —*Tr.*

economic development with long-term thinking. In the industrial civilization, we are willing to sacrifice the environment to merely pursue rapid economic advance. However, the long-term thinking and the scientific development concept attach great importance to the protection of nature and the balance of ecology, advocate green manufacturing and recyclable development, and realize the harmonious coexistence between man and nature. On the issue of coordinating economic development and environmental protection, the government must play a leading role in increasing financial input, improving laws and regulations, and cooperating with enterprises to achieve harmonious development of the economy and the environment.

(3) *Promoting the transition from isolated thinking to holistic thinking*

The universality of connection means that all objects, phenomena, and processes are not isolated, and they interact, influence each other and restrict each other. Development is also connected. The development of any object is inseparable from other objects. Therefore, this requires us to make full use of holistic thinking in the process of understanding the world and transforming the world. In the new situation, the Five-sphere Integrated Plan put forward by the Chinese Communist Party is to fully use the holistic thinking to solve social contradictions, which properly manifests the social development and operation. For example, coordinating urban and rural development is to pay more attention to rural development issues at both theoretical and practical levels, to make policies favorable for rural areas, and to look at urban and rural development from a holistic perspective. It is to promote the philosophy of enhancing agriculture with manufacturing development, cities supporting the countryside narrowing the gap between the urban and the rural, and to promote the joint development of urban and rural areas. Coordinating regional development is to consider multiple aspects and various factors of regional development from multiple aspects and angles, thereby promoting the integration and coordination of regional development. Coordinating economic and social development means realizing coordinated economic and social development, taking into account the progress of the economy and the harmony of society from the perspective of the entire society. Coordinating the harmonious development of man and nature means that it not only satisfies the material and cultural needs of the people but also protects the natural environment and ecological balance and achieves sustainable development. To coordinate domestic development and opening up to the outside world, we must avoid risks, meet challenges, seize opportunities, and fully utilize the two markets and resources in the complicated international and domestic situations. To sum up, only by standing at the height of comprehending the overall situation and using holistic thinking to coordinate the unity and development of all aspects can we better solve complex social contradictions and promote the overall and coordinated development of society. Fundamentally speaking, the Five-sphere Integrated Plan reflects the objective laws of socialist modernization and manifests the strategic concept of the all-round development of the socialist society.

(4) *Promoting the transition from linear thinking to non-linear thinking*

Linear thinking is the abstraction of matter rather than the abstraction of the essence of the matter, which is the one-sided, straight line, and intuitive thinking. People have been affected by this linear thinking mode for a long time. They tend to have the wrong tendency of being one or the other, right or wrong and do not consider the correct and effective things in other options. They choose between two alternatives. The linear thinking model equates social development with economic development, which easily triggers some related social problems. Non-linear thinking is interconnected, non-planar, three-dimensional, acentric and borderless network structure, which is similar to the human brain and vascular tissue. The world we live in is a non-linear system. In addition to the most important human factors, there are natural and social factors that are closely related to human life, which affects one another and maintains the operation of the world. In the current society, opportunities and challenges coexist, but social contradictions are more prominent. If these contradictions are not handled well, it is easy to trigger the Butterfly Effect of society. Therefore, we must deal with social affairs with a non-linear thinking model, and study the development model, mechanism of action, and the form of expression of the entire society. Taking all factors into consideration, we will fully embody non-linear thinking in all aspects of our social production and life, and better run the society and the world where we live in.

(5) *Promoting the transition of material-oriented thinking to people-oriented thinking*

Material-oriented thinking believes that development equals growth and human being is a tool for development. This is a one-sided and unscientific understanding, which ignores the environmental problems that may arise in the process of economic development and the contradiction between man and nature. More importantly, it ignores the value of human beings, leading to the "value added to the world of objects is directly proportional to the depreciation of the world of human beings".[1]

---

[1] Chen Yaonian, Qin Zheng'ai, "The Transformation of the Scientific Outlook on Development and the Way of Thinking", *People's Tribune,* 2006(11), pp.60-61.

Therefore, we should advocate the concept of scientific development in the whole society to guide social construction, firmly follow the people-oriented point of view, pay attention to the role of people in advance of green manufacturing, and adhere to the people-oriented thought. The masses of the people are the decisive force for social change and reform. China's development and growth cannot be separated from the efforts of the people. All developments in China are aimed at realizing the interests of the broadest masses of the people. We must ensure that development is for the people, that it is reliant on the people, and that its fruits are shared by the people. If we do not adhere to the humanistic thought or promptly and consciously emphasize and implement the essential principle of development for the people, on the people, and by the people, this development trend may deviate from the Party's fundamental purpose and the will of its people. Therefore, the transformation from the material-oriented thinking to the people-oriented thinking determines the nature, results, and significance of development as well as the future of socialist development.

Chapter 5
Practical Exploration of Green Manufacturing in China

5.1 The vision for the development of China's manufacturing industry

The manufacturing industry is a pillar industry of our country, which processes manufacturing resources into industrial products, household goods, consumer goods, according to market requirements and through a systematic and skilled manufacturing process. It takes an essential position in national economic development and has a high economic contribution rate. At present, China is in a critical period of social transformation. Since the founding of the People's Republic of China, its manufacturing industry can be divided into two stages. The first stage was from the founding of the People's Republic of China in 1949 to the reform and opening up in 1978. During this period, China had adopted five-year national economic plans, introduced important manufacturing projects from the Soviet Union and other manufacturing powers, and comprehensively upgraded its manufacturing industry. The second stage was from the reform and opening up to now. Through unremitting efforts and development, China's manufacturing output has ranked first place in the world but still has a long way to go to catch up with the advanced manufacturing of the developed countries. The current mission of China's manufacturing industry is to improve the quality and level of manufacturing and move toward a manufacturing power.

The promulgation of *Made in China 2025* (also known as the "China Version of Industrial 4.0 Plan") reflects the determination and courage of our country to stride forward to a strong manufacturing country. *Made in China 2025* is of great significance in the process of China's industrial development. It promotes the development of manufacturing industry, realizes stable economic growth and optimizes the allocation of manufacturing resources. *Made in China 2025* is the program of action for the first ten years of implementing the strategy of manufacturing power in China. Its fundamental purpose is to realize the transformation of China's manufacturing industry from big to strong, to enhance the international competitiveness of its manufacturing industry, and to realize the great rejuvenation of the Chinese nation through the prosperity and development of the manufacturing industry. The State Council has made a major strategic plan to enhance China's overall national strength, enhance its international competitiveness and safeguard its national security. It has made greater policy efforts than before and has made new arrangements and regulations on industry access, taxation, finance, and industrial system.

5.1.1 *Made in China 2025* is in the background of the global division of labor

5.1.1.1 The new trend of the global division of labor

(1) *The international division of labor within products based on production links and processes is becoming increasingly prevalent*

The final production of products is no longer a sign of production relations between countries. There are production links in R&D, design, manufacture, sale, and operation. The factor concentration of each link of the value chain determines the division of labor in each link of production rather than the average factor density of the product. Therefore, the international division of labor goes deep into all links of the same industry and the same product value chain with specific factor density requirements, forming regional or global processing bases, manufacturing bases, R&D bases, procurement or marketing bases serving the global production network. It changes the so-called concentration of developed countries in high capital and high-tech intensive production while developing countries focus on the division of labor in labor-intensive industries. The potential implication of this trend is that specific countries can expand their advantages in particular factor-intensive links to all sectors.

(2) *The internalization trend of the world market is increasingly strengthened*

Countries at different levels of productivity can develop the same industry at the same time, but because of the internalization of the world market in this industry, there is a huge gap between countries' profits. The value of assets created by specialized knowledge, management skills, and brand management is much higher than the value of tangible goods. Countries with knowledge-intensive product design, research and development, management services, marketing, and brand management rely on controlling patents, standards, and brands, and through the value chain layout, have achieved monopoly income distribution in the production process rather than in the circulation process. The ability to allocate global elements beyond the borders has become an important support for ensuring the benefits of the international division of labor. The potential implication of this trend is that countries or regions that act as global regulatory centers, global laboratories, global R&D bases, and global logistics bases have distinct value-added advantages over global manufacturing bases and global processing bases.

(3) *There is a hierarchy of non-equity linkages around the world*

The universality of subcontracting activities has caused more and more independent manufacturers to be involved in the internal part of the network, which is dominated by multinational companies. The global production network has increasingly integrated into the national economy and disintegrated the international division of labor by countries. Although there is no equity link between companies, there is a relationship between "leadership" and "subordinate". The micro-form of the international division of labor is reflected in the hierarchical relationship between the leading enterprises in the industry and the controlled suppliers. The underlying meaning of this trend is whether or not an industry-led enterprise has a significant influence on whether or not a country can have a dominant position in the international division of labor.

5.1.1.2 Three major demands for global manufacturing development

(1) *Ecological demand*

Manufacturing is a pillar industry that creates human wealth. The traditional manufacturing industry has brought enormous economic benefits and material enjoyment to humankind in the process of industrialization. However, it is undeniable that it has also led to an ecological crisis and a waste of resources. Faced with the deteriorating living environment, people begin to reconsider how to utilize nature and protect the earth. As an essential carrier of the manufacturing industry, enterprises not only need to gain profit but also pay for the environment. Sustainable development of the manufacturing industry and green manufacturing trend of thought has shown strong ecological demands. On the one hand, enterprises are urged to make full use of resources in the manufacturing process as much as possible. On the other hand, it is necessary to avoid pollution to the greatest extent. The traditional manufacturing industry is highly intensive in wasting resources in the production process, regardless of the environment, and the understanding of the product is the process of from designing to scrapping, regardless of its worthiness. Therefore, it poses a great threat to the global environment in which we live and pollutes the living space of human beings. The severity of this problem has been attached great importance to at all levels of society, and it is imminent to solve it. Especially in today's rapid advancement of technology, product updates are faster, and resource abandonment becomes another problem that needs to be solved. In this way, manufacturing companies will inevitably bear most of the responsibilities, and they need to change the current predicament by taking the green manufacturing path through transformation.

The ecological demand of manufacturing industry needs to change the development model that the manufacturing industry takes the interests as the ultimate pursuit. The traditional manufacturing industry does not consider the environmental and pollution issues, only takes economic benefits into account in the production and manufacturing process, which also makes the development of the manufacturing industry very difficult. The manufacturer makes the raw materials into products, discards the products into the environment after they are used, and discharges a large amount of exhaust gas, and waste residue into the environment during the industrial production process and the use of the products. These substances are the main environmental pollutants. Therefore, the sustainable development of the manufacturing industry has put forward a demand for environmentally friendly and resource-saving production models, which regards ecological benefits as its benefit output. At present, the scientific and technological revolution is in full swing. New achievements have emerged in the frontier fields of science and technology, such as new materials, nanotechnology, and biotechnology, and will be further applied to production activities. Information technology, such as big data and the Internet of Things are gradually developing in cooperation with the manufacturing industry, which makes manufacturing industry acquire new manufacturing model with the support of information technology. The development of science and technology has led to the transformation of the traditional manufacturing industry with faster speed and better quality. At present, the manufacturing industry has followed the trend and is gradually moving towards green manufacturing. Therefore, the new manufacturing model of green manufacturing, which optimizes the use of resources and integrates with environmental protection, is a positive response to the ecological demand for manufacturing development. It will also become the fundamental approach to solve the sustainable development of the manufacturing industry and the only way to the development of manufacturing industry in the 21st century.

(2) *Innovative demand*

Innovation is the inexhaustible motive force for development. Countries all over the world have begun to carry out enterprise innovation in response to the demand of the manufacturing industry to change the innovation model. To improve their overall competitiveness and master the core of technology, developed countries are committed to technological innovation so that they can play a leading role in the new round of competition. For example, the United States is proactively building a manufacturing innovation network, and the UK has stepped up its efforts to build an "Industrial Technology Innovation Center", all of which aim to input incentives through scientific and technological innovation, while at the same time advancing the transformation of technology into products at a faster rate. These actions in developed countries are aimed at creating an emerging manufacturing ecosystem with innovation at its core and promoting manufacturing transformation. China must be keenly aware of this essential trend and actively promote the creation of an innovative manufacturing model at the national level to minimize the gap between China and the developed countries to seize the initiative in competition. It is generally believed that the manufacturing industry rather than the virtual economy is the vital support of the national economy and the basic industry of national development. Especially after the global financial crisis in 2008, the importance of the real economy has been recognized. The developed countries such as the US, Germany, the UK, France had put forward the strategy of "re-industrialization". Developing countries such as India are also speeding up their planning and layout. China has put forward the strategic plan of *Made in China 2025*, focusing on promoting the construction of manufacturing power. Countries are attaching great importance to the transformation of the manufacturing industry. China also keeps up with the mainstream of the times and proposes *Made in China 2025* to vigorously promote the transformation from a big manufacturer to a strong manufacturing power.

Innovation is the core driving force of *Made in China 2025*. In the future, with the further integration of the new generation of information technology and manufacturing industry, the mode of production, enterprise organization and product mode of manufacturing industry will be significantly changed. Enterprises may face many bottlenecks in the traditional process of manufacturing development. Innovation helps enterprises find the right path for their development. The manufacturing industry includes the production of daily necessities, industrial products, military products, etc. It is an important pillar industry for economic growth. In the manufacturing industry, an essential factor that cannot be ignored is the manufacturing capacity of human beings, which determines the strengths and weaknesses of manufacturing development. The world today is undergoing rapid development and a critical period of transformation. All walks of life are undergoing accelerating changes. Manufacturing as a basic industry is no exception. The manufacturing model is gradually changing. One is product-centered, and the other is customer-centered. With products as the center, we produce products that meet the needs of people with quantity and quality. With customers as the center, all of the products meet the requirements of customers and design and produce different products for different groups. These two models guide the current manufacturing concepts and processes of manufacturing enterprises worldwide. In-depth thinking, we will find that whether it is product-centered manufacturing or customer-centered manufacturing, it is built around products and human life. In this process, there is much waste of resources, environmental deterioration, and ecological crisis and other issues. In particular, the modern manufacturing industry has produced a large number of large-scale productions, which has caused severe environmental problems. When all these threaten the survival and development of human beings, we begin to reflect on and seek a new mode of manufacturing development, so green manufacturing is formally proposed.

(3) *Economic demand*

Manufacturing is also the pillar of economic growth, and the development of green manufacturing must have its economic demand. At present, the concept of green manufacturing has been widely recognized all over the world. For China, it is still a long-term process to truly penetrate the concept of green manufacturing into the hearts of every Chinese person and apply it to practice. At present, China is still in the initial stage of application. In the future development of manufacturing industry, we should take innovation as the core to develop green manufacturing, to reduce the use of resources and energy on the largest scale, to reduce the pollution to the environment, and weaken the ecological damage to the maximum extent. The development of manufacturing industry is transforming into green manufacturing and approaching international standards. At present, green manufacturing has been implemented as national strategies in many countries and regions. A very representative point in practice is the introduction of a low-carbon economy. In 2003, the UK government released the energy white paper *Our Energy Future: Creating a Low-Carbon Economy*. A low-carbon economy is a low-energy, low-pollution, low-emission development model with the concept of sustainable development which is opposite to the "three-high"[1]

---

[1] High-pollution, high-emission, high-energy consumption —*Tr.*

model of industrial development in the past. The low-carbon economy has become the basic demand for green manufacturing.

The economic demand for green manufacturing is to develop a low-carbon economic development mode. Promoting green manufacturing means to reduce waste of resources and energy, reduce pollution, and improve the efficiency of resource utilization in the process of product production and manufacturing. For the public, they enjoy both high-quality products and high-quality environment. For enterprises, it not only improves the efficiency of enterprises but also no longer needs to pay for environmental pollution. For the employees, they enjoy a good working environment, and their work efficiency improves. Therefore, the implementation of green manufacturing will be a win-win result. The basic demand of green manufacturing is the low-carbon economy, which is to create new production technology to eliminate the "three high" model through technology integration, technology innovation, technology research, and development. To maximize resource utilization, minimize energy consumption and promote the harmonious development of ecology and economy, green manufacturing, intelligent manufacturing, and advanced manufacturing technology are needed to ensure the smooth development of the low-carbon economy. At present, many multinational corporations, such as SIEMENS in Germany, Toyota Motor Corporation and Hitachi Limited in Japan, and Ford Motor Company in the United States, have started to implement green manufacturing strategy to develop green products in different degrees. "Green manufacturing will be one of the biggest strategic challenges for the industry in the near future, from engineering, business to market perspectives." *The Journal of Manufacturing and Technology News* pointed out in a headline report entitled Green Manufacturing Is A Strategic Priority.

5.1.1.3   The domestic background of *Made in China 2025*

(1) *Resource and energy in manufacturing are overconsumed*

After the constant development in recent years, China has gradually become a manufacturing center in the world with its export continuing to increase. Since 2010, the ratio of China's manufacturing output among the whole world has ranked first in a four-year cycle. Besides, there are more than 220 kinds of product made by China among over 500 major industrial products, ranking first through the world. At present, there are 24 industries in total, and the excess capacity problem has been seen in 21 industries of which metallurgy industry, clothing industry, and steel industry are representatives. Making steel industry as an example, according to the statistics from the China Iron and Steel Association, at the end of 2010 the capacity of steelmaking had reached 800 million tons, while in 2011 the newly putting capacity of steelmaking was 80 million tons with about 30 million tons of backward capacity being sifted out and at the end of 2011, and the crude steel production capacity was around 850 million tons. According to the statistics from China Metallurgical Industry Planning and Research Institute, by the end of 2011, the capacity of crude steel production was around 900 million tons. However, in 2011, 683 million tons of crude steel was produced in China, which resulted in a severe excessive production. On a wider perspective of the current situation, other manufacturing industries also face the same risk.

(2) *The driving force of innovation is insufficient*

Since the reform and opening up, we have adopted a method of exchanging technique with our market and massive introduction of foreign capital and technologies to alleviate the situation of rapid development. In return, our domestic market was occupied by multinational enterprises from export by a foreign investor with large usury of our profit. However, those advanced technologies and core technologies that we have been longing for a long time were very few. Products with strong export competitiveness such as textiles, garments, shoes, toys as well as home appliances, electronic parts, electromechanical products, are low value-added. Few products with innovative technologies only need to be processed with supplied materials or to be assembled by supplied components. In the joint venture, foreign companies control the core technology and sales channels. We have to pay high patent fees and low-cost labor to exchange meager profit. In the international market, low-price, lack of self-IPR are the label of Chinese products. Lack of independent innovation, we are not a powerful manufacturing country but a country as a production base for other countries.

(3) *The construction of the basic Internet infrastructure is deferred*

It is emphasized in *Made in China 2025* document that the development of the manufacturing industry should be driven by the mutual integration of IT application and industrialization, and the deep integration of industrialization and information technology is an important driving force for building a manufacturing powerhouse, taking a new path to industrialization, and changing the mode of development. Currently, our country has been in a relatively under-developed situation around the world due to poor industrialization, a low combination of industrialization and urbanization, inadequate basic information facilities. From the Networked Readiness Index announced by the Global Information Technology Report 2015, China has dropped from 51 in 2012 to 62 in 2015, severely lower than Singapore, the United States, Japan, etc. One of the remarkable features is the big regional difference in the coverage of information service. The basic information infrastructure and coverage of Internet are outdated in the western region. If the basic information networks are inadequate, our capacity cannot keep pace with the new trend of "Internet Plus" and integrate the industrialization and IT application.[1]

(4) *The population dividend is waning*

According to the statistics, every dollar put in Europe and America developed manufacturing industry will receive triple output and 5.8 times in Southeast Asia countries. However, there are only 2.8 times in China. It shows that human resource advantage begins to disappear. China has gradually entered the aging society. Therefore, the southeastern coastal areas have met the challenge of labor shortage, particularly in the labor-intensive industries and manufacturing. It is obvious that our country has lost our previous advantages in the labor force for many big manufacturing factories. Nike and Foxconn have their new factories in the Southeastern Asian countries to make full use of their cheap labor force. With some foreign-funded enterprises transferring their factories from China, it is obvious that our population dividend is waning.

(5) *Low efficiency in natural resources utilization*

China has put the focus on the heavy industry while it needs to consume plenty of resources and energy with serious environmental pollution. Many corporations with low technology aimed to pursue economic profit, therefore, they cost more resources and energy, which results in low efficiency. According to the data, China's energy consumption per unit of GDP is about 1.9 times of the world average, 2.4 times of that of the United States, 3.65 times of that of Japan, and even higher than that of developing countries such as Brazil and Mexico.

5.1.1.4　The international context for the publication of *Made in China 2025*

(1) *The influence of re-shoring manufacturing in developed countries*

From 2009 to 2012, the American government has carried out a series of policies to attract the reshoring of manufacturing and promote economic growth. For example, "Buy American" and "National Export Initiative" have made remarkable achievement. Caterpillar listed in the Fortune Global 500 has transferred its overseas excavator production back into Texas. The General Electric Company has transferred its

---

[1] Miao Wei, "Do a Good job of in-depth Integration of Informatization and Industrialization", *People's Daily*, Nov.13, 2014.

outsourced jobs from China and Mexico back to Louisville and added a new high-density battery factory. Whirlpool Corporation has invested US$2.1 billion in Tennessee to build a new factory, and Apple Inc. has put US$100 million to remove parts of its production line back into America, etc. Benefiting from cheap energy caused by salary stagnation, the weak dollar and the breakthrough of shale gas technology, America has become the ideal places for the investment of large multinational corporations. SIEMENS has built a gas turbine factory; Airbus has invested US$600 million in building a new assembly plant in Alabama; Samsung has spent US$4 billion to expand Texas-based enamel chip factory. Based on the relevant data, the number of US manufacturing employment has increased 489,000, reaching 11.9 million, an increase of 4.3 percent in 2011, at the same time, large multinational corporations reduced its investment to developing countries, only in the first half of 2012 China's index in attracting FDI has reduced 3 percent compared with the previous years. At present, America has closed its gap in the cost of manufacturing industry with China to 5 percent. The Boston Consulting Group once said that American metalware, machinery industry, computer, and spare parts industry could realize self-supply in 2020 instead of importing from China. [1] Faced with the gradual shrinkage of the traditional market, China's manufacturing industry must take instant action to solve the problem of surplus productivity and open a new market for products.

(2) *The impact of the investigation of "anti-dumping and countervailing duty" in European and American countries*

Based on the SWOT analysis of all manufacturing industries, the developed countries in Europe and America, unexpectedly, chose "the advanced manufacturing" as the main breach of industrial recovery. As for life-based manufacturing (textiles, garments, furniture, and shoes, etc.) and resource-based manufacturing (such as minerals, steel, paper, etc.), they build tariff and a non-tariff barrier to protect and enhance their investigation for "anti-dumping and countervailing duty" to reverse their trade deficit. According to The 1930 Tariff Act, from 2010 to 2012, United States International Trade Commission initiated 112 investigations in the name of "337 Rogatory", 39 of which were for Chinese companies, accounting for approximately 38.42 percent. The EU has gradually launched more "anti-dumping and countervailing duty" investigations to China including photovoltaic products, coated fine paper, soy

---

[1] Zhang Lidong, "Research on the Path of Manufacturing Transformation and Upgrading in the Background of *Made in China 2025*", *Jiangxi Social Sciences*, 2016(4), pp.43-47.

protein products, stainless steel seamless pipe, ceramic product, bathroom products, aluminum foil products, screw-thread steel, etc. [1] Chinese manufacturing enterprises are busy with various trade investigations, while European and American companies can seize the opportunities and vigorously explore the global market, even strive to squeeze the living space of China's manufacturing industry. The photovoltaic industry is the first to bear the brunt and suffer heavy losses.

(3) *The resistance of overseas acquisitions*

Developed countries in Europe and America have been keeping high alert towards China's overseas expansion in manufacturing. According to Dealogic, the failure rate of overseas acquisitions by Chinese companies in 2010 was 11 percent, ranking first in the world, while the rate of the US and the UK was only 2 percent and 1 percent. As known to all, cross-border investment is an important way to allocate global resources rationally. Overseas direct investment in the US reached a peak of US$421.5 billion in 1990. Even in the economic downturn in 2010, it can also maintain a high level of US$325.5 billion. However, It is late for China to start cross-border direct investment, which did not exceed US$100 billion until 2013. Only we learn from foreign experience and reduce our failure rate in overseas investment and acquisition can we make full use of global resources, energy, and technology, etc. to further support the in-depth integration and development of our country's industrialization and IT application. Faced with a global industrial revulsion, China's manufacturing is in a crossing road. In 2014 the industrial added value achieved RMB22.8 trillion, accounting for 35.85 percent of the global GDP. The enormous industrial economic stock is a "Sword of Damocles": [2] the negative impact brought by excess capacity and weak manufacturing for China is worse than those developed countries in Europe and America. A hard landing may threaten our economy without the support of our lower-end. However, if we cannot reach a high level in high-end, it is possible for China to suffer from the engine and power of economic growth. To focus on the realistic need through changing the way of economic growth, Chinese government has proposed the strategy of *Made in China 2025* in March 2015: we should attach importance to some key fields including endogenous growth driven by innovation, advanced manufacturing, high-end equipment, and smart technology to accelerate the transformation and upgrading of manufacturing industry.

---

[1] Zhang Lidong, "Research on the Path of Manufacturing Transformation and Upgrading in the Background of *Made in China 2025*", *Jiangxi Social Sciences*, 2016(4), pp.47-48.

[2] Zhang Lidong, "Research on the Path of Manufacturing Transformation and Upgrading in the Background of *Made in China 2025*", *Jiangxi Social Sciences,* 2016(4), pp.49-50.

5.1.2 The vital deployment of *Made in China 2025*

5.1.2.1 The overall framework

Made in China 2025 is a cooperative achievement guided by Ministry of Industry and Information Technology, working together with National Development and Reform Commission, Ministry of Science and Technology, Ministry of Finance, General Administration of Quality Supervision, Inspection and Quarantine and Chinese Academy of Engineering. The framework of *Made in China 2025* can be concluded as "one, two, three, four, double five and ten."

"One" means one goal. It is not our ultimate goal to become a big manufacturer, but we should strive for being a strong manufacturer.

"Two" means that our country should take full advantage of industrialization and informatization technology when we head for being a powerful manufacturer country. This is the general tendency based on the guidance of the 18th National Congress of the CPC, and it is also the principle and direction for the development of China's manufacturing industry.

"Three" means we must undergo "three steps" in the development strategy of manufacturing. In general, it should take 30 years in three steps to realize the goal, to upgrade China from a big manufacturing nation to a powerful manufacturing nation.

"Four" means four principles. The first principle is to emphasize the market's priority and the government's role in guidance. The second principle is that China's manufacturing industry should be based on both the current and the long-term. The third principle is to adhere to both comprehensive advancement and critical breakthroughs. The fourth principle is to stick to both self-development and win-win cooperation.

"Double five" is to carry out two "five" principles. The first "five" refers to five guidelines: namely, innovation-driven, quality-first, green development, structural optimization, and people-oriented; the second "five" means the five major projects, including the construction of the manufacturing innovation center, facility strengthening we call it as the firm foundation project, the intelligent manufacturing project, the green manufacturing project, and a high-end equipment innovation project.

Based on the overall framework, breakthroughs are required to focus on ten key areas, including innovative materials, biology, and information technology. *Made in China 2025* provides a solid guarantee and support for the development of green manufacturing in the future, and points out the direction of the development of manufacturing industry in the future. The whole society should make concerted efforts to study and implement the *Made in China 2025*, focusing on enterprises, in order to upgrade China from a great manufacturing nation to a powerful manufacturing nation.

5.1.2.2 Strategic guidelines and guiding principles

Made in China 2025 was proposed by the expert team of the Chinese Academy of Engineering after almost three years of research and demonstration. To achieve the ultimate goal of this strategy, our country needs to make concerted efforts to collaborate in all sectors of the society to complete the transformation in the next 30 years so that China can become a manufacturing power. *Made in China 2025* is the action plan of the first decade for China's implementation of manufacturing power, and it plans the path and schedule for the next manufacturing development. The deployment of the *Made in China 2025* means that our country will cost 30 years effort to construct a manufacturing power, promote international influence and enhance the economic foundation of the Chinese Dream to pay tribute for the 100th founding anniversary of the People's Republic of China. Therefore, the guiding ideology of *Made in China 2025* is mainly three "Persistence", namely, adhering to the basic policy of "innovation-driven, quality-first, green development, structural optimization, and people-oriented". We should adhere to the basic principle of the market playing the main role, government-led, staying firmly rooted in the present while looking ahead to the future, considering the overall situation, making breakthroughs in key areas, sticking to independent development, opening up, and cooperation. Besides, adhering to the goal of becoming a manufacturing powerhouse through the strategic deployment of "three steps": the first step is to enter the ranks of manufacturing powers by 2025; in the second step, by 2035, China's entire manufacturing industry will reach the middle level of the world's manufacturing powers; in the third step, by the time the 100th founding anniversary of the People's Republic of China, the status of China's manufacturing powerhouse has become more consolidated, and its comprehensive strength has entered the forefront of the world's manufacturing powers.

5.1.2.3 The key points of task

Made in China 2025 clearly defines its strategic goal, which is based on the guidance of the government and the integration of resources strategic goals and tasks are implemented. The critical tasks of this plan show that we should firstly improve the national innovation capability in manufacturing, and try to improve the innovation system of manufacturing that makes enterprises as the mainstay, focuses on market-oriented and the combination of government, industry, education, and research, and enhances the independent innovation capability in core links and important areas. Secondly, to make the production process more intelligent, it is necessary to enhance the integration of informatization and industrialization. Therefore, a new production model can be set up. Thirdly, to consolidate the foundations of the industry by working to break through bottlenecks in four areas: core basic spare parts, advanced fundamental techniques, critical basic materials, and basic industrial technologies, and finally weak foundation can be settled. Fourthly, to lay a solid foundation for quality, establish brand advantages, and form domestic brands with independent innovation capabilities. Fifthly, to implement green manufacturing in the process of manufacturing development and establish a manufacturing production system that is energy conservation, environmental protection, and circular development. Sixthly, to focus on new generation of information technology, high-end equipment, new materials, biomedicine, and other strategic priorities, guide the community to gather all kinds of resources, and promote the rapid development of advantages and strategic industries. Seventhly, to promote the restructuring of the manufacturing industry, push the traditional industry forward to the middle and high-end, gradually dissolve excess capacity, facilitate the coordinated development of large and medium-sized enterprises, and further optimize the layout of the manufacturing industry. Eighthly, to enhance the joint development of manufacturing and services, stimulate business model innovation and business form innovation, give impetus to the transformation of production-oriented manufacturing to service-oriented manufacturing, vigorously develop producer services closely related to manufacturing, and speed up the construction of functional service areas and service platforms. Ninthly, to promote the development of key areas, strengthen the top-level design of the manufacturing industry, and enhance the overall competitiveness of manufacturing enterprises.

5.1.3   The contribution of *Made in China 2025* to sustainable development

5.1.3.1   Innovation-driven strategy contributes to sustainable development

Innovation is an inexhaustible driving force for the development of enterprises, and manufacturing is no exception. Innovation is one of the key links in China's efforts to implement *Made in China 2025* and build a manufacturing powerhouse. At present, China's R&D and scientific and technological innovation investment have been at the forefront of the world in recent years, and its importance placed on innovation has dramatically increased. Although there are certain innovative technologies and achievements, after all, it started late, and it is inevitable to encounter difficulties during its development. From the overall perspective, there is a relatively large gap between China and developed countries. According to the analysis of relevant data, the ratio is over 50 percent in our country's dependence of technology for foreign countries, which is relatively high, so we must attach great importance to innovation, strengthen our ability of independent innovation, and speed up the breakthrough and research and development of core technology.

5.1.3.2 The allocation of resources in the real economy

Facing a situation of "deviating from reality" in the manufacturing industry, our country also suffers from market competition pressure imposed by developed countries. Therefore, China must accelerate the revitalization of the real economy and create a better environment for enterprise development through reform and innovation in the new situation. Only in this way, can enterprises develop faster and the manufacturing industry becomes stronger. *Made in China 2025* needs to introduce relevant supporting policies, provide financial subsidies and preferential policies to new high-tech industries, support and help small and medium-sized enterprises, improve multi-level personnel training system, expand the opening of manufacturing industry and other safety precautions to create a favorable environment for the transformation and upgrading of manufacturing industry.

5.1.3.3 Dynamic adjustment in key technologies and industrial fields

In the last round of the strategy of developing emerging manufacturing industries, the Chinese government has proposed seven major areas including photovoltaic and wind power industries, but the expected results can't be reached owing to the overcapacity and big competitive pressures caused by the expansion in scale and inefficient growth. In response to this historical lesson, *Made in China 2025* adopted a strategic deployment of "1+X". In addition to the existing plans, there is also "X planning". The key fields of "X planning" should be dynamically adjusted and updated in real time based on changes and developments of the world market.

5.1.3.4 The goal of industrial power in *Made in China 2025*

Made in China 2025 not only stipulates the development direction of our country's manufacturing industry in general but also subdivides into various production fields. Experts and scholars believe that manufacturing industry is currently at a critical stage of transformation and upgrading, and we must strictly abide by *Made in China 2025* program of action to achieve the strategic goal of becoming a manufacturing power. *Made in China 2025* is the action plan for the first decade of China's strategy of becoming a manufacturing powerhouse. It lays out the path and time for the development of the manufacturing industry in the following years. The deployment of *the Made in China 2025* and efforts mean that our country will cost 30 years effort to construct a manufacturing powerhouse. At the same time, the economic foundation of the Chinese Dream was consolidated. At present, the core technologies that China's manufacturing industry needs to break through including the manufacture of core components, the development of key basic materials, and advanced technological processes. Therefore, given the current disadvantages and problems of China's manufacturing enterprises, the most important task of the current manufacturing development is to organize the implementation of industrial strong foundation projects through innovation-driven strategy and cultivate a group of internationally competitive manufacturing enterprises to occupy the international market better.

5.1.3.5 The sustainability of development promoted by the transformation and upgrading of the manufacturing industry

The developed manufacturing countries' determination and courage to respond to the industrial change are reflected in Germany's "Industrial 4.0" plan, Japan's "Industrial Revitalization" strategy, or the EU's "Industrial Revitalization" strategy. To be able to seize the opportunity for change better and become the leading power in competition, China has also promulgated the "Industrial Revitalization" strategy, *Made in China 2025*, to promote the development of China's manufacturing industry.

Firstly, a sound and multi-level manufacturing industry system needs to be established to promote the research and development of core technologies, encourage industrial innovation and transformation in the manufacturing industry and prepare for taking the path of innovation-driven manufacturing in the following stage. The promulgation of *Made in China 2025* is of great significance to promoting the innovation and development of China's manufacturing industry, improving quality and efficiency, and is bound to cause worldwide debate.

Secondly, the most critical task in the current development of China's manufacturing industry is to accelerate the integration of informatization and industrialization, and to improve the intelligence of manufacturing equipment. The combination and development of "informatization and industrialization" should be toward the goal of intelligent manufacturing. To promote the transformation of "Made in China" to "Created in China" in a wide range, in 2014, Haier Group used intelligent production equipment. Due to the application of intelligent equipment, nearly 20,000 employees were laid off, which has caused a heated discussion among netizens. Actually, we should face squarely up to this realistic problem. If we apply intelligent equipment on a large scale, how can we resettle the surplus labor force? China has a large population in itself, but Germany has a relatively small one. When implementing the "Industry 4.0" strategy, Germany also focused on the issue of surplus labor. Therefore, when our country implements *Made in China 2025* strategy, we should also pay more attention to human factors and reflect our care to human. Besides, small and medium-sized enterprises are very concerned about the upgrading and transformation of China's manufacturing industry. The government needs to consider how to cultivate a number of outstanding small-and medium-sized enterprises that are full of innovation and vitality.

Thirdly, local governments in China need to take measures to follow the strategy of *Made in China 2025* vigorously. The manufacturing industry is the mainstay of China's national economy and the primary source of national taxation. The smooth transformation and upgrading of the manufacturing industry are closely related to the fiscal revenue of the national government and the local governments at all levels. Through an in-depth interpretation of the document, *Made in China 2025*, we can understand the tasks and priorities of China's implementation of the strategy of manufacturing a strong country, accelerate the transformation and upgrading of China's manufacturing industry, and focus on a new round of technological revolution and competition, and create a new chapter in China's manufacturing industry.

5.2   The lessons learned in green manufacturing

5.2.1   Relying on a new round of technological innovation

At present, the competition is becoming increasingly fierce all over the world. It is essential to ensure that all countries remain invincible in the fierce international competition by improving production efficiency and innovation ability, resources and energy consumption and various forms of capital investment. In terms of technological development and demand-driven, green manufacturing has influenced and guided the direction of today's technology development, from product design to manufacturing technology, from enterprise organization management to marketing strategy formulation, many green manufacturing technologies and concepts are in the process of development.

5.2.1.1　Environment-friendly technology

Environment-friendly technology is a general term for pollution reduction, rational use of resources, energy conservation, and environment compatibility. It includes both production process technology and end treatment technology, covering the entire process of know-how, production process, products and services, equipment, organization, and management, with the purpose of minimizing waste emissions and pollution in an environmentally acceptable manner. In the Global Agenda 21, our work in this area has begun by explicitly encouraging enterprises and sectors to develop, use and disseminate environment-friendly technology, and also support the establishment of a cooperative network for the transfer of environment-friendly technology.

5.2.1.2　Clean production

Clean production is practical production methods and measures that can not only meet the needs of people, but also make rational use of natural resources and energy resources, and protect the environment. Its essence is the planning and management of human production activities with the least material and energy consumption, quantifying, recycling, and innocuous waste, or eliminating it in the production process.

5.2.1.3　Industrial ecology

Industrial ecology is an innovative and sustainable industrial strategy. It involves in the design of industrial systems to minimize waste and improve the recycling of materials and energy, emphasizing that production systems should be as close as possible to prevent the loss of energy or useful materials. Industrial ecology attempts to shape industrial systems according to natural systems. Therefore, one biological product becomes the investment of another and maximizes the benefits of the whole process. In this way, many interacting companies and enterprises can be seen as an ecosystem, reducing waste emissions and increasing resource utilization. Besides, major car companies around the world are racing to develop energy-efficient and pollution-reducing technologies, offering low-pollution and even zero-pollution vehicles. According to the US General Motors Technology Development Center, 50 percent of the center's development projects are related to the environment. At the same time, the development of energy-saving materials technology and comprehensive utilization technology of resources is also changing with each passing day.

5.2.2 Transforming traditional design concepts

5.2.2.1 The history of green design

In the history of industrial design, fuel vehicles, electric machinery, chemical, and steel raw materials have become the main way of industrial production. The combination of these means and the socialized modes of production has created a good material living standard for humankind, and achieved the goal of "people-oriented." But at the same time, a serious ecological crisis occurred caused by the large consumption of resources and energy and the severe environmental pollution. Over-commercialized industrial design misleads people to consume blindly and excessively, which makes industrial design receive much criticism. It is under the background of the serious crisis of industrial design that green design emerges as the times require. Green design is a design method that comes into being gradual with the birth of the concept of "green product". [1] The earliest green products were born in the former Federal Republic of Germany. In 1987, the country implemented a plan called "BLAUER ENGEL", whose main purpose is to: (1) to appeal to consumers to use goods that have less impact on the environment; (2) to promote manufacturers to produce environment-friendly and energy-saving products; (3) as an important factor in the industrial production process and a market-oriented tool, environmental standards must comply with environmental protection requirements throughout the product life cycle, and will not excessively consume resources and energy and dispose a large amount of waste.

5.2.2.2 The redefinition of the traditional design concept

Green design refers to the green design from the very beginning of the product in the production process. It not only refers to a series of traditional design ideas such as product function, quality, and cost but also integrates low carbon, low energy consumption, and low pollution so that with such a design concept the entire life cycle of the product has a minimal negative impact on the external environment.

Research shows that compared with traditional design, green design put more emphasis on ecological design with low energy consumption, low carbon, and low pollution. It integrates the concept of sustainable development into all aspects of products, and even the process of recycling and re-manufacturing of product life terminal is designed in the stage of product research and development. Green design has revolutionized the way of thinking, which firmly rejects the old path of polluting first and fixing it later and adopts a new environmentally protected strategy with emphasis

---

[1] Lu Lan, Qi Ershi, "Developing green manufacturing is imperative", *Mechanical Design*, 1999(5), pp.37-39.

on prevention and treatment. Therefore, green design plays a vital role in the manufacturing industry.

Green design refers to the integration of environmental awareness in product planning, design positioning, and design methods. To achieve the sustainable development of the product design process, environmental protection standards must be met throughout the product life cycle to minimize resource and energy consumption and environmental pollution. The natural ecosystem is an organic whole. If we want to keep nature in its original state, we must maintain its original appearance without artificial interference. [1]

The "4R" (reduce, reuse, recycle, regeneration) principle of green design is mainly embodied in the "circulation of substances" and "flows of energy". In the actual operation process, macro-planning is disintegrated in the micro-development, in a sense contrary to the original intention of protecting nature. Designers from NGO, who devote to sustainable development, firmly believe that design can be a key factor in promoting social transformation and upgrading, and promote the establishment of a resource-saving and environment-friendly society. Their design standards may give some enlightenment to green design.

[re] duce—designs that minimize waste and raise awareness of resource use

[re] source—designs using renewable natural materials, managed to ensure a sustainable long-term supply

[re] make—designs that allow easy, cost-effective disassembly and re-use of parts at the end of life

[re] create—customized designs-encouraging a lasting bond between owner and object

[re] spond—sociable design which invites interaction with others

[re] mind—designs given character by their history-reminding us to treasure what has lasted

[re] use—designs making creative use of ready-made objects and components

[re] cycle—designs from reprocessed waste materials

[re] claim—designs using waste materials in the raw

This series of standards adds vitality to green design. Green design is no longer just a simple "4R" principle nor an empty slogan. Designers impress customers with

---

[1] Hu Rong, Hu Rufu, "Green Manufacturing Technology and Development Trends in Product Development", *Machine Tool and Hydraulic Pressure*, 2003(5), pp.137-138.

innovative ideas and designs so that people can have a bright feeling when they see the products.

5.2.3 Establishing a green social system

The legislation of our country has set up a series of rules and regulations on the green process and green design, which has a positive effect on the prevention and control of environmental pollution. However, an overview of our country's environmental protection laws and regulations, especially the laws and regulations on green manufacturing, is still relatively scarce. However, the rise of green manufacturing will lead to the green of the whole social system.

5.2.3.1 To strengthen the legal construction of green design

The establishment of the "three synchronizations"[1] system regulates green design to a certain extent, but this system is mainly focused on the design and construction of the factory, and there is no relevant specification for product design. We need to clarify the three principles of green design: environment-oriented principle, recyclable principle, and detachable principle.

5.2.3.2 To identify the entry threshold for raw materials

The quality of materials will have an important impact on all aspects of green manufacturing. If poor quality materials are selected, it will have a series of negative impacts on the entire green manufacturing process; On the contrary, if the manufacturer attaches great importance to environmental protection and green manufacturing in the raw materials selection, it is the product which is conducive to environmental protection and resources and energy conservation so as to alleviate the burden of environmental pollution. However, on the selection of raw materials there isn't any laws and regulations in China, and there are only sporadic regulations. The Clean production Promotion Act provides that non-toxic or low-toxic raw materials should be chosen instead of highly toxic and hazardous raw materials. Because it is a very general concept between high toxicity, high harm or low toxicity and low toxicity, and an accurate standard cannot be found. China needs to raise the entry threshold of raw materials and introduce specific standards for selecting raw materials and specify the list of prohibited raw materials. These specific and accurate standards will help to ensure the smooth completion of the whole green manufacturing process.

---

[1] Facilities for preventing and controlling environmental pollution and destruction shall be planned, constructed and put into use at the same time as the main production projects. —*Tr.*

5.2.3.3 To establish the green product evaluation system

Improving the green market system and increasing the supply of green products are essential components of the ecological civilization system reformation. Establishing a unified green product standard, certification, and labeling system is an inevitable requirement for promoting the development of a green and low-carbon cycle and cultivating a green market. The government should establish a green product evaluation system. This green evaluation system should include: (1) an eco-label certification system, also known as a green labeling, means that government departments or public or private organizations issue certificates to relevant manufacturers in accordance with certain environmental standards to prove that the production, use, and disposal of their products are all in line with environmental protection requirements and are environmentally sound or harmless, and are conducive to the regeneration and recycling of resources. (2) To implement a unified green certification in order to adapt the products to the requirements of the international market, China's quality inspection departments should uniformly set up green product identification, standard list and certification catalog, and organize green product certification according to the standards in the standard list. The product certification catalog implements periodic assessment and dynamic adjustment mechanisms to make certification more standardized. (3) In accordance with the requirements of the international market, our country should cultivate a number of green product standards, certification, testing professional service institutions, improve the technical ability, work quality and service level so that our products can meet the green evaluation requirements of the international market.

5.2.3.4 To establish a sound legal system of product packaging

In recent years, the total output value of China's packaging industry has grown averagely of 20 percent per year. What kind of hidden worries are accompanied by packaging while it is driving economic growth and improving human life? According to statistics, the total amount of garbage in China is more than 6 billion tons per year. In urban solid waste, packaging accounts for 30 percent. Only in Beijing, packaging waste accounts for about 3 million tons annually, such as cartons, paper bags, plastic bags, glass bottles and metal boxes, a waste of 830,000 tons. Over-packaging has brought great waste of resources and ecological pollution. However, there is no relevant legal regulation in China to manage product packaging. Product packaging has always been a legal grey area. Therefore, it is urgent to establish a sound green packaging system for products. We can take action from the following aspects: (1) To define precisely the standard of product packaging and strengthen supervision. Our country should set the standard of packaging according to the value of the product, stipulate that the price of the package should not exceed a certain proportion of the price of the product to prevent excessive luxury packaging. We should choose the packaging materials carefully to present the product with the most economical materials, the most practical value, and the most beautiful design by considering environmental protection and practicality. (2) To implement a system of recycling and utilize packaging resources, our country should establish a system of recycling and utilize packaging resources adapting to China's actual conditions, stipulate the management principles, channels and methods for recycling and utilizing packaging wastes such as paper, wood, plastic, metal and glass, and establish a special recycling and processing institution to maximize the utilization of packaging materials.

5.2.3.5 To establish an economic incentive system for environmental protection

In the process of administrative management of environmental protection, the government exerts the macroeconomic regulation and control role of the market, and enables the manufacturing enterprises to actively carry out environmental protection through the regulation of the market itself and the combination of reward and punishment measures. The following steps can be taken: (1) To levy the environmental tax. An environmental tax is an economic means of internalizing environmental costs of environmental pollution and ecological destruction into production costs and market prices, and then distributing environmental resources through market mechanisms. The introduction of environmental taxes requires the promotion of various supporting reforms. Otherwise, the environmental tax will only become a small tax to raise funds. (2) To increase the fines. Our country should carry out measures to deal with the environment with heavy punches, impose high penalties on those enterprises with excessive emissions, and use the fines as the national funds for pollution control. Enterprises that commit crimes against the wind should be heavier, stricter, and faster, and raise the cost of crimes for enterprises. For those SMEs with more serious pollution, they can reduce their production scale and waste by paying high fines for the massive punching mission.

5.3 Successful examples of green manufacturing in China

5.3.1 Huawei Technologies Co. Ltd: advanced manufacturing mode supports green manufacturing

The global value network established by Huawei is characterized by advanced manufacturing mode, and its path is as follows: breakthrough in R&D of the most advanced product, cultivation of a series of products, a moderate expansion, and global value chain modularization.

5.3.1.1 Breakthrough in R&D of the most advanced product

Founded in 1987, Huawei was initially registered with RMB20,000 with 24 employees. It can be said that it was a tiny manufacturing company. In just 30 years, Huawei experienced a leap and transformation from agent switch to production of high-end technology products. It has to be said that it has become a leader in the manufacturing sector and a model of successful green manufacturing.

In the 1990s, multi-national enterprises have monopolized China's electronic equipment market, and electronic products were once dependent on imports. Even if they had their own brands and manufacturing enterprises, they could only carry out basic operations. The key parts of the core technology are in the hands of developed countries. Thus, China's electronic equipment development is very tough. At that time, Huawei seized the business opportunities in the market and initially gained profit by selling the agency exchange. In 1992, Huawei invested all the benefits of the proxy switch into the research and development of JK1000, a half-mechanical, half-digital entry-level product. As soon as it entered the market, it achieved sales of RMB100 million. Over the next two years, Huawei took this as an example and developed two types of switches with considerable benefits. [1]

The switch developed by Huawei is superior to foreign products in price, quality and user experience, and has gained market and won good fame, which has laid a solid foundation for the enterprise to develop high-end technology products and open up a broader market.

---

[1] Huang Haifeng, "Create More Intelligent Products with Passion and Multiple Management of Huawei Terminals", *Communication World*, 2012(22).

5.3.1.2 Cultivation of a series of products

Huawei's rapid growth and development are closely related to the importance attached to technology. Every year Huawei invests at least 10 percent of its revenue in research and development of its products. However, despite the increasing emphasis and investment, the efficiency of R&D and innovation of Huawei is declining every year, and the phenomenon of "increasing production without increasing revenue" has led to a severe decline in corporate profits. In recent years, Huawei spent tens of millions RMB to develop the second generation of cordless phones (CT2), digital enhanced cordless telecommunications (DECT), and other wireless products, and cutting-edge technologies such as ATM switch products but it proved that poor research and development is not very good for the market, so many products haven't had lost its commercial value in production. At the same time, many products developed by Huawei are extraordinarily complex and large product systems, such as C&C08 switches, GSM, WCDMA. Their software scale exceeds 10 million lines of code. It needs thousands or even tens of thousands of staff in various fields and industries to complete the research and development task after two or three years. Therefore, how to speed up the entry of products into the market has become another problem.

Huawei has introduced the integrated product development process system (IPD) from IBM. An IPD can be seen as a small independent company and operating costs and financial indicators need to be calculated. Huawei has more than 100 production lines, and how to manage them is very challenging. Take the relatively large production line for example, it has a special product research and development management committee composed of experts who are familiar with the product and its operation. They monitor and evaluate the R&D activities of each production line, deciding whether product development is worth continuing or terminating.

The monitoring and evaluation activities of the expert group mainly focus on the investment in product research and development and the market benefits that may be obtained, and at the same time evaluate whether the various elements of the product line, such as talents and technologies, are feasible in the R&D process. Huawei fully adopted the IPD model to promote product development and speed up product market entry. IPD made Huawei shift from technology-driven to market-driven. In the process, Huawei completed market research, demand analysis, pre-research, project design, product development, intermediate experiments, manufacturing, production, marketing, sales, engineering, product line manufacturing management in the sense of a complete process from installation, training, and service to user information feedback. Customer managers of each product line must be responsible for whether their products respond to market demand and sales benefits or not. By receiving effective feedback from the market, they can understand the different needs of different customer groups and make appropriate adjustments. Through the joint efforts of all parties, Huawei's R&D has become increasingly sophisticated and gradually approached the international market.

5.3.1.3　A moderate expansion

The investigation shows that Huawei has established a relatively complete value chain with IPD, and has divided the value chain into modules, established marketing service module, manufacturing module, and R&D module. Huawei is looking around the world for the lowest cost module manufacturers, outsourcing low-value modules, and focusing on core modules, strengthening its control position on core modules and increasing the added value of the core module.

(1) *R&D module*

Since its establishment, Huawei has realized the importance of R&D and has always paid attention to the cultivation of research talents. It has long been cooperating with well-known universities at home and abroad and has obtained a lot of research results. To further innovate and develop new technology products, Huawei actively learns from Intel Corporation and Microsoft Corporation. To expand the scale of research and development, more researchers are trained. Huawei has established a large number of research institutions in Silicon Valley in the United States, Bangalore in India, Moscow in Russia, and domestically, Beijing, Shanghai, Guangzhou, Hangzhou and other places to support and establish new production lines, research, and development of new products, and enhance market competitiveness and international influence. India Institute, Nanjing Institute, Central Software Department and Shanghai Research Institute have passed CMM5 international certification, which indicates that Huawei's software process management and quality control have reached the advanced level in the industry. Huawei is also actively engaged with the top 36 operators in the world to collaborate on innovation and increase R&D investment.

(2) *Production operation module*

By studying Huawei's production history, we find that the whole process of production was completed within the company, and different tasks were assigned to different production workshops to complete the production together in the past. Now Huawei has changed that mode and assigned different tasks according to its comparative advantage to different enterprises in different countries and regions, and different enterprises divided work to complete the production tasks together. In this way, the task is divided into various modules, which is conducive to improving efficiency and ensuring quality. In 1999, IBM experts demonstrated that Huawei's core competitiveness lies in R&D and the advantages of leading the market. In the process of supply chain management, as long as the core competitiveness is firmly grasped, the remaining non-core parts can be completely outsourced, allowing professional firms to subcontract. Therefore, Huawei has carried out the internal division of labor adjustment, existing integrated resources, in order to reduce production costs, eliminate inventory as soon as possible, the company's production department, planning department, and other tedious departments merged, forming a new supply chain. It improves the efficiency of the company's operation, reduces the operating cost of the company, at the same time unifies the overall management of the various departments, speeds up the speed and quality of production and manufacturing, and further improves the competitiveness of the company. To further concentrate the whole company's efforts to develop core business and improve the independent innovation ability of enterprises, Huawei further transferred non-core business through outsourcing in 2000. In fact, in the whole country, especially Shenzhen and other places, Huawei's outsourcers are even tens of thousands of people who take their advantage to provide services to Huawei at a lower cost and a faster speed. The operating model of splitting tasks into outsourced companies has made Huawei's supply chain more competitive. At present, Huawei's inventory can reach zero standard, and the speed of product delivery has improved significantly, having a good result in the market. The way of non-core product outsourcing has created new opportunities for the development of enterprises. Following this line of thinking, Huawei has continued to expand its market, search for suitable outsourcing companies around the world, and gradually shift production of some components to overseas factories. Working closely together both in international and domestic, a dynamic, global production network has emerged.

(3) *Marketing service module*

In the early days, Huawei lagged behind other enterprises in the market, in other words, it did not have any advantages. Facing the problem, Huawei has expanded its market to Africa, Europe, America, and other countries and regions. Since 2000, the global communications market has shrunk, and China has inevitably been affected. Instead of further expanding the market, the market has tended to shrink. Facing such a situation, Huawei promptly adjusted its strategic strategy. Since 2005, Huawei had changed its strategy towards internationalization for promoting the international R&D,

production, services, and operations, while at the same time opening up foreign markets as far as possible. At first, Huawei continued its strategy and thinking of entering the markets of developing countries and gradually moving towards the markets of developed countries when opening up overseas markets. In addition to broadening the marketing market, Huawei has also made efforts in marketing, which of course are basically in line with its domestic marketing thinking through advertising, participating in the relevant conference forums, inviting customers to conduct field research and other ways to deepen social understanding of the company. By modularizing its marketing services, Huawei has made its own distinctive brand in a relatively short period of time by increasing its international sensitivity and wide recognition. By the year 2017, Huawei's markets have spread all over the world, especially in China, Asia Pacific Region, the Americas, the Middle East and Africa. The establishment of four sales regions has greatly enhanced international influence.

5.3.1.4　Global value chain modularization

The investigation and research show that Huawei accelerates the construction of global network system based on modularization. On the one hand, it pays close attention to the changing market; on the other hand, it seeks for suitable partners to establish strategic cooperative relations with scientific research institutions, multi-national enterprises, suppliers, distributors and customers by means of community of interests, substantial transfer of profits, product compatibility, capital integration, equity participation and cooperation, so as to complement each other's advantages and build a global value chain.

In Japan, Huawei chose NEC to help it quickly achieve the sales of its data communications products. In North America, Huawei and its well-known brand 3COM jointly invested in its world-class network marketing channels to sell Huawei's data communication products, greatly improving its sales on products in North America. Meanwhile, Huawei has partnered with telecom operators to provide network operations for the carriers. Huawei has provided high-quality services for 320 wireless networks and 220 fixed networks of 180 operators and gradually realized the integration of manufacturing and service areas. China has set up a joint venture with Siemens to focus on R&D, production, sales, and service of TD-SCDMA to promote the further development of TD- SCDMA. A joint UMTS R&D center with Motorola has been set up in Shanghai to provide a more powerful, comprehensive UMTS product solution and High Speed Packet Access (HSPA) solution to global customers. Besides, Huawei has also established joint ventures in Egypt, Russia, and Brazil, and in Saudi Arabia, Iran, India and other countries, through cooperation with local manufacturers, it has successfully achieved local production. Huawei's services spread globally.

Huawei's current service organizations are located all over the world, with technical support to provide customers with timely and high-quality service needs, and professional training centers to provide training services to customers. There is also a large and systematic team of professionals who provide different needs and meet the different needs of different customers. In these service organizations, there are both Chinese and overseas employees. It not only ensures the quality of service but also fully takes the needs of customers into account. Customers can put forward their requirements through the sharing platform and gain the corresponding services and information they need. Huawei has made full use of the opportunity to cooperate with large science and technology companies and higher education institutions at home and abroad to build a mature network system and to provide timely services for Huawei's customers at home and abroad, at the meantime it is committed to building the best team to meet the high-end client-to-end service requirements.

Under severe competition, Huawei has a rational recognition and adopt a multi-party cooperative approach to construct a mature global value network. It must be said that it is an inevitable choice in the face of the current situation. In this process, on the basis of adapting to market changes and user needs, Huawei has worked closely with various enterprises, colleges, and subcontractors to form valuable interest groups and build up mutual trust and interoperability with each other. Under increasing market pressure, it ensures the overall competitiveness of the global value chain.

5.3.2   Lenovo Group: the advantageous management model helps green manufacturing

Lenovo is one of the Global 500 companies. Its R&D innovation team and advanced management model are at the forefront of the world. Users can safely and boldly use the products and services provided by Lenovo. Its products, like personal computers (the classic Think and the All-in-one YOGA), storage, smart TV, and a range of mobile Internet products such as smartphones (including Lenovo and Motorola), tablets and applications have been well received and respected by people from home and abroad. In recent years, Lenovo's market has been expanding, its market has been continuously expanded, and its business capabilities have been steadily improved. Lenovo's brand has been recognized by more and more people at home and abroad. In this process, the quality management model of twin-engine drive plays a crucial role.

The modern quality management model has experienced several stages such as quality inspection, statistical quality control, total quality management, and excellent performance quality management. Also, the theoretical breakthrough at each stage has played a positive role in improving quality. No matter in which stage of development, the theory must be combined with the development of the enterprise itself in order to guide the practice, so that the quality management of the enterprise can fully reflect its characteristics. The twin-engine drive is Lenovo's application of the quality management theory to the management model of enterprise development. This model has been deeply branded as "Lenovo". The twin-engine drive quality management model was established in 1984. It started with a scale of a dozen people and RMB200,000. It has experienced Wan Yuan Pentium (In 1996, Lenovo and Intel launched the price battle of Wan Yuan Pentium, the PC price was around 20 thousand Yuan.), millions of Lenovo lepad taping out, sponsoring the Beijing Olympic Games, acquiring IBM PC department, and acquiring IBM X86 server department and Motorola. Those events made it more and more international.[1] With the rise of the Internet and the increasing number of products being introduced to the market, customers are paying more attention to the user experience brought by the product instead of the product performance. To cope with this change, Lenovo timely transferred the focus of quality management from products to customers and combined with Lenovo's unique tools and complexes to form a twin-engine drive quality management mode which was established with product and customer as the center and the link of multiple plates.

5.3.2.1 Continuously improving product driving engine

The quality management of product driving engine is a stage that many enterprises must go through. At this stage, the enterprise's focus is on the internals of the enterprise and the product itself. Enterprises often improve the stability and reliability of products through full participation, process improvement and application of new tools. Lenovo's product-driven engine takes the product as its core and integrates the product delivery process as its guarantee. It ensures the competitive power of Lenovo's product quality by means of careful control and rigorous decision-making of product development concept, planning, development, validation, intelligent manufacturing, and the rational use of quality management plan, early warning mechanism and other tools and methods.

---

[1] Wang Huiwen, Suo Shengjun, Li Jicheng, Zhai Yingchun, "Double-engine Drives Quality Management Model to Help Lenovo from Made in China to Created in China", *Quality Miles,* 2015(12), pp.66-68.

Moreover, the company's leading strategy, culture, mission vision and so on, are the basis for the engine to fully function. After years of development, the quality management of Lenovo's product engine rive has become increasingly sophisticated. As a guarantee, the mainstream business process has been upgraded from Integrated Product Development (IPD) to integrated product delivery (IOD), and a quality management plan has been introduced into the process to enhance project risk identification, control and the optimization design of the products. In terms of smart manufacturing, Lenovo has established a complete closed loop from customer customization to resource management, manufacturing scheduling, logistics and transportation to customers. This closed-loop coverage has customers in more than 160 countries, and Lenovo has invested thousands of servers. The servers built a new IT system to efficiently manage hundreds of suppliers, 11 owned factories and 20 partner factories. Moreover, it has built a global end-to-end finished product logistics network through cooperation with more than ten regional logistics partners. As a result, an end-to-end closed-loop efficient system has been formed, and the multi-dimensional customization including name implemented by Motorola mobile phone is the representative embodiment of the system.

5.3.2.2 Gradual improvement of the customer-driven engine

Total quality management (TQM) theory puts customers into the category of quality management for the first time, but it is challenging for enterprises to find out in the process of implementation. The main reason is that quality is what customers feel, but objective management tools and measurement indicators are what we are short of. The quality management is driven by the product engine only contacts and interacts with the customer in the two aspects of product design and sales. The two traditional quality indicators, one- time pass rate, and maintenance rate can only reflect the stability of enterprise production and the reliability of the product. Therefore, there will be contradictions that product quality indicators are good, but the number of product sales is limited, and customers complain a lot. With the deepening of Lenovo's understanding of customers and the rise of the Internet, a customer-driven engine has been introduced to solve the quality problem.

The quality management under the customer engine is based on the customer as the core, the enterprise and customer interaction process as the guarantee. Moreover, it is to improve customer satisfaction in the contact, purchase, use, and participation in the product design stage through the means of big data, user experience research and other means. The customer satisfaction index consisting of net recommendation value, total return rate, customer satisfaction, new product indicators and other aspects are the objective measures of customer-driven quality management results. The introduction of the customer-driven engine provides Lenovo with more opportunities for quality improvement and a relatively objective evaluation system to ensure the correctness of its quality improvement direction. Big data is one of the most powerful tools of the customer-driven engine. As a new tool in the Internet era, Lenovo has established corresponding IT systems, which can capture customers' feedback information from such places as technical websites, social media, and forums, and use special tools to process the data preliminarily. A professional team makes an in-depth analysis of the data and forms analysis reports. Each team can apply the results to product design improvement, quality or service improvement, and product promotion and marketing activities according to their own needs. Customers' demands can be grasped more quickly and accurately through the use of big data tools.

The dual-engine-driven quality management mode is associated with Lenovo's characteristics. It is Lenovo's new management mode to cope with the "Internet Plus" era and assess the situation. It closely connects products with users and improves user experiences and market competitiveness. To a certain extent, it promotes the innovative development of Lenovo and sets a model for other enterprises to learn from at the same time.

5.3.3 Haier Group: user-driven mode is the focus of green manufacturing

Founded in 1984, Haier Group started from the manufacture of refrigerators and gradually developed into the manufacture of the water heater, television, fax machine and other household appliances, which is popular among the Chinese public and has become a leader in the white goods manufacturing industry in China. After more than 30 years of development and expansion, Haier has established 24 industrial parks, five research and development centers and 66 trading companies in the world. Haier has gone through five strategic changes in the past 30 years, which are divided into four stages according to its background and characteristics of change corresponding to the life cycle of Haier's commercial ecology.

The first stage is development period. At the beginning of the establishment of Haier Group in 1984, the total number of employees was less than 800, and the company did not have any profit, and the deficit was RMB1.47 million. At that time, it was a good time for reform and opening up. Many domestic manufacturing industries learned to introduce technology and experience abroad to promote the development of their enterprises. Haier also seized the opportunity in its tough time. As the leader of Haier, Zhang Ruimin was aware of this trend with a keen eye. Moreover, with resolute determination, he introduced German refrigerator production technology, increased the scale, improved the quality, promoted the production, and brought Haier through the crisis.

The second stage is expansion period. In the 1990s, China encouraged enterprises to merge and reorganize. Under the call of the state, Haier merged 18 enterprises through the restructuring of assets, holding joint ventures and other means, and employed 1.5 thousand people from 1991 to 1997. After the merger and reorganization, Haier's market has been further expanded, the production scale has been further increased, and the products have been more diversified. From refrigerators as its initial production to 27 categories such as water heaters, fax machines, and televisions, it has brought convenience to people's daily life.

The third stage is the period setting the pace. From 1998 to 2012, Haier expanded its overseas field to conform to the development trend of globalization. In 1999, the company established its first overseas factory in the Philippines and then established a factory in the American hinterland of South Carolina. In 2001, Haier acquired the Italian Meneghetti Refrigerator, established design centers in Lyon, France and Amsterdam, the Netherlands, and set up a marketing center in Milan, Italy. Thus it realized the localization tactics in Europe. In 2002, Haier bought the Greenwich Bank Building in Midtown, New York as the North American headquarters. In 2005, Haier's Middle-East Industrial Park opened in Amman, Jordan. In 2011, Haier and Japan Sanyo Electric Co., Ltd. signed an agreement to acquire Sanyo Electric's various businesses, and form two research and development centers, four manufacturing bases and six regions of the localization market structure in Japan and Southeast Asia.

The fourth stage is reconstruction period. In 2012, Haier implemented a network strategy, transforming traditional manufacturing companies into Internet platform-based enterprises. In 2014, it officially launched the "U+ Smart Life Operating System". In 2015, it launched "U + App" and developed more than 300 corporate partners to build a smart life ecosystem. At this stage, the business model of creating customers in the Internet era explored by Haier is the Rendanheyi Model, ie., the win-win model of staff and customer (The staffs realize their values by creating values for the customers). Haier has transformed its enterprise from a managed organization into an investment platform. Moreover, the employees have been changed from passive labors to self-driven innovators on the platform. The driving of employee entrepreneurship is the continuous interaction of user needs. Enterprises, employees, and partners changed into a small and micro business ecology of win-win cooperation.[1]

In 2012, Haier began to transform into intelligent manufacturing and gradually built a relatively mature system. In the process of transformation, Haier adhered to the concept of the customer first and promoted the interaction between products and users. In the process of transformation, to provide users with good experiences, Haier has been able to customize the production of air conditioners, refrigerators, washing machines, and water heaters, and achieved large-scale customization. "Zero distance from the users" has become Haier Group's business philosophy and broad consensus.

5.3.3.1　Users are designers

Haier can carry out large-scale customization, and on this basis, Haier has carried out a related study, that is, the entire process of product production into the user factor for giving customers a better experience. Users only need to make relevant choices, and then the company can match the suitable products, and meet the needs of users more quickly and conveniently. In Haier's Zhengzhou Interconnection Factory, more than 200 customization schemes can be assembled through 11 general-purpose modules and four personalized modules. Users can choose suitable products for their own needs. It provides users with various choices and also meets the needs of users' special requirements so that the connections between product and user are getting closer and users also trust the company more. Eventually, a win-win situation is achieved. This selective customization is only the first step for Haier's development of intelligent manufacturing capabilities. Haier divides the customization mode into three types: module customization, crowd-sourcing customization, and exclusive customization. Module customization is decomposed into different modules, including both general and personalized modules, and the schemes will be customized through the combinatorial matching of the modules. Some users initiate crowd-sourcing customization, and other users can participate in a wide range of patterns. This pattern will directly connect the user requirements into the intelligent production system. Exclusive customization is customizing products and solutions for users to meet their needs.

---

[1] Shi Jinping, Liu Jili and Hu Ying, "Empirical Study on the Relationship between Equity Incentive and Corporate Performance of Listed Companies on Small and Medium-sized Plates", *Operating Managers*, 2014(4).

5.3.3.2 Zero-distance contact of the whole process

The Industry 4.0 we are committed to building not only requires enterprises to achieve development through transformation and upgrading, but also requires users to rise to a new level of purchasing and experiencing products, and enterprises should enhance the user's product experience through customization. Haier Group always believes that the entire R&D, production and delivery process from product design to the actual use of the product can enhance the user experience through "zero distance from the user". In the process of product design, module business, research and development of small and micro, and production of small and micro, are organized around users and their specific needs to form a set of personalized solutions in multipartite, real-time and zero-distance interactions. When the plan is confirmed, the user can directly enter into the production system of the interconnected factory to check the production state and logistics status of the product at any time until the product is delivered to the user. Haier believes that opening up the whole process of customized production to users to make the production of personalized products under the control of users is a major improvement of user experience. The synchronous sharing of users' personalized demands and the cooperation of production line depend on the digital integration of "one horizontal and one vertical". Horizontal integration refers to the integration of the whole process supply chain system, including user demand, product design, manufacturing, logistics, and service, through the application of interconnection technology. Vertical integration refers to the construction of the Internet of Things to realize the interconnection of enterprises, factories, workshops, equipment, and people.

5.3.4 Shenyang Blower Works Group: cloud manufacturing is the key point of green manufacturing

Shenyang Blower Works Group Corporation (SBW) was founded in 1934. Its predecessor was Shenyang Blower Factory. It became Shenyang Blower Works Group after completing the corporate restructuring in 2004. It is a pillar state-owned enterprise in China's manufacturing industry. It is mainly engaged in the R&D, design, manufacture, and sales of products such as fans, pumps, and compressors. It is now one of the most powerful manufacturing enterprises in China. SBW has a long history and strong scientific and technological strength, excellent product quality and large market share. It is in a leading position in the manufacturing industry nationwide and is constantly improving its level to get closer to international standards. In recent years, in response to national policies and strategies, it has promoted the integration of industrialization and informatization in the development process, continuously enhanced the independent innovation capability of enterprises, researched and developed innovative technologies, and established market-oriented management in enterprise management. The modern management model based on management innovation, technological innovation, and cultural innovation focuses on innovation and breakthrough in both technical and management operations, strives to improve competitiveness, cultivate corporate culture, and enhance corporate efficiency. In 2014, SBW won the China Industry Awards, which fully reflected its strength and status in China's industrial field.

5.3.4.1 The construction backgrounds of cloud manufacturing

Although SBW has been promoting the integration of industrialization and informatization in the process of development, there are certain gaps and contradictions in the promotion of IT application in some of its auxiliary enterprises.[1] Some subordinate companies' application systems of SBW are backward, including the inconsistency of management and application software such as CAX^2, PDM, and ERP. As a result, the IT application of the enterprise is seriously backward, resulting in the backward use and allocation of resources and hindering the progress of the whole enterprise. As a large manufacturing enterprise, it has many problems, such as low operating efficiency, unreasonable resource allocation, and poor information exchange. At present, the manufacturing industry is facing a situation with a rapidly changing market and environment. If the transformation and upgrading cannot be completed in time, it is easy to be left behind by enterprises with advanced manufacturing technology. As an important pillar enterprise in China, SBW urgently needs to complete industrial transformation through innovation and breakthroughs in innovation and core technologies.

At present, with the rapid development of cloud computing, it is widely used in data processing and information mining in military, biological, IT industry, e-commerce, and other fields. Manufacturing group enterprises are paying more and more attention to the IT application in data processing, process optimization, resource allocation, collaborative manufacturing, remote monitoring, and other aspects in the production and operation process. They are also trying to introduce cloud computing into the

---

[1] Ma Shaokui, "'The Cloud Manufacturing' of the Shenyang Blower Works Group", *China Information Technology*, 2012(2), pp.26-28.

[2] CAX is the general name of Computer Aided Design (CAD), Computer Aided Engineering (CAE), Computer Aided Manufacturing (CAM) and Computer Aided Process Planning (CAPP).

manufacturing industry to further improve the IT application level in the production and operation process. As one of the critical technologies for cloud manufacturing model application, cloud computing plays a crucial role in promoting the transformation and upgrading of China's manufacturing industry. Cloud manufacturing mode is a networked manufacturing mode that focuses on cloud computing combines advanced information technologies such as the Internet of Things and utilizes network and cloud manufacturing service platforms to organize online manufacturing resources according to users' needs to provide them with various kinds of on-demand manufacturing services.

The emergence of cloud manufacturing mode has brought opportunities for SBW's transformation and upgrading. Firstly, it is helpful to satisfy the information needs of its auxiliary enterprises, improve the overall IT application level of the group, and completely change the backward situation of information construction of some auxiliary enterprises within the group. Secondly, it is necessary to construct the mechanism of resource sharing and distribution within the group to optimize the allocation of resources and to improve the efficiency of resources. Thirdly, it introduces the advanced idea of "manufacturing as service", innovates the business model of the group, and promotes the change of the group from traditional manufacturing enterprise to manufacturing service enterprises. Fourthly, it creates a virtual resource cloud pool, realizes the dynamic transfer of data between servers, and improves the security of group data information. To promote the application and popularization of cloud manufacturing mode in Shenyang's manufacturing industry, Shenyang promulgated the "Shenyang Cloud Manufacturing Platform Construction Plan". Considering the local manufacturing environment and the level of information construction of manufacturing enterprises in Shenyang, SBW was taken as the first phase of cloud manufacturing platform construction, and then to the success of full application of its cloud manufacturing platform, to create a intensive, cross-regional cloud manufacturing platform, so that more small and medium-sized enterprises will be served.

SBW has earnestly grasped the important historical opportunity of constructing cloud manufacturing service platform in Shenyang. It pays attention to the application of advanced technologies such as cloud computing and Internet of Things in industrial production and builds a manufacturing platform based on "private cloud" to promote IT application as a group. The important content of the construction will continuously improve the overall level of the Group's IT application to enhance its ability to adapt to external dynamic and complex environments quickly.

5.3.4.2 Cloud manufacturing enhances the group's mastery of opportunity

The cloud manufacturing platform of SBW intelligently manages the needs of users, strengthens customer relationship management, dynamically grasps customers' potential needs, improves the group's ability to identify opportunities, promotes the group to discover potential market opportunities, provides innovative ideas for the group, guides the group's product development and design, and enables the group to meet customer needs. At the same time, SBW uses cloud manufacturing platform to provide real-time monitoring services for the user equipment to help users prevent and eliminate seedling failures of equipment, effectively ensure the safe operation of the user equipment and reduce the maintenance pressure on the equipment and the loss caused by equipment failure. For example, SBW provides 24-hour uninterrupted remote monitoring and fault diagnosis services for 37 users and 139 units by using cloud manufacturing service platform, which reduces the economic losses of hundreds of millions of dollars[1] and greatly improve customer satisfaction. It can be seen that the cloud manufacturing platform of SBW has improved the group's ability to identify opportunities and promoted the group to take active measures to meet the potential needs of customers, so as to realize the improvement of customer satisfaction.

5.3.4.3 Cloud manufacturing improves the group's capability to integrate and restructure

SBW's cloud manufacturing platform integrates and optimizes the group's manufacturing resources and application software, realizes the auxiliary enterprises' on-demand allocation of resources, and promotes the group's integration and reconstruction capability. On the one hand, SBW promotes the informatization process of its auxiliary enterprises and realizes the standardization of information management of its auxiliary enterprises. For example, CAX, PDM, ERP, and other informatization application software are brought into the unified management under SBW, which enhances the standardization of subordinate enterprise management and upgrades the overall informatization level of the group. On the other hand, SBW can effectively avoid the redundant investments of IT infrastructure, application software and related IT personnel of the group's auxiliary enterprises, reduce the cost pressure of the auxiliary enterprises, and urge the auxiliary enterprises to concentrate capital to carry out

---

[1] The Joint Research Group of the Second Bureau of the Central Organization Department, the Organization Department of the Liaoning Provincial Party Committee, and the Organization Department of the Shenyang Municipal Committee, "The 'SBW Code' of Enterprises Core Competitiveness", *Guangming Daily*, Nov. 26th, 2013.

specialized production operations. In conclusion, cloud manufacturing model improves the capacity of group integration and reconstruction and promotes the reduction of group cost.

5.3.4.4 Cloud manufacturing improves the group's technical flexibility

Based on cloud manufacturing platform, SBW applies various cloud technologies to the whole life cycle of manufacturing, such as R&D, design, production, processing, and sales. It has enhanced the group's technical flexibility, provided a virtualized R&D environment for the research and development of the products of SBW, promoted the integration of information technology and R&D, greatly enhanced the R&D and innovation strength of the group, and greatly shortened the product development cycle and the design cycle. For example, the research and design cycle of SBW's products has been shortened from 6 months to 1-3 months, close to the advanced level of the international industry. It can be seen that the cloud manufacturing platform can enhance the group enterprise's technical flexibility, so as to shorten the product development cycle.

5.3.4.5 Cloud manufacturing improves the group's organizational flexibility

Based on the cloud manufacturing platform, SBW carries out intelligent management of the production and operation of its auxiliary enterprises to enhance inter-enterprise collaboration. Moreover, it has improved its flexible ability, promoted the seamless connection of cooperation among the group's auxiliary enterprises, enhanced the coordination and agility of the production and operation of the group's auxiliary enterprises, and enabled the group to realize agile manufacturing, thus significantly shortening the manufacturing cycle of products. For example, its product manufacturing cycle has been reduced from 5-8 months to 1-4 months. The product delivery capacity has been significantly enhanced, which is conducive to the early launch of the product and effectively improves the overall market reaction capacity of the group. All in all, SBW has improved its organizational flexibility and achieved the shortening of the product manufacturing cycle based on the cloud manufacturing model. It can be seen that its cloud manufacturing has improved the ability of the group's opportunity identification, managing customers effectively, discovering and excavating potential customer demands, and providing suggestions for product innovation and production process improvement. It effectively met the customer's individual needs and monitored user equipment in real time. To protect the customer's property equipment and improve customer satisfaction, cloud manufacturing improves the group's ability of integration and reconstruction, realizes the centralized integration of the group's superior resources, distributes according to needs, and reduces the group's cost. Cloud manufacturing improves the group's technical flexibility, applies cloud technology to product research and development, and shortens the product development cycle. It also enhances the group's flexible organizational capability, promotes the cooperative manufacturing and agile manufacturing of the group's auxiliary enterprises, and shortens the product manufacturing cycle. Therefore, the cloud manufacturing model can greatly improve the dynamic capability of SBW, so that the enterprise performance is improved.

5.3.5 High-speed railways: China's calling card in manufacturing

Since the 21st century, global environmental and ecological problems have become more and more serious, which has aroused widespread consensus and high concern. In all industries, especially in the transportation industry, through the analysis of energy consumption, waste of resources, nature protection, and security and other aspects, the railway has distinct advantages, especially high-speed railway. Therefore, high-speed railway enjoys an important opportunity for development. Developed countries have gone through difficult explorations after industrialization. Through the readjustment of transportation policies, they have shifted the focus of development to railways, especially the construction of high-speed railways. In the past two years, the world is stepping into the golden age of high-speed railway development. According to the high-speed railway development plan of each country, it is estimated that by 2020, the total length of the world high-speed railway will exceed 50,000 kilometers, and the new mileage will reach 30,000 in the next seven years. Above the meter, the resulting direct investment in high-speed rail will exceed US$1.1 trillion. According to the added value of the whole industry chain, the development of high-speed rail will have a greater impact on the world economy. China's high-speed rail has thus gained unprecedented historical opportunities.

China's high-speed rail industry is making rapid progress, and its technology has been making breakthroughs. It is on par with developed countries and has strong advantages. At present, China has the longest high-speed rail operation in the world. China's high-speed rail network has grown rapidly, becoming the world's longest high-speed rail network in just a few decades. Of course, the development of China Railway High-speed has also gone through a difficult stage of exploration.

5.3.5.1 The development of China's high-speed railway

At present, the high-speed railway is one of the most popular transportation in China, which brings great convenience to the people. What is high-speed rail? The International Railway Alliance defines high-speed railway as a new transport line with the speed of 200 km/h and 250-300 km/h. The definition of high-speed rail is different in different countries. The National Railway Administration of China defines high-speed railway as a newly designed passenger train with a speed of 250 km/h and above, with an initial operating speed of not less than 200 km/h. [1]

China's high-speed railway started relatively late but has been developing rapidly, with roughly four stages of development. The first stage is the beginning stage of China's high-speed railway. China's high-speed rail started late, mainly starting with preliminary planning in 1990, and then began to explore the road gradually. In the second stage, the Chinese railway sped up six times. In the course of the development of China's high-speed rail, the six times of acceleration in speed increase of China's railway has laid a solid foundation for the development of China's high-speed rail. After six- speed increases by the railway, the speed has been increased from 90 km/h to more than 200 km/h. The third stage is rapid development stage. China railway experienced six times of acceleration, and the speed reached 200 km/h, which can be called quasi-high-speed railway. Since then, China has indeed embarked on the path of high-speed rail development, during which the speed of China's railways has been stabilized at the level of 200 km/h and further developed to higher speed technologies. In 2003, Qinhuangdao-Shenyang special railway line, China's first passenger line, was officially opened for operation. The line is designed to run at a speed of 200 km/h, with 50 km/h to spare. In 2004, China put forward a medium- and long-term railway plan, putting high-speed rail construction on the agenda. The fourth stage is the large-scale development stage of China's high-speed rail. At this stage, in accordance with the medium and long-term railway planning, China began to build high-speed rail on a large scale, and gradually formed a comprehensive and efficient high-speed rail operation network. From 2003 to 2015, the construction speed of high-speed rail has been on the rise, eventually reaching 23,603 kilometers. In addition, Hainan Western Ring High-Speed Railway was also opened in 2015, becoming the first high-speed railway operation line around the island. So far, the railway construction plan was completed in

---

[1] Gan Gouxian, Mao Yan, "The resurrection of the Silk Road: An Analysis of China's High-speed Railway Diplomacy", *Journal of the Pacific*, 2010(7), pp.66-67.

2015. [1]

5.3.5.2 The technology development of China's high-speed railway

China's high-speed railway started late, but its development speed is fast, and its development scale is enormous. It has only surpassed developed countries in just over a decade. This remarkable development achievement lies in the unique development model of China's high-speed rail. China's high-speed rail is innovating and perfecting on the premise of drawing on the technology of developed countries, and gradually forming high-speed rail technology with Chinese characteristics.

The technological development of China's high-speed rail can be divided into three stages. The first stage is about China's early high-speed rail technology. The EMU trains before 2004 were the representatives of China's early high-speed rail technology. The high-speed rail technology during this period is mainly through the self-developed EMU series, mainly representing the models of "Great White Shark", "Blue Arrow" "Central Star" "Zhonghua Star" "Pioneer" "New Dawn", etc. Among them, "Great White Shark" is the first generation of electric vehicles, with a design speed of 200 km/h; "Blue Arrow" is the first batch of EMU models for mass production, with a speed of 200km/h; "Pioneer" created a record of 292.8 km/h in the operation of the Qinhuangdao- Shenyang Passenger Line; "Zhonghua Star" broke the record of "Pioneer" and reached a speed of 321.5 km/h, which became the "first speed of China railway" at that time. In the second phase, China is currently operating an EMU online. This stage mainly refers to the series of EMU produced by China through the process of introducing digestion, absorption, and innovation. The EMU at this stage can be roughly divided into two parts: one is the EMU series which is led by the technology of absorbing and introducing innovation, and has series 1, series 2, series 3, and series 5; the second is CRH380 series which is called "a new generation". The third stage is the EMU series currently under development or will enter operation. At this stage, the EMU series technology is more perfect, and the advantages of the previous stage are more prominent. It mainly includes CRH2H, intelligent high-speed train, permanent magnet transmission high-speed train, etc., and gradually move toward higher-end technology. The development of China's high-speed rail technology has continued to progress along with the expansion of high-speed rail construction and has also formed an independent research and development system. Although the research and development of CRH

[1] Yan Xiaosu, Li Fengxin, "The Road to Technological Innovation in China's High-Speed Railways—Based on Statistical Analysis of Patent Data", *Science Focus,* 2013(5).

series mainly adopt the imported technology, absorbs the fusion and recreates the new model, it also creates the integration advantage of China's railway, which is also a prominent feature of China's Railway High-speed.

Three crucial factors China Railway High-speed entering the international market are cost-effectiveness, technical content, and safety factor. According to authoritative research reports, the cost per kilometer of high-speed rail construction abroad is US$0.5 billion, while the construction cost in China is US$33 million. The cost difference of 1/3 makes "Made in China" more popular. Yan Hexiang, director of the Science and Technology and Legal Department of the National Railway Administration, said in an interview that China is already the fastest growing country in the world, with the longest operating mileage and the largest scale of construction. From August 1st, 2008 (the Beijing-Tianjin intercity high-speed railway was opened to December 2013, the mileage of China's Railway High-speed operation is almost the sum of the mileage of all other countries. The scale of operation development and accumulated experience are difficult to be surpassed by other countries. At the same time, China has unique construction experience in the construction of a high-speed railway under the conditions of high altitude and extremely cold climate. China's Railway High-speed technology is "eclectic". Based on the technology of developed countries such as Germany, France, and Canada, it has been digested, absorbed and combined with Chinese characteristics for innovation. High-speed rail has achieved 70 percent localization rate. Relevant patent issues have been solved. Strong technical, managerial talents and experience of the whole industrial chain have been formed in engineering practice. From public works engineering, communication signals, traction power supply to bus manufacturing, China can export a package, which is difficult for Germany, Japan, and other developed countries to achieve. China's Railway High-speed technology can be retrofitted with existing lines at 250 kph or new lines built at 350 kph.

5.3.5.3 China's high-speed railway diplomacy and the Belt and Road Initiative

China's Railway High-speed diplomacy is a part of the Belt and Road Initiative, which focuses on two areas. First, the construction of cross-border high-speed rail (with China as the main fulcrum and the starting point), thus developing close ties with countries connected with the high-speed railways. Most destinations countries are neighboring countries. The land is adjacent or close to each other; the second is a direct investment in overseas high-speed rail market, which together constitutes high-speed rail diplomacy with Chinese characteristics. At present, the connection and communication on a global scale are increasingly strengthened, and most countries strongly urge to cooperate with other countries. From this aspect, the construction of transportation facilities is particularly important, which can provide convenient transportation means for national and regional connections. Whether the construction of a cross-border high-speed railway or direct investment in overseas markets, it is a concrete manifestation of actively cooperating with the implementation of the Belt and Road Initiative, and further expanding and developing its connotation.

China's overseas railway high-speed diplomacy is of great significance to China and other countries. Through this diplomacy, China's Railway High-speed has developed a broader market and gained a lot of profits. More importantly, many countries have realized China's current technology and innovation capacity through the influence of high-speed rail and reviewed "made in China". In this process, we can promote communication among countries, develop a good friendship, and achieve a shared development of all countries. The diplomatic objects of China's high-speed rail will gradually step out of Eurasia, open up a broader market, and make a tremendous impact on the world. We will promote the implementation of the Belt and Road Initiative. When President Xi Jinping visited the UK in October 2015, he pointed out at the UK-China Business Summit that the "Belt and Road" is open to all countries. It was originated from the ancient Silk Road but not limited to the ancient Silk Road. In the west, the European economic circle is a broad "friend circle" that crosses Africa and connects Asia and Europe. All interested countries can join the "friend circle". China's high-speed rail diplomacy has promoted the joint development and prosperity of China and neighboring countries, enhanced the friendship between the countries, deepened the ties between the people of all countries, and further improved the Belt and Road Initiative.

Chapter 6
China's Green Manufacturing: A Tough Work Ahead

6.1 Challenges to and opportunities for China's manufacturing industry

6.1.1 New ideas on green manufacturing since the 18th CPC National Congress

At present, China's equipment manufacturing industry is in a critical period of development. Transformation and upgrading, and the structural adjustment will be the main theme of the future development of China's equipment manufacturing industry. Green manufacturing, integrated manufacturing, service-oriented manufacturing, and ultra-normal manufacturing will become the trend of China's manufacturing industry, and transformation and upgrading must be determined. Thus, relevant departments have put forward a series of new thoughts and new ideas to promote green industrial development according to the general requirements of the 18th CPC National Congress for achieving industrialization and ecological civilization construction by 2020.

6.1.1.1 Implementing system engineering for green manufacturing

The implementation of green manufacturing means that through the development of technological innovation and system optimization, the concepts of green design, green technology, green production, green management, green supply chain, and green recycling will be integrated throughout the product lifecycle to realize the whole industry chain with the slightest environmental impact, the greatest resource and energy utilization efficiency, and the coordinated optimization of economic, ecological and social benefits, which is a long-term and systematic work. In order to implement *Made in China 2025*, accelerate the greening of production methods, and build a green manufacturing system, the Ministry of Industry and Information Technology, the

Committee of National Development and Reform, the Ministry of Finance, and the Ministry of Science and Technology jointly issued the Implementation Guideline for Green Manufacturing Engineering (2016-2020) (hereinafter referred to as "the Guideline").

The Fifth Plenary Session of the 18th CPC Central Committee put forward five development concepts of "innovation, coordination, green, openness, and sharing". These concepts were implemented in the overall thinking of the green manufacturing project implementation guide. Green development is the core concept of green manufacturing. The goal of manufacturing is to establish a manufacturing system with the green and low carbon cycle. The Guideline sets out the specific objectives of implementing green manufacturing projects: by 2020, the overall level of green industrial development will be significantly improved. Compared with 2015, the traditional manufacturing materials consumption, energy consumption, water consumption, pollutants, and carbon emission intensity are significantly reduced. The emission intensity of major pollutants in key industries will decrease by 20 percent, the comprehensive utilization rate of industrial solid waste will reach 73 percent, and some heavy chemical industry resource consumption and emissions will peak. The industrial energy consumption per added-value of enterprises above designated size will decrease by 18 percent, the carbon dioxide emissions per unit of industrial added value and water consumption will drop by 22 percent and 23 percent respectively. The energy conservation and environmental protection industry have increased substantially, initially forming a new engine of economic growth and a new pillar of the national economy. Building hundreds of Green Industrial Parks and thousands of Green Demonstration Factories has promoted 10,000 kinds of green products, initially established a relatively complete green manufacturing system and formed a market-oriented promotion mechanism, etc.

The Guideline puts forward specific work deployments, such as demonstration and promotion of green manufacturing transformation of traditional manufacturing industry, demonstration and application of green development of resource recycling, demonstration and application of green manufacturing technology innovation and industrialization, and pilot of green manufacturing system construction. According to the current situation of the industry and the prediction of the effectiveness of the existing advanced and applicable technologies, the specific objectives of each work were determined.

6.1.1.2 The internal requirements for developing a manufacturing power

Industry is the foundation of our country, the foundation of our economy, and the main battlefield to promote economic development. Industry should take the initiative to adapt to the "new normal" and take the green low-carbon transformation and sustainable development as the focus of building a strong manufacturing country, put it in a more important position, significantly improve the level of green and low-carbon manufacturing, and accelerate the formation of new engines of growth in economic and social development. The full implementation of green manufacturing is an inevitable choice to participate in international competition and enhance competitiveness.

China's manufacturing industry as a whole is at the middle and low end of the industrial chain, with high consumption of resources and energy and weak labor cost advantages. Since the current economy has entered the stage of medium and high- speed growth, the downward pressure is greater. In the global "green economy" reform, it is imperative to build a strong manufacturing country, make overall use of two resources and two markets, speed up the green development of manufacturing industry, vigorously develop green productive forces, and rapidly enhance the overall green national strength and the green international competitiveness. This requires us to form the industrial structure and production mode of saving resources and protecting the environment, change the traditional production mode of high input, high consumption and high pollution, and establish a resource-saving and environment- friendly industrial system with low input, low consumption, light pollution, high output and good benefit, which is the basic feature of a manufacturing power. Levy is also the essential requirement of manufacturing power. Only when the manufacturing industry realizes the green development, can it not only create the material wealth of invaluable assets for the society, but also maintain the "green mountains and clear waters" of the natural environment, and realize the dream of upgrading of the country's manufacturing.

6.1.1.3 The only way to achieve eco-environmental advancement

The 18th National Congress of the CPC has made a strategic plan to promote the eco-environmental advancement, bringing the task into the overall layout of the Five-sphere Integrated Plan. The Third Plenary Session of the 18th CPC Central Committee pointed out that we should deepen the reform of ecological protection system closely around the construction of beautiful China, speed up the establishment of good ecological system, and promote the formation of a new pattern of harmony between man and nature. The Opinions on Accelerating the Construction of Ecological

Progress (hereinafter referred to as the Opinions) is the first document in China to make a special arrangement on the construction of ecological civilization in the name of the Party Central Committee and the State Council. It is the top-level design and general plan for the eco-environmental advancement at the 18th CPC National Congress, the Third and Fourth Plenary Sessions of the 18th CPC Central Committee. It specified the overall requirements of ecological progress, the goal vision, the key tasks and the direction requirements of establishing a complete institutional system. It is the programmatic documents of promoting the ecological progress in China in the future. It is the first time in the Opinions that "greening" is regarded as one of the "new five modernizations" (i.e., new industrialization, informatization, urbanization, agricultural modernization, and greening). It requires that green development be transformed into a new comprehensive national strength and a new international competitive advantage. This is the latest summary and concentrated expression of the all-around green transformation of China's economic and social development. The Fifth Plenary Session of the 18th CPC Central Committee established the concept of innovation, coordination, green, openness and sharing of development, and pitched the green development as one of the five major development concepts. All these put forward new and higher requirements for China's industrial development. On the one hand, we should accelerate the process of industrialization and strive to build China into a manufacturing power leading the development of the world's manufacturing industry through three decades of efforts. On the other hand, we should firmly establish and implement the concept of green development, unswervingly change the mode of development, promote the formation of resource-saving and environmental protection spatial pattern, industrial structure, production and consumption modes, and achieve green and sustainable development.

With the acceleration of China's industrialization process, the overall quality of industry has obviously improved, the industrial system is complete and independent, and the international status has been significantly risen. China has become a real industrial power. Among more than 500 major industrial products, more than 220 kinds of products rank first in the world. However, China's industrial development still has not shaken off the extensive model of high input, high consumption, and high emissions. The industry is still the main area of energy consumption and emissions. The bottleneck of energy resources has become increasingly prominent. From industrial development to ecological protection has become an inevitable trend in social development.

Ecological protection is a new stage in the industrial development, and it promotes a sustainable and high-quality development for the latter. The ecological progress is not only a simple sense of pollution control and ecological restoration but also to overcome the drawbacks of traditional industrial growth and explore a resource-saving, environmentally friendly green development path. Ecological progress is a kind of advancement form of harmonious coexistence, benign interaction, and sustainable development between human society and nature. It is a logical result of industrial development at a particular stage. Its essence is to build a resource-saving and environment-friendly society based on carrying capacity of resources and environment, taking the natural law as a criterion and sustainable development as the goal. A new pattern of modern construction of harmonious development between man and nature is formed in society. This puts forward new and higher requirements for China's industrial development. On the one hand, we should accelerate the process of industrialization and basically realize industrialization by 2020; on the other hand, we should pay more attention to ecological protection, change the mode of development, and form a resource-conserving and environmentally friendly spatial distribution, industrial structure, and mode of production and livelihood. To achieve the ecological advancement, green manufacturing must be carried out in an all-around way, the gap between green manufacturing capacity and the world's leading green manufacturing capacity must be narrowed continuously, and the advanced international level of green development must be accelerated and surpassed. Promoting green manufacturing in an all-around way, speeding up the construction of industrial structures and modes of production with high scientific and technological content, low resource consumption and low environmental pollution, and realizing the "green" mode of production can not only effectively alleviate resource and energy constraints and ecological and environmental pressures, but also promote the development of green industries and enhance energy conservation and environmental protection.

6.1.2 Green transition: the primary challenge facing China's manufacturing

6.1.2.1 The consideration from industrial development

Environmental problems are one of the most critical problems facing the world today. Since the industrial revolution in the early 20th century (especially in the last 50 years), environmental problems have become a major problem in human society. Environmental pollution and ecological damage have become increasingly serious, and continued to deteriorate. The problems have even evolved into related economic and political contradictions and crises, thus threatening human survival. In the process of modern industrialization, economic development and environmental protection are often considered incompatible with each other and even considered as two kinds of things that can not exist simultaneously. According to this logic, it will inevitably lead to the contradiction between economic development and environmental protection, as well as ecological problems arising from economic development outside the constraints of environmental protection. There was a wrong view in the theoretical circle that economic growth inevitably consumes resources and discharges waste. Therefore, economic development and environmental protection are in opposition. The main reason for this conclusion is to narrowly understand environmental protection as a way to repair environmental problems through end-to-end treatment, which will inevitably consume economic costs, thereby reducing economic benefits. Therefore, the paradox between economic development and environmental protection, which has puzzled the western world and even China since the modern industrial revolution, was once deduced into the theoretical hypothesis of "Environmental Kuznets Curve". Through the process of industrialization in western countries since modern times, including the beaten path of pollution first, treatment afterwards they have adopted in dealing with the problems of economic development and environmental protection, we can see that an isolated and mechanical view of the relationship between economic development and environmental protection is a fundamental cause of the current global ecological problems. It can be said that the environmental problem in today's world is caused by the separation of economic development and environmental protection.

From the perspective of human economic and social development, the excessive exploitation of natural resources and the deterioration of the ecological environment are issues that deserve attention. The problem left over from the industrial economy is the exchange of material values and commercial values with natural values. Although the material richness can be obtained, it will face the depletion of natural resources. If we compare the technological development of human society and the accumulation of material well-being at this stage with the economic level of 5,000 years ago, human beings may be proud of what they have achieved today, but the picture of the world may not become better, nor will it increase the human happiness because of the improvement of the material gains, and the relationship between different races of human beings has not become more harmonious. On the contrary, wars, barrenness, environmental pollution, and terrorist activities have repeatedly discouraged us. If people would sacrifice for some of the achievements of the present for a peaceful, calm, and even backward life, they would not have been dismayed at the messy world today. That is because the economic development we enjoy now is at the sacrifice. The cost of this unstrained development makes people start to reflect on whether the achievements and pride we have are rational. Are we in right mind if we pursue the material gains at the cost of our environment? In this process of reflection on the beginning of the modern development model, the rationality of green development must become the focus of people's consideration.

Green development refers to transforming the current industrial civilization into environment-friendly industrial development. While developing, we should also consider the carrying capacity of the environment, reduce the resource consumption of development, and at the same time carry out specific restoration and protection of the damaged environment. Moreover, the concept of the circular economy and low-carbon technology are incorporated into the concept of development, which will inevitably lead to the coordinated development of the social economy and the natural environment. Green, circular, and low-carbon development aims to form resource conservation and environmental protection, so as to achieve the progress civilization. As far as the connotation is concerned, green development covers a broader range and includes both cyclic development and low-carbon development. The latter two are just development are the concrete manifestations of green development, so we can use green development to express it in a unified way. In today's world, different countries and regions are practicing the connotation of green development with varying concepts of development. It can be said that green development is the trend of future world development. The connotation of green development is not sticking to conventions, but with the growth of world economy and knowledge level, aims to break through the environmental carrying capacity and limitations, seek a coordinated development model of economic growth and natural resources consumption, and achieve a win-win result.

6.1.2.2　The urgency of green development

The green development concept is regarded as a concept of sustainable development at the beginning of its being put forward. However, its content usually only stays in harmony between economic development and resource environment, and the ecological environment that carries economic development is often ignored. It can be seen that the initial stage of this concept is also incomplete and unsystematic. Of course, the concept of green development is constantly enriched itself with the growth of economy, the upgrading of knowledge, and such emergence of negative social phenomena as the economic crisis, scarcity of natural resources and loss of biodiversity.

Then, its epochal connotation is given in this process. In terms of connotation, the concept of green development first regards the ecological environment capacity and resource carrying capacity as the basic conditions for development and sums up the defects of the traditional economic development model. It creates a new type of development mode which can achieve sustainable development and ecosystem balance in order to realize innovation.

The concept of green development is a scientific and comprehensive development concept derived from the concepts of circular economy, sustainable development, and low- carbon development. Its ultimate goal is to achieve people's happiness and social stability, and it emphasizes the coordination of environmental carrying capacity while maximizing economic development. As a result, it is a sustainable development that resource conservation, environmental friendliness, and social progress have been achieved. Green development requires not only improving the utilization patterns of energy resources but also protecting and restoring natural ecosystems and ecological processes so as to achieve the harmonious coexistence and coevolution between human and nature. Green development is a higher concept of development which is formed by the academic community and the government on the basis of summarizing the experience of the past extensive development model. Under the dual requirements of ecological capacity and resource carrying capacity, it can realize important development concepts based on economic development, environmental protection, and social progress.

Green development can achieve a win-win model of economic development and resource conservation based on the experience of the past extensive development model, and it emphasizes efficiency, harmony, and sustainable development. Green is vital, healthy and lasting, and it is coordinated, fair, orderly and diverse.[1] Green development regards the ecological environment as an intrinsic factor of economic development, and also considers ecological benefits while developing the economy. Its ultimate goal is to achieve sustainable development of people and nature, and people and society. It requires ecologicalization and greenization of economic activity process, so we must not only focus on the increase in the amount of social wealth but also pay more attention to its qualitative improvement. Green development aims to develop environment-friendly industries, reduce resource consumption, protect and restore the ecological environment

---

[1] Liu Yanhua, "Strategic Thinking on Several Issues Concerning Green Economy and Green Development", *China Awards for Science and Technology*, 2010(2).

as well as develop the circular economy and low-carbon technology to make economic and social development coordinate with nature.[1]

Under the scrutiny of the green development concept, people pay more attention to the concept of efficiency in the process production. The efficiency here also includes the use of natural resources, access to resources within the capacity of the ecological environment, and maximize utilization. It should be noted that the concept of green development takes environmental protection and the utilization of natural resources as a priority. It must be the goal and principle of green development that the harmony and health of the ecological environment are maintained while the economic growth is guaranteed. Compared with the development concepts left over from the industrial civilization period, the green development concept is a complete set of development concepts. This concept emphasizes that people should get rid of the simple material interests and the accumulation of social wealth, and adds the harmony of the ecological environment into the concept of coordination in order to realize the ecological progress and follow the development of natural laws. People can finally achieve healthy development without the sacrifice of the environment and resources. To achieve development on the basis of maintaining environmental health, we must attach much importance to the technological innovation and change of production mode.

6.1.2.3 The 13th Five-Year Plan for China's green development

Green development is a reflection and surmounting of the rapid industrialization process of human society in modern times. It is "good medicine" for treating the binary opposition of economic development and environmental protection. It is used to cope with the current global climate change and solve the ecological resources problem of economic and social development. The Communist Party of China has accumulated rich practical experience in green development after having explored for more than 20 years. In 1995, in the 9th Five-year Plan proposal of the Fifth Plenary Session of the Fourteenth CPC Central Committee, it was stated that the "sustainable development strategy" should be implemented. This can be regarded as the initial plan for green development; the 10th Five-year Plan and 11th Five-year Plan have both set up the concrete plan for building a "two-type" society of resource-conserving and environment-friendly in the process of implementing the sustainable development strategy; the 12th Five-year Plan clearly defines the theme of Green development for the first time, and

---

[1] Hu Jintao, "A Speech at the 15th Academician Conference of the Chinese Academy of Sciences and the 16th Academician Conference of the Chinese Academy of Engineering", *Guangming Daily*, Jun.8, 2010.

puts forward "establishing a green, low-carbon development concept". In the 13th Five-year Plan, green development has once again become an important strategy to guide China's economic and social development, and the core concept and important model of national ecological civilization construction.

In general, green development mainly refers to a new development model that regards environmental protection as an essential pillar for achieving sustainable economic and social development under the constraints of ecological environment capacity and resource carrying capacity. As a social consciousness, the core concept of green development lies in dealing with the relationship between man and nature, and between people correctly. The concept of green development comes from the historical practice of human social development, and it will guide the future development of human society. The "green development" in a narrow sense is to develop environment-friendly industry, reduce energy and raw material consumption, protect and repair the ecological environment, develop the circular economy and low-carbon technologies in order to harmonize economic and social development with nature. The "green development" in the broad sense has a richer connotation. It is an innovative development pattern that combines the eastern and western cultures and combines the Marxist ecological theory with the characteristics of the times of today's world development based on the traditional pattern of development. On the whole, "green development" is the combination of "green" and "development", emphasizing the unification of economic and social development and ecological environmental protection. As a Chinese model of ecological advancement, the green development is profoundly reflected in the overall layout of the overall plan for promoting the all-around economic, political, cultural, social, and ecological progress of China's economic and social development. In political construction, green development requires perfecting the laws and regulations for protecting the ecology, strengthening the law enforcement supervision mechanism and improving the administrative system; In economic construction, green development requires a green layout of industrial development to enhance human well-being and social equity through low-carbon, recycling, and sustainable development; In cultural construction, green development requires cultivating green values in society, so that the green concept is deeply rooted in the hearts of the people; In social construction, green development is the symbol of progress in modern society, and it is the hope and aspiration of human beings for a better future; In the construction of ecological civilization, green development requires the rational use of natural resources so as to improve the ecological environment of human society and harmonize the relationship between humans and nature.

During the 13th Five-year Plan period, the green development path of China will be a road to modern social civilization that is different from Western values and sparkles with Eastern wisdom. China's green development takes the sound institutional system as a guarantee and scientific innovation as important support. It actively mobilizes all citizens to participate by creating a green cultural atmosphere of society. In accelerating the ecological progress, we must improve the property rights system of natural resources assets; In implementing the innovation-driven development strategy, it is necessary to formulate systematic technical solutions around the ecological protection; In the formation of a new pattern of "co-governance and sharing" in green society, we must actively promote the participation of the public in ecological protection. In short, China's green development is not only a Chinese model for its own ecological progress but also contributes to the rest of the world.

6.1.3   China's manufacturing industry at a new historical starting point

6.1.3.1   China's manufacturing industry: navigating the "new normal"

The word "new normal" was first proposed by President Xi Jinping in May 2014. At the Central Economic Work Conference ended on December 11, 2014, the trend in changes of China's economy were analyzed and compared in detail for the first time from nine aspects including consumer demand, investment demand, export, international balance of payments and so on, and then concluded that China's economy was evolving to a stage of superior form, more complex division of labor, and more rational structures. China's economic development has entered a "new normal". In recent years, China's GDP growth has slowed down, from the rapid growth of the past to the "new normal" of medium and high-speed growth. However, China's manufacturing industry, influenced by various internal factors and external pressures, has also begun to enter the "new normal" of manufacturing. Compared with booming Internet industry, the manufacturing industry is now struggling with difficulties. In 2015, China's GDP growth rate was 6.9 percent. From the data of nearly 20 years, the GDP growth rate of China's economy reached 14.2 percent in 2007; it is close to the previous peak 14.3 percent in 1992. It started to decline after 2007. Although it returned to 10.6 percent in 2010, it has not rebounded to its original height since then and has continued to fall in recent years. It can be seen that China's economic growth rate has slowed down markedly. China's economy has entered a new stage that is different from the rapid growth period of the past 30 years and has entered the "new normal" of economic development.

Under the guidance of the concept of "new normal", Chinese manufacturing has also entered a new stage. The past development model of China's manufacturing industry is mainly driven by factors, especially demographic dividends and investment drivers. In recent years, we can see that China's manufacturing is confronted with double pressures: internal labor costs and operating costs continue to rise, the external economic situation continues to slump. Trade data is deteriorating. Low-end manufacturing faces low-cost competition in Southeast Asia and other developing economies. High-end manufacturing needs to withstand the impact of developed countries.

Under the internal and external pressures, Chinese manufacturing has also begun to enter a "new normal": first, the cost advantage is gradually weakened. According to a report released by the Boston Consulting Group (BCG), China's manufacturing costs are almost the same as those in the United States. Among the top 25 economies in terms of global exports, if taking the manufacturing cost of the United States as a benchmark100, the cost index of "Made in China" is 96. As a result, it aroused widespread concern and a great disturbance. The labor cost advantage of "Made in China" and the competitiveness of traditional labor-intensive manufacturing industry have already gone. The second is transformation and upgrading of the value chain. On the one hand, the original labor-intensive industries are shifting to countries with lower labor costs such as Southeast Asia and India; on the other hand, China's manufacturing is extending to the higher end of the value chain. *Made in China 2025* is the guide for China's manufacturing strategy during the coming decade. It has designed a plan for the transformation and upgrading of China's manufacturing industry, and promoted "Made in China" to "Created in China". Third, the Internet and manufacturing industries are closely integrated. The deep integration of the Internet and traditional industries will become the commanding height of a new round of "Made in China". Such things as the Internet of Things, cloud computing, big data, industrial Internet, mobile Internet, e-commerce and so on will become key technologies to boost the development of manufacturing. The fourth driving force is demand from consumers. Consumer demand is becoming more diversified, seeking for high product quality and innovation. There are more and more personalized demands and shorter and shorter response time to requirements. The demand for service quality is getting higher and higher. Meanwhile, consumer demand is constantly changing. Whether the product can meet the needs of consumers and satisfy their experience to a great extent determines the success or failure of the enterprise. Fifth, export growth slowed down. The growth rate of export data of "Made in China" slowed down due to the sluggish global economy. It used to be double-digit growth but now dropped to a single digit and even negative growth in some months. Sixth, environmental and resource challenges. The rapid development of China's manufacturing industry in the past decade has consumed not only a large amount of energy but also brought a huge impact on the environment. The problem of high pollution and high energy consumption in the manufacturing industry has become more prominent. We need to start with two aspects to solve this problem. On the one hand, enterprises need to strengthen the green management of the whole life cycle of products and strive to build its system that featuring efficient, clean, low-carbon and recycling. On the other hand, under the guidance of the government, we should adjust the industrial structure, develop clean energy and enhance the research and application of various energy-saving technologies and equipment.

From the perspectives of steel, machinery, automobiles, home appliances, food, medicine, and other major industries, China's manufacturing pressure is not diminished, and it is urgent to transform to cope with the "new normal". Factors, especially the demographic dividend mainly drive the past development model of China's manufacturing industry. The key to guaranteeing the "new normal" is to switch the new dynamic mechanism from factor driven to innovation driven. Therefore, for China's manufacturing industry, only by actively adapting to the "new normal" of China's economic development, and making adequate preparations, seizing opportunities, and strengthening independent innovation, can we achieve sustainable development and cultivate new competitive edges manufacturing.

6.1.3.2 Innovative development of China's manufacturing industry

It has been more than half a century since the emergence of China's manufacturing industry, and it can be said that China has a relatively independent and full-fledged manufacturing structure with complete categories. In this process, China has accumulated a strong product foundation and technical level, and now it has become the world's first manufacturing country. However, it should be recognized that the innovation system of traditional manufacturing industry is difficult to maintain the demand for future economic development, and three profound changes that need to be achieved: first of all, an innovation chain should be created to realize the transformation from the current technology innovation oriented by technology introduction to independent technology innovation. It is the early performance and the primary approach for developing countries in its push for manufacturing development. Experience shows that this innovative model is unsustainable, especially in the post-industrial civilization era. It is difficult to achieve the catch-up of the manufacturing industry by the current development model, and an independent and innovative model must be created. Therefore, we must adapt to the development trend of global industry change, hold the innovative carrier of self-service features, improve the independent manufacturing mode in different areas, and exploit new technology innovation chain. In doing so, the disconnection and deficiency of traditional innovation industrial chain will be improved, and the independent innovation mechanism will be gradually completed to solve the problem of insufficient supply of core technology in the manufacturing industry. Secondly, it is necessary to build a new industrial chain and realize the single technological breakthrough towards the omnidirectional technological innovation. The global competition is in the phase of the transformation from product competition to the industrial chain, that is to say, the competition and integration capability of the overall industrial chain directly determines the overall level of the manufacturing industry. At present, confronted with a phenomenon of "isolated techno-island" that refers to lack in technology and a series of problems such as multiple deployments and decentralized investment in many industrial chain elements of innovative resource elements, it is difficult for some key areas in China to achieve overall breakthrough and development. Therefore, China's manufacturing industry needs to establish an innovation carrier. That is, we should make an overall planning and coordinate allocation of various innovative resource factors, gather and integrate with single technical results, and deploy the innovation setup around the industrial setup as well as the capital setup around the innovation setup. As a result, a breakthrough in the industrial chain will be achieved. We will create an innovative ecosystem and gradually transform a single local innovation into an integrated and cross-disciplinary collaborative innovation. China's manufacturing innovation has long been a long-term development from the deployment of scientific research projects to breakthroughs in technology research and development, and to the linear model of innovation in the product industry. This model has been difficult to sustain the new development of technology and industry cross-border integration. Therefore, it is essential to create a manufacturing innovation ecosystem that covers the integration of technology, talents, policies and international cooperation. The innovative culture atmosphere is created, and various types of innovative operators played its role in breaking the boundaries of units, organizations, regions, and industries. Alongside that, it has formed a high-level characteristic of the collaborative innovation network platform of manufacturing industry and has shaped the new advantages of China's manufacturing industry international competition.

6.1.3.3 The green development of China's manufacturing

As China became the world's largest manufacturer, the existing resources are difficult to coordinate the relationship between traditional industrial development and natural resource consumption. Therefore, we must improve the existing economic growth mode and development mode. The concept of green manufacturing covers the concept of circular economy and the connotation of sustainable development. If we want to choose a road with high technical level, and little environmental pollution, and at the same time achieve good economic benefits and low resource consumption, we must adhere to the road of green development. Green manufacturing refers to the development model that adds the factors of environmental impact and resource utilization into the consideration system without affecting the regular performance, structure, and characteristics of the product. Through green manufacturing, whether in the design, manufacture, transportation, after-sales, recycling, etc., the environmental bearing capacity is fully considered, as well as the human hazard and social impact of the full consideration. Moreover, it can also guarantee the survival and profitability of the enterprise itself. Green manufacturing means to embed key technologies in the life cycle of product design, product manufacturing, product marketing, and product recycling. It can simultaneously apply green, environmental, and energy-saving manufacturing concepts to related manufacturing processes. In this way, a set of green development processes has been developed, and China's manufacturing industry has been at the forefront of global manufacturing. *Made in China 2025* pointed out that China should comprehensively promote green manufacturing, strengthen research and development of advanced energy-saving and environmental protection technologies and processes and equipment. In addition, China should accelerate the green transformation and upgrading of manufacturing industries, actively promote low-carbonization, recycling, and intensification, and make energy use more efficient in manufacturing. Besides, China should also strengthen the green management of the whole life cycle of products, and strive to build a green manufacturing system with high efficiency, clean, low carbon and recycling. However, the current situation in China is that industry accounts for more than 70 percent of the country's energy consumption. Therefore, in terms of green development, it will take a long time of technology accumulation and transformation. All in all, China has a long way to go in the course of green development. We should start with green manufacturing to open the road of green development in China. As a result, it is imperative to implement green manufacturing project in all industrial sector.

The green development of China's manufacturing industry should vigorously promote the application of information technology. The new generation of information technology has become a powerful guarantee and inevitable choice for manufacturing enterprises to achieve green manufacturing through the monitoring and management of the whole process of product formulation, process and raw material procurement, manufacturing, warehousing, transportation, use, overhaul, and scrap. It can be said that the use of information technology to promote industrial green upgrading is imperative and should be listed as a "must-action" for corporate development. For example, the establishment of an energy management center is an important means for enterprises to improve the information level of energy management. Statistics show that enterprises that have built energy management centers save an average of 1.5 to 10 percent of their energy. From the operation of more than 20 enterprises that have been built energy management centers in Hebei, it can save nearly 1 million tons of standard coal, 2.6 million tons of water and 21.4 million kWh, and reduce carbon dioxide emissions by 1,078 tons and mercury emissions by 60,000 tons. As a result, the energy-saving effect is remarkable, and the atmospheric emissions are reduced obviously. It is estimated that if all enterprises above the Bohai rim area implement the construction of enterprise energy management center, the coal consumption is expected to exceed 100 million tons. At the same time, the promotion of green manufacturing projects must also take into account China's industrial base. From a global perspective, although China's industry has certain competitive advantages in some fields such as power equipment and construction machinery, generally speaking, China is still in the 2.0 and 3.0 stages of industry. Compared with Germany and the United States, we still have certain distance. Therefore, the foundation of information technology application in some industrial enterprises in China still needs to be improved. Under the background, the promotion of green manufacturing engineering should be guided in the light of the actual situation as it seeks to set the goal of differentiation. In this connection, more enterprises can apply the new generation of information technology to practice green manufacturing, and then promote the overall green manufacturing goal of China's manufacturing industry.

6.2 China's confidence in green manufacturing

Although China's green manufacturing is in a critical period of co-existence of challenges and opportunities and many problems are urgently to be solved, as a major manufacturing country that is transforming into a manufacturing power, China should not shrink back from difficulties or underestimate its capabilities, but should show its "green confidence" in this strategic opportunity. "Green confidence" is a positive development attitude and a new requirement for the development of China's manufacturing industry. It is not a blind confidence, but a new concept based on the current level of development and innovation and development potential. Through the innovation of green technology, the green transformation of development paradigm, and the integration of enterprise production with green technology, the foundation of "green confidence" will be reflected in every aspect of China's manufacturing industry.

6.2.1　Green innovation: a strong push for green manufacturing in China

6.2.1.1　Weak capacity for technology innovation of China's manufacturing

Since the founding of the People's Republic of China, especially since the reform and opening up, China has become a big manufacturing country. However, it is not strong or competitive enough despite the big size. The cause is that our capacity for independent innovation is insufficient, and key and core technologies are still heavily reliant on imports. The industry generally has a shortage of technology supply, and the innovation and industrialization results are poor. The main reasons for these problems are the lack of innovative platforms and pilot systems for the transfer of laboratory technology to product technology, the lack of industrial common technology supply systems, basic materials for industrial development, and essential technical support. China's manufacturing industry is facing a new historical task to achieve a manufacturing industry from large to strong. To address this challenge, innovation is the key but not easy to fulfil. Building a new innovation carrier and network is an important way to enhance the sustainable competitiveness of the manufacturing industry comprehensively. Focusing on the primary needs of manufacturing innovation and development, we should actively learn from the strategic deployment and successful experience of developed countries, and build the innovation center as a way to integrate and reorganize innovative resources, technology, organization, business, capital allocation and barriers, promote innovation mechanisms, model innovation and management innovation, and further ensure the smooth transition of innovative technologies into commercial commodities. This is an urgent and arduous task for us.

The so-called "challenge" is also in innovation, because the weak capacity of technological innovation is the biggest constraint of China's upgrading in manufacturing industry. On the one hand, China's manufacturing enterprises rely heavily on technology introduction in the development process, but cannot be well digested and absorbed after that. No innovation has been done to those productions. When new products and technologies appear in foreign countries, we can do nothing but to introduce them again. On the other hand, it relies heavily on foreign products in manufacturing equipment. Even some equipment that can be produced in China is difficult to generate economies of scale due to the lack of system integration capabilities, and our equipment manufacturing enterprises are nothing but supporting enterprises for foreign-related equipment manufacturers. The weak capability of China's technological innovation stems from the following two reasons: first, there are problems in technology introduction. Second, there are insufficient technological innovation activities. Technological innovation does not mean that the technology introduction is unnecessary. On the contrary, technology introduction provides a good chance for learning the sophisticated technology for domestic enterprises. Through the digestion and absorption of imported technologies, the gap between domestic technology and advanced international level can be narrowed, and the cost of technological innovation can be reduced. In today's highly specialized labor division, any major technical innovation is based on existing technologies, and there does not exist any independent innovation in the full sense of the world. Re-innovation on the basis of technology introduction has also become an important way for late-developing countries to achieve catch-up. The success of re-innovation after technology introduction, as represented by Japan, demonstrates the importance of technology introduction for industrial upgrading in late-developing countries. However, the introduction of technology is only the first step in technology introduction. The complete technology introduction includes the whole process of introduction, digestion, and absorption. In this process, the input of digestion and absorption is far greater than the introduction of technology. Research indicates[1] that Japan and South Korea have invested 5-10 times more money in technology digestion and absorption than in technology import, and the input of technology digestion and absorption in our country is less than 1/10 of the technology import. That is to say, after the introduction of the same technology, Japan and South Korea spend 50-100 times of investment on re-innovation than our country. This also explains the following phenomenon from one angle to some degree: China and South Korea's auto

---

[1] Yang Yonghua, "Research on the Evolution Mechanism of 'Adaptation Learning' in Technology Innovation Dispersion, and the Relationship between Technology Introduction and Independent Innovation", *Modern Economic Research*, 2010(3), pp.44-48.

industry have adopted the "first introduction, post-innovation" approach to technological innovation, but South Korea has achieved independent innovation and become one of the world's auto powers, China is caught in a vicious circle of "import, fall behind, reintroduce". Relying on the introduction of technology, car manufacturers will inevitably be reduced to vassals of the world's automotive giants.

The key to strengthening the development momentum of the manufacturing industry is to implement a strategy driven by innovation. [1] In recent years, an enterprise-based innovation system combining production, teaching, research, and use is emerging, showing strong vitality and momentum, and major innovations. For example, the ARJ21700 new turbofan branch passenger aircrafts have been officially put into commercial operation, and the C919 large passenger plane will complete the first flight after numerous ground texts. While affirming the achievements, we must be fully aware that China's manufacturing innovation system is still not perfect. There are still some short links and drawbacks that restrict innovation. From the point of view of supporting policies, some policies and measures are not being satisfactorily implemented in practice to encourage enterprises to innovate. The entry barrier of high-tech enterprises is high, and it cannot benefit most of the manufacturing enterprises; from the perspective of the incentive mechanism, the institutional environment for the full mobilization of innovative talents still needs to be improved, and the mechanism for free flow and efficient allocation of innovative elements such as talents, information and venture capital needs to be improved; from the perspective of the service system, the number of public service platforms that support enterprises to develop and innovate is still small, with inadequate capacity are not strong. The large-scale scientific research equipment and innovative resources are not available to the public; from the perspective of the social environment, the social atmosphere that encourages innovation and tolerance failure has not yet formed. The social status and income of industrial workers are at a low level. Therefore, to solve the weak links in innovation, we need to work together from many perspectives, such as building innovation system, improving innovation and incentive mechanisms, and creating a good social environment.

6.2.1.2 Green innovation: a new kinetic energy for manufacturing in China

China's manufacturing industry, driven by innovation, should gradually move towards green upgrading and smart manufacturing. The green upgrading refers to the

---

[1] Miao Wei, China and the World: Economic Transformation and Structural Reform, http://money.163.com/17/0319/14/CFT8FC84002580S6.html.

green development model of the manufacturing industry proposed above, which is the demand for ecological development and the inevitable choice of China's manufacturing to high-end development. Smart manufacturing refers to the use of the "Internet Plus" model to integrate industrialization and informatization to achieve mutual transformation and promotion. Green manufacturing must follow a path featuring high-tech content, low consumption of resources, and less environmental pollution. Smart manufacturing focuses on improving quality and efficiency, emphasizing interconnection, automation and intelligence, and personalized service. The two complement each other, promote each other, and are inseparable. The application of information technology in smart manufacturing, such as smart grid, intelligent building, multi- network integration, etc., not only enables the interconnection of production and sales but also helps reduce resource consumption and promote energy conservation and emission reduction. New materials and energy-saving technologies to be promoted in green manufacturing also have many new products and technologies that need to be launched in smart manufacturing. In the process of improving quality and efficiency in China, green development and smart manufacturing are important directions, and in many ways, they have the same goal. At the same time, green manufacturing requires upgrading of product equipment, technology, and production processes, thereby nurturing new areas of economic growth and new development momentum.

The 10th Five-year Plan specifically proposes to promote the traditional transformation of the manufacturing industry, promote the establishment of an industrial system for green and low-carbon recycling, and encourage enterprises to upgrade their technical equipment. The key to the implementation of green manufacturing lies in the continuous innovation and promotion of green technologies and green products, covering the needs of upgrading traditional industries and emerging industries from a high starting point of development. Traditional manufacturing industries such as steel and textiles use efficient green production technologies and technical equipment to transform traditional manufacturing processes. Emerging industries such as information and communication and high-end equipment will have to start from green design and build a green industrial chain.

6.2.1.3 The implement innovation projects of high-end equipment

The green development of China's manufacturing has a huge demand for green technology. China needs to promote the development of a new generation of green industry technology and manufacturing technology, and green manufacturing and smart manufacturing as the main direction of deep integration. Our goal is to reduce the operating cost of pilot demonstration projects by 30 percent, the production cycle of products by 30 percent and the rate of defective products by 30 percent by 2020. Chen Ji, director of the Institute of Industrial Economics of Capital University of Economics and Business, said that China's manufacturing industry faces many constraints, the first of which is rising labor costs. Smart manufacturing is conducive to extending the competitive advantage of China's manufacturing industry. Developing smart manufacturing can improve production efficiency, help enterprises cope with rising labor costs in the future, and accelerate standard production and maintain a competitive advantage.

In 2010, China surpassed the United States to become the world's largest manufacturing country, large but not strong, especially the competitiveness of high-end equipment manufacturing has not been strengthened. Taking the integrated circuit industry as an example, nearly 80 percent of integrated circuit chips depend on imports, and the high-end chip import rate exceeds 90 percent, highlighting that China's manufacturing capability for independent innovation is not strong and lack of key and core technologies. In this regard, the future development of China's manufacturing industry needs to organize a number of innovative industrial special projects such as large aircraft, aero engines and gas turbines, energy and new energy vehicles, and achieve independent research and development in the above areas by 2020, and high-end equipment by 2025. The market share of independent intellectual property rights has increased substantially, the core technology of external dependence has dropped significantly, the basic supporting capacity has been significantly improved, and the important fields of equipment have reached the leading international level. *Made in China 2025* puts forward that the key to changing China's large but weak manufacturing industry is to make breakthroughs in high-end manufacturing. At present, China still has a certain gap between its brand and technology and advanced international level in high-end manufacturing. As far as the current development of domestic manufacturing industry is concerned, high-end medical equipment, high-end CNC machine tools, offshore engineering equipment, and civil aerospace are not only the current areas where high-end equipment is concentrated but also represent the direction of future development of emerging industries. There is still a certain foundation in the field, and it is not too late to catch up. Due to the relatively large investment in these areas and the difficulty in starting to make profits, it is necessary for the state to provide support to help them through the initial stages of development. Therefore, the government-supported high-end equipment innovation project is an essential part of China's manufacturing green development plan.

6.2.1.4 The institutional underpinning for innovation

At present, green manufacturing has become a trend in international development. With the improvement of environmental awareness, consumers are willing to spend more money to purchase low-carbon, environment-friendly green products. Under the premise of good response from the masses, green manufacturing, which reflects an orderly and healthy development concept, has been accepted by more and more countries and will become an important embodiment of corporate competitiveness and social responsibility. Wang Jun, vice minister of the consultation and research department of the China Center for International Economic Exchanges (CCIEE), told *Beijing Business Daily* that China's manufacturing industry has gone through a path of high energy consumption and high pollution. Therefore, it is necessary to improve the "green quality" and "green benefits" of China's manufacturing industry. The Chinese government should promote the green upgrading of the manufacturing industry and build an institutional guarantee for innovative development.

(1) *More favorable industrial policies*

Industrial policies usually play a powerful role in optimizing the allocation of resources in society. As the market is unpredictable, the industry needs strong backing from favorable industrial policies to respond to market changes and make up for market failure at any time. China's industrial policy is formed in a long-term exploration. The government has a strong, decisive role in the formulation of the policy, and plays a decisive role in it. From all industries, the industrial policy is more prominent in the automobile industry. In 1994, China introduced the "Industrial Policy for the Automotive Industry". After its promulgation, China's automobile industry is increasingly expanding, and it has gradually become the main development direction of the production industry. Since then, the emergence of a joint venture car factory has accelerated the rapid development of China's auto industry. In 2004, the "Policy on Developing the Automobile Industry" was promulgated. The promulgation of this policy advocates "independent innovation". Although the policy is very targeted and requires self-reliance and self- development of automobile industry technology, it lacks specific operating rules for their implementation. Although the two auto industry policies have promoted the development of the automobile industry in a practical sense, it can be seen that it also has serious defects. The excessive intervention of government and inadequate investigation and research on different markets has led to a failure to make good use of the policy to promote the development of the automotive industry.

As can be seen from the above industrial policies, China has the following characteristics in the formulation of industrial policies: first of all, the characteristics of the planned economy run through the entire automobile industry policy, and the government has strong direct intervention capability. Secondly, the government does not make directions by studying market trends, but rather blindly makes the policies, which results in rigidity and failure to response to the uncontrolled market. In this kind of policy environment, some enterprises have a sense of initiative, passively implement the industrial policy, which will only lead to disasters in production. Even if the enterprise itself is highly innovative, the result will not be able to adapt to the rapidly changing market, and it will be difficult to achieve sustainable development. As a result, industrial policies cannot benefit all enterprises as a whole. Those policies are only in favor of the large enterprises, but many small and medium ones are ignored, which finally weakens the market. Consequently, many small and medium-sized enterprises fail to play their role as innovation subjects. It is not difficult to see that China's industrial policies have excessively interfered with enterprises' management for a long time, and they cannot make good use of the "invisible hand" of the market. If the market allocation of resources cannot be rationalized, the Chinese enterprises cannot have strong competitiveness in the global environment. To make up for the above-mentioned industrial policy deficiencies, the China's industrial policy should be emphasize on how to promote effective competition in the market and provide enterprises with the favorable conditions for scientific research, talents, and information.

(2) *To provide economic means for innovation and development*

Economic means are mainly divided into two types, one is market means, and the other is non-market means. Market means refers that the concept and method of industrial policy should be determined by the market, that is, adopt a more market-oriented approach to guide industrial development. For example, pollution rights trading system is an excellent example of the government's adoption of market means to promote green development. The pollution rights trading means that the government, according to Coase's theorem, gives pollution rights to polluters by means of sales, lease, auction, gift, etc., and establishes the pollution rights trading market to allow the pollution rights to circulate like market commodities. Trade in pollution rights has the advantages of minimizing the cost of pollution control and strong operability, which can encourage enterprises to adopt green technology innovation. For pollution enterprises that have not carried out green technology innovation, buying the share of pollution rights not only increases the production cost but also pushes them to the disadvantaged position of production competition. Therefore, pollution rights trading system effectively promotes the transformation and upgrading of emission enterprises.

Non-market means refers that the government uses economic leverage such as price, tax, fee, credit, subsidy, mortgage and insurance to force enterprises to include the external costs generated in their economic decisions. These means mainly include:

(i) Environmental resource tax is levied. Enterprises with serious pollution environment will not be able to obtain high profits due to high pollutant discharge tax, fuel tax, pollution product tax, etc., but have to carry out green technology innovation and adjust their product structure. (ii) Direct funding. The enterprises and relevant research institutions receiving the funding directly from the government must adhere to the will of the government and devote themselves to green technology innovation, which is also convenient for the government to manage. (iii) Preferential Credit. The government financial sector provides low-interest, interest-free concessional loans to companies from research and development of green technologies to commercial applications. (iv) Government purchases. Direct purchase of green technologies and products developed by enterprises, especially for new products in the public sector, and their application to public social utilities not only promotes the ability of enterprises to enhance green technology innovation, but also guarantees the benefits of the government and the public, which plays a role in the social benefits of green technology and products.

(3) *Policy means for innovative development*

For the development of green manufacturing innovation in China, the Chinese government mainly redesigns their policies instruments in three categories. First, patent protection means. In the information age, Internet technology has accelerated the spread of science and the promotion of technology, and green technology has become a commercial technology that is easy to share. It is necessary for enterprises to give priority to the patent protection of technological innovations when researching and developing, not only to protect the exclusiveness of enterprise technology, but also to stimulate the innovation power of enterprises. The second is the legal framework. Since the long-term development, our laws and regulations on ecological and environmental protection have been built from scratch, and gradually formed a systematic, legal system on ecological protection. However, it is still not perfect, and we need continuous reform to construct a scientific and rational legal system. The third is the approach to macro-regulation. The government needs to give guidance to enterprises to keep them on the track, guide enterprises to a green and sustainable production mode, and follow the principle of flexibility and change in policy formulation. Enterprises that are conducive to the construction of ecological civilization shall be encouraged to provide resources such as capital, technology, and market information.

(4) *Green manufacturing standards, green product certification system and incentive mechanism*

The standard of green manufacturing has been in a relatively vague state in China, so we first need to clarify green manufacturing standards and establish corresponding technical standards systems. The technical standard system not only requires clearing its standards in all aspects of green manufacturing but also should be consistent with the requirements of the quality management system standards and the link management system standards. Secondly, we lack awareness of the identification of green products. In the past, we did not pay attention to whether the products are green. This leads to a looser certification system for green products. We need to strengthen our awareness of green products and establish a strict green certification system. This system can strictly control manufacturers' production from the process to the final product to be green, realize such goals as low energy consumption, low pollution, low carbon and so on, and reduce environmental pollution as much as possible. Finally, the government should establish an incentive mechanism to encourage enterprises to innovate green products and set up a special fund to solve various environmental pollution problems facing the manufacturing industry. In particular, we will increase innovation and development of green technologies such as low energy consumption, high efficiency, low pollution emissions, and low carbon. By using policy support and incentives to stimulate enterprises, enterprises will go further and further along the road of green manufacturing.

6.2.2 "Green technology paradigm": a leader of green manufacturing

At the period of two or three hundred years from the 18th century to the present, technology has been fully developed in all fields of society. The technological products have gradually replaced the original nature and formed an environment that completely encloses human beings. Under this gradual uncontrolled technological order, various technological malpractices and social consequences have gradually emerged and even began to threaten the survival of humankind seriously. Strictly speaking, the modern technology model has been challenged as never before.

6.2.2.1 The green turn of the traditional technology paradigm

From the 1960s to the 1970s, technology penetrated into the society in an all-around way, accompanied by the brilliant success of the road. Crisis and disasters also expanded and affected the whole world, and the anti-technology, anti-culture and anti-civilization ideological trend began to take shape in the world. However, in the view of scholar Zhao Jianjun, the radical technology pessimism is irrational. Modern technology cannot solve ecological problems in a real sense, but we can do nothing in this field without it of technology. Therefore, completely giving up technological fixes to solve environmental problems is tantamount to giving up for nothing. The urgent task of restoring the real existence of humankind and solving the contradiction between economic development and ecological environment is to re-examine the technology and explore a progressive technology with ecological orientation. Green technology is the result of the green development of modern technology. The so-called greening is a dynamic process, which represents the state in which things lead to the unification of ecological nature and human world values, internalizing ecological natural views and values into ways of thinking, and externalizing into concrete actions. The greening process of modern technology should comprehensively reflect the progress of the economic dimension, the progress of the political dimension and the progress of the cultural dimension. In the modern technology paradigm, the advancement of the economic dimension has become the main goal and criterion for technological development; The green technology is from a systemic point of view. Under the guidance of the green concept, it fundamentally links economic, natural and social factors together, and realizes the joint development of human interests and environmental interests. The technology is to realize the long-term development of human technology better. It is a modern technology that only pays attention to the immediate material interests of human beings, and does not pay attention to the inheritance and criticism of the values of society, life and culture. It can be said that the emergence and rise of green technology is not only the result of the logical progression of the technology itself but also the inevitable development of human history, reflecting the new direction and new trend of society.

The formation of green technology paradigm first needs to solve the relationship between man and nature. The human-centered concept of development has caused devastating damage to the existence of nature, society, and people, distorting the relationship between man and nature, making the ecological crisis inevitable. To harmonize the relationship between man and nature, we must reflect on the past road of industrialization. Following the principle of ecology and the law of ecological economy, being able to protect the environment, maintain ecological balance and save energy and resources is all effective means and methods to promote the harmonious development of mankind and nature.[1] Only when people put priority to ecological protection can the green technology paradigm play a positive role, thus maintaining a sustainable development.

Nowadays, the whole world has realized the predicament of industrial civilization, started the new exploration of modern industrialization, and put forward the green technology paradigm of ecological civilization and sustainable development. The scientific paradigm in the era of sustainable development should be a new paradigm integrating environmental knowledge-ecological knowledge-scientific knowledge, namely scientific knowledge-ecological knowledge paradigm and scientific knowledge-environmental knowledge paradigm, which can be further summarized as "green knowledge paradigm". Technology is also a technological paradigm that contains environmental philosophy and green culture, that is, technology-environment paradigm and technology-ecological paradigm, and can be further summarized as "sustainable technology paradigm" or "green technology paradigm".

In the process of a paradigm shift, a group of scientists, engineers, politicians, and ordinary people who seek to solve the harmonious development of society, economy, politics, environment, and ecology, and realize the harmonious coexistence between man and nature form a green knowledge and technology community. They exchange information and knowledge with each other. The green knowledge and technology community will pay more attention to the ethical, ecological or environmental responsibility of science and technology, attach importance to the evaluation and analysis of the ecological value, environmental value and sustainable development value of technology, and consciously apply to the development of technology. Based on these characteristics, green technologies cannot only rapidly support the great and rapid development needs of the industry civilization, but also take social benefits into account while considering economic benefits, and promote social development to a sustainable and environmentally-friendly state.

6.2.2.2 Dividend from green technology innovation

At present, one of the main reasons for the low overall benefits of China's

---

[1] Qin Shusheng, "Philosophical Thinking of Ecological Technology", *Science and Technology and Dialectics*, 2006(4), p.75.

ecological economy of enterprise is the severe shortage of green technology innovation and diffusion. Moreover, through the green technology innovation and diffusion, we adopt green technologies that harmonize economy and ecological environment with ecological positive effects. By implementing ecological and clean production methods, we can recycle raw materials and waste, reduce pollutants at the source and in the production process as much as possible, and realize a virtuous cycle between economic growth and ecological environmental protection. In the face of new technology individual or scientific paradigm, enterprises and companies do not immediately apply it directly to production. They also need to consider whether the various technologies within the enterprise match the new technology, or whether they can be integrated into the organization and business of the enterprise to get higher profits and broad market prospects. The enterprise needs to consider the possible reactions of industry, commerce, society and other aspects in the face of new technologies, the degree of acceptance of the public and the risk of the old technology being abandoned. It takes much time for all new technologies to be developed and approved by the market. The old configuration must accept the new domain and be familiar with its internal practices, which means that the engineers working with the old syntax have to regroup and face the new domain. It is not easy to make this transformation. All this has to be done in collaboration with finance, institutions, management, government policies, and people skilled in new areas.[1]

Technological progress and innovation will continue to be one of the decisive factors to implement green manufacturing fully. It is necessary to highlight the strategic supporting role of green engineering technology, strengthen green technology innovation, and accelerate the development of applied technology with advanced technology and economic feasibility. We will actively organize and implement integrated and systematic green solutions for energy conservation, consumption reduction, emission reduction, and pollution control. Green manufacturing puts more emphasis on the technological innovation of the whole life cycle, that is, it innovates the traditional design, manufacturing technology, and production mode, comprehensively realizes the greening, and constructs a green manufacturing system, including promoting ecological design, building green factories, implementing green manufacturing, increasing recycling and advocating green consumption. For example,

---

[1] Brian Arthur, *The Nature of Technology: What It Is and How It Evolves*, translated by Cao Dongming and Wang Jian, Hangzhou: Zhejiang People's Publishing House, 2014, p.177.

the Ministry of Industry and Information Technology of China is vigorously promoting ecological design. It starts to consider the impact of the whole life cycle of products on the environment and resources from the point of scheme design, so as to coordinate the development of green manufacturing in the selection of raw materials, production process, green consumption, and effective recycling.

Green technology is of great help to the comprehensive ecological effects. It should pay attention to the creation and diffusion of green technologies, which is also the foundation for manufacturing companies to create permanent power. A metal manufacturing companies, for example, before the use of green technology or ecological technology, it used resources poorly. At the output side, heavy pollutants are released, such as wastewater or waste containing heavy metals like mercury and chromium, which are discharged without treatment. Consequently, it wastes the natural resources and causes irreparable damage to society on the one hand. If the company follows the principle of ecological optimization or the law of ecological economics, rationally uses green technology, upgrades the traditional production line, and builds an ecological closed-circuit circulation process, it can realize the waste recycling, thus greatly improving the efficiency of the resources and relieving the pressure of the ecological environment.

Facts have proved that green manufacturing technology innovation is not only conducive to energy saving and consumption reduction in the industry but also brings enormous benefits. The air blast energy recovery apparatus developed by Xi'an Shaangu Power Co. Ltd can save RMB56.8 million for each user, and the expected annual benefit of the product is more than RMB2 billion. Suzhou Dihill Green Technology Co., Ltd. developed the "Intelligent Recycling System of Cutting Fluid", which has been successfully applied in Jianghuai Automobile and other companies, is expected to form a market scale of RMB20 billion, and save RMB8 billion - RMB10 billion per year for processing enterprises; Anshan Iron & STEEL CO., Ltd. is the "leader" of metallurgical slag treatment technology and equipment. Last year, the total solid waste was 6 million tons, and the annual output value reached RMB850 million. Today, the government and enterprises attach great importance to green manufacturing. Green manufacturing technology companies have already become aware of the benefits of this development. In the future development process, companies that respond to green manufacturing will inevitably further expand their advantages and share the dividends brought by green innovation.

6.2.3 The tremendous vitality of green technology innovation released by enterprises

Green technology innovation and diffusion is the key to achieving sustainable development for Chinese enterprises. The environmental pollution, ecological destruction, and the depletion of natural resources caused by the application of existing traditional technologies are among the most serious negative effects. [1] With the available technical and economic model, the production process of Chinese enterprises is linear and non-circular, consuming and wasting a lot of resources and energies, as well as discharging a large amount of waste to pollute the ecological environment. Now people are increasingly aware of the limitations of the model of "available technology system + end-of-pipe treatment" in sustainable development. Therefore, we put forward the requirement of developing green technology with a positive ecological effect through innovation and diffusion, to achieve the sustainable development of corporate eco-economy. Driven by this development approach and model, the increasing innovation activities of enterprises and the growth of high-tech industries have effectively promoted the technological progress of enterprises and the development of economy and society, releasing tremendous vitality.

6.2.3.1 Task-oriented green technology innovation

Technological innovation is a systematic process involving technological research and development, diffusion, marketing, and other steps. The continuity of these steps marks the completion of the technological innovation process. The single green technology innovation process is primarily to meet market demand. To describe a single green technology innovation, due to the complexity of corporate green technology innovation activities, we can abstract it into a linear process. The research and development that the enterprises are doing are aimed to develop new products and processes with competitive advantages. They can either provide new products with new features or low cost, or develop processing technologies to guarantee product quality, to ensure fast and stable production, and to save materials, energy, and labor. At present, the reality of energy shortage has put forward new requirements for enterprises' research and development. This requirement is a driving force for real needs reflected in the research and development of new products and new technologies. Looking back on the history of green technology innovation and development, it is also that the greening

---

[1] Zhang Xiaojun, Research on the Driving Factors and Achievement of the New Strategy of Green Innovation of Enterprises, Hangzhou: Zhejiang University, 2012.

of consumption has led to changes in production field. Human beings' reflection on their behaviors, especially their economic behaviors, has enabled humans to gradually establish a viewpoint of sustainable development and introduce green into daily life, which has triggered a chain reaction between green technology and green design. As a result, they have developed technology to prevent and control environmental pollution, benefit the comprehensive utilization of resources and the reduction of the waste resources, and balance the ecological natural resources. It can be said that this is a task-oriented green technology innovation.

6.2.3.2 Increasing enterprises' capacity for independent innovation of green technology

With China's constant efforts in green technology development, transformation and promotion, new green technologies, processes, and products are emerging one after another. However, in general, China's green technology development capacity is still weak with low-tech products. To reverse this situation, the independent innovation capacity of Chinese enterprises is expected to be improved, especially those large enterprises with capital and technical resources advantages. They should be encouraged to actively carry out green technology innovation and respond to the favorable situation of the current green industry development. For some large enterprises that can integrate with the world, they must also have a forward-looking awareness, implement a high-start development strategy, and meet the requirements of internationalization to make their products enter into the international market. Aiming at establishing an international enterprise group and breaking through in the center of the world market, they have to focus on the advantages to cultivate quality products. We must strive to cultivate a team of corporate talents for innovation, especially to cultivate a large number of entrepreneurs who are full of entrepreneurial spirit and good at innovative management; we must establish technology development centers among qualified enterprises and provide internal technical sources for corporate innovation in order to vigorously improve their capacity of independent innovation; we must increase the investment in technological innovation of enterprises and establish a multi-channel capital investment system to make sure the enterprises can raise enough innovation funds so that the overall investment efficiency of innovation can be improved.

6.2.3.3 The micro-ecological economic management of modern enterprises

The implementation of the micro-ecological economic (green) management of modern enterprises is one of the essential ways and countermeasures to promote corporate green technology innovation. Practice has shown that China's weak micro-economic management not only causes a series of severe microeconomic and macro-ecological economic contradictions, but also hinders green technology innovation, which requires enterprises to innovate management system, implement modern corporate micro-economic management, establish a coordinated eco-economic management model, improve corporate comprehensive ecological benefits, and accelerate corporate green technology innovation. For example, Qingdao Haier Refrigerator Co., Ltd. implements the ISO14000 environmental management standard series. Its financial department updates the accounting method, extends the green accounting to the corporate eco-economic activities, internalizes the eco-environmental cost, promotes the enterprise to continue to develop green products and carries out corporate green innovation. To implement modern corporate micro-economic management, we must adjust and reform internal organizational structure and functions, and establish specialized institutions, internal ecological management systems. At the same time, we must set up self-improvement and environmental management self-restraint system, participate in the decision-making of corporate green technology innovation, and strengthen the environmental audit in the process of corporate green technology innovation. The implementation of modern corporate micro-economic management will lead to a modern corporate management revolution, promote corporate green technology innovation, and realize sustainable development of Chinese enterprises.

6.3 Strategic response to promoting green manufacturing in China

Since the launch of reform and opening up, China's manufacturing industry has been developing rapidly. With the undertaking of global industrial relocation, it has gradually become a world manufacturing power. The evolution of the global manufacturing pattern is causing an increase in labor costs and environmental carrying pressure and a shortage of energy supply. These difficulties have forced the developing concepts and models of China's manufacturing industry to change. China's manufacturing industry must go out of the difficulties, no longer rely on factor-driven and developing at the cost of polluting the environment, and turn to a rising green road that combines technological innovation with the transformation and upgrading of traditional industries. At present, the innovation capacity and transformation and upgrading of China's manufacturing industry still face complex internal and external environments. How to overcome these difficulties and successfully realize the rise from being a big manufacturer to a strong one has become a significant issue facing China's green manufacturing development.

6.3.1 The connection between the Belt and Road Initiative and *Made in China 2025*

Made in China 2025 released by the State Council is China's first ten-year program of actions to guide the implementation of the strategy of being a manufacturing power. It focuses on the next generation of information technology, high-end equipment, new materials, biomedicine, and other strategic priorities; it guides the gathering of various resources in the society to accelerate the development of competitive and strategic industries. *Made in China 2025* was signed by Premier Li Keqiang and released by the State Council in May 2015. Some scholars called it the "Industry 4.0" plan of the Chinese version. In this plan, the "three-step" strategic goal to be a powerful country is put forward, and the first step is to be a part of powerful countries in the world's manufacturing industry. Currently, China is still in the process of industrialization and facing enormous pressure of competition from abroad. The core technology and high-end equipment manufacturing still need international technical support, and China is still on the stage of catching up with advanced international countries. Therefore, China should attach great importance to the high integration of its manufacturing system with foreign advanced technology and initiate the path with its unique characteristic.

The Belt and Road Initiative, is short for the Silk Road Economic Belt and the 21st Century Maritime Silk Road which was proposed by President Xi Jinping in 2013. The Belt and Road is not an entity and mechanism, but a concept and initiative for cooperation and development. It relies on the existing bilateral and multilateral mechanisms between China and the countries along the Road and uses the existing and effective regional cooperation platforms, aiming to jointly build a community of shared interests, destiny and responsibility featuring political mutual trust, economic integration and cultural inclusiveness by borrowing the historical symbol of the ancient Silk Road, holding high the banner of peace and development, and actively developing economic partnerships with countries along the Road.

During the period of the booming development of the Belt and Road, we can link the cooperation vision of the Belt and Road with the industry of *Made in China 2025* to make China embrace a major opportunity for the development of green manufacturing.

6.3.1.1 The development of China's manufacturing industry facing both challenges and opportunities

The manufacturing industry is an essential cornerstone of China's economy. At present, China's economy is undergoing growing downward pressure; it faces not only various challenges but also many opportunities. Taking the Belt and Road Initiative as an example, because it complies with the global trend of a new round of industrial relocation and infrastructure construction, it has brought about major strategic opportunities to the development of China's manufacturing industry, particularly the rise of green manufacturing.

(1) *"China's manufacturing" is in urgent need to transform and upgrade*

The manufacturing industry involves various fields in the national economy and is the pillar industry of the national economy and the engine of economic growth. It is the basic carrier of high-tech industrialization, serving as an important way to absorb labor and employees. Therefore, it is the main force of international trade and also the important safeguard for national security. After three decades of industrialization in China, and "Made in China" has become a new label for China's foundation in the world. The Belt and Road has connected China's major industrial bases, where the manufacturing factories have made outstanding contributions to the development of China's manufacturing, while also facing the pressure of structural and technological aging and low-carbon restrictions. Thus, manufacturing factories need prompt transformation and development. With the industrial development policy in the Belt and Road Initiative, some industries with overcapacity, such as steel, electrical, automotive and equipment manufacturing, can be exported to Central Asia, West Asia, and Southeast Asia. At the same time, the green development of the local manufacturing industries along the Road can be effectively realized by using modern technology to transform traditional manufacturing and increasing investment in the green low-carbon transformation of these industries. Similar to other countries in the world, China is currently facing the impact of a new round of industrial and technological revolution, which generates many opportunities and poses challenges. How to accelerate the upgrading of technology, industry and global value chain, reshape the national innovation system and innovation capacities, and rebuild the national competitive advantage has become the prevailing direction of countries along the Road. On this background, Chinese enterprises urgently need to go abroad, and open up a new Silk Road to the shared prosperity between themselves and countries along the Belt and Road through technical cooperation and resource sharing, which is also the common wish of countries along the Belt and Road.

(2) *Green manufacturing must have "Chinese Standard"*

In recent years, China and the countries along the Silk Road Economic Belt has had much close cooperation in many fields of manufacturing. In the context of the Belt and Road Initiative, China and many neighboring countries have shared much cooperation in high-speed automobile machinery, microchips, steel industry, non-ferrous metals industry, rare earth metals mining, deep conversion refineries, silicon production, drip irrigation equipment and other fields. In the future, more and more countries will choose to cooperate with China. With this opportunity, the green development of China's manufacturing industry is also transforming into a service-oriented and knowledge-based one in the process of "going global". To enhance the attractiveness, accelerate the green development of China's manufacturing, speed up the building of FTA, and gather the manufacturing industry that represents the level of global competitiveness, "Made in China" still needs to be equipped with its standards. To respond how to carry out the work of technical standards in the industry in the future, "The Plan for Furthering the Standardization Reforms" released by the State Council in 2015 puts out the measures of "adhering to the integration with the world with Chinese characteristics" "enhancing the international influence of Chinese standards" "creating a standard Chinese brand" and "using Chinese standards to drive China's products, technology, equipment and services to go global". To fully play its role, China's green manufacturing and industrial transformation and upgrading need to integrate with the world and get more recognition of the countries. It will not be long before Chinese standards go global, and the world is in line with Chinese standards. The process of formulating technical standards is a complicated process, which usually requires the participation of the entire association or even the whole industry. After completing the standards, it needs to be approved via standard application channels. Therefore, it is necessary to actively organize the action plan in advance in the industry to make the technological standards authoritative, feasible, forward-looking and inclusive, as well as applicable. While China's manufacturing is reaching out to the world, we must also ensure that the standards of China's manufacturing industry go global, especially the standards of green manufacturing. As a result, the relevant enterprises in green manufacturing play a certain leading role in building excellent technology, establishing alliances in relevant fields, and even obtaining domestic and foreign financial support to promote the added value of enterprises.

(3) *Using the Belt and Road Initiative to make a big push to develop "Made in China"*

Manufacturing cooperation is a vital field because the countries along the routes of the Belt and Road Initiative have different industrialization level. The differences will inevitably lead to complementarities, which stimulate the potential of cooperation. With the implementation of the Belt and Road Initiative, cooperation between China and neighboring countries, as well as the countries along the Road, will be further expanded and deepened. Green manufacturing promotes industrial upgrading and actively participates in international cooperation to promote Chinese manufacturing to go global. For example, China's green equipment and technology of renewable non-ferrous metals are integrating with the world through the non-ferrous metals industry. With the speed raising on the Europe-bound China Railway Express trains and the development of Chongqing-Xinjiang-Europe railway, the expansion of the overseas market of the renewable non-ferrous metals industry and the industrial transfer will be further accelerated, which will drive the export of high-end technical equipment for renewable non-ferrous metals and play a leading role in the international market of high-end technical equipment. Besides, under the Belt and Road framework, the Chinese government has done a series of work to strengthen the connectivity on development plans and strategies with relevant countries, and to negotiate projects that are suitable for all parties. Meanwhile, China also pushes forward the establishment of an Asian Infrastructure Investment Bank and set up a Silk Road Fund to make possible the development of an overseas development model with Chinese characteristics of "Investment + Trade + Technical Equipment + Engineering Design + Engineering General Contract".

Green manufacturing is the main direction of manufacturing transformation and drives the green transformation in the entire manufacturing industry. The Fifth Plenary Session of the 18th CPC Central Committee proposed the new vision of green development and placed green development in a critical position. *Made in China 2025* adopted by the State Council has fully implemented green manufacturing as an important part of achieving the strategic goal to be a manufacturing power. It requires to step up efforts to research and develop the technologies, processes, and equipment of advanced energy-conserving and environmental protection technologies, speed up the green transformation and upgrading of the manufacturing industry, and strive to build an efficient, clean, low-carbon, and circular green manufacturing system. Green growth has become the commanding height of global economic competition, and green manufacturing development will become the prevailing trend. In *Made in China 2025* "green" appeared 46 times as a keyword. To fully implement green manufacturing, we must focus on the theme—"green", innovate traditional design, manufacturing technology, and production methods, fully realize "greening" and accelerate the construction of a manufacturing system characterized by "green" in accordance with the concept of the whole life cycle.

Green upgrading is a highlight of China's manufacturing. *Made in China 2025* explicitly states that the green transformation and upgrading of manufacturing industry should be accelerated, manufacturing resources are used more efficiently by actively extending low carbonization, circulation and intensification, meanwhile, efforts should be stepped up to create a green manufacturing system characterized by efficient, clean, low-carbon, and circular through green product lifecycle management. By 2020, the emission intensity of major pollutants in key industries would have fallen by 20 percent. By 2025, world-class advances would have been achieved in the green development of manufacturing industry and unit consumption of major products, and the green manufacturing system would have been initially established. Joint research by the Ministry of Industry and Information Technology and the Academy of Engineering shows that China's industry is still the main area for consuming energy resources and generating emissions. Compared with developed countries, there still exists a gap in industrial energy efficiency and water efficiency. For example, the average domestic energy efficiency level of the steel industry is 6 percent to 7 percent lower than the advanced international level; the building materials are 10 percent behind, and the petrochemical industry is 10 percent to 20 percent behind. The water use of China's industry with the added value of over ten thousand US dollars is 569 cubic meters, which is much higher than that of Japan and South Korea.

In the context of the Belt and Road Initiative, the traditional industry will speed up the green transformation and upgrading by utilizing the industrial development plan of *Made in China 2025*. We need to comprehensively boost the green transformation and upgrading of traditional manufacturing such as iron and steel, nonferrous metals, chemicals, building materials, papermaking, printing, and dyeing, accelerate the research and development of a new generation of circular processing technologies, vigorously develop and promote processing technologies featuring energy efficient use, pollution reduction, recovery of resources and safe disposal of waste materials, actively adopt advanced equipment such as high-efficiency motors, boilers, transform traditional manufacturing processes through efficient and green production processing technology and equipment, and speed up the green upgrade in key industries. We are expected to widely apply clean and efficient casting, forging, welding, surface treatment, cutting and other processing technologies to achieve green production, strengthen the application, research and development of green products, popularize lightweight, low-power, easy recycling and other technological processes, and continuously improve the energy efficiency level of end-use energy products such as motors, boilers, and internal combustion engines, and electrical appliances.

The transformation and upgrading of traditional industries will guide emerging industries to become a high starting point for green development. We will create green supply chains through technical means such as "green design, green materials, green processes, green production, green packaging, and green recycling". We will accelerate the development of green information and communication industry, work energetically to greatly reduce the production, use, and operation energy consumption of electronic information products, promote lead-free production processes and develop new green components to control lead, mercury, cadmium and other toxic and hazardous substances effectively. We will actively build green data centers and green base stations, comprehensively apply energy-saving emission reduction, green technology, and equipment carbon reduction effects, and ensure the renewable energy and proper distribution of energy supplies. Also, we will facilitate to develop new materials, new energy, high-end equipment, as well as bio-industry green low-carbon development, rapid prototyping, surface engineering, and other green materials technologies, vigorously research and develop high-performance, lightweight green new materials, green biotechnology, and green biological products. Moreover, we will extend the application of information and communication technologies and quicken the construction of smart grids, intelligent buildings, multi-network integration, intelligent logistics and so on to promote energy conservation and carbon reduction.

In promoting the efficient recycling of resources, the green transformation of traditional industries needs to rely on enterprises to strengthen technological innovation and management. By continuously improving the ratio of using green low-carbon energy, we will build a balanced distribution of green smart micro-grids in industrial parks and enterprises, enhance green lean manufacturing capabilities, significantly reduce energy, material and water consumption, and control and cut down fossil energy consumption. We will encourage circular production across the board, establish symbiosis between enterprises, parks, and industries, and establish links among raw materials to achieve shared resources. We will also boost the standardization and large-scale development of resource recycling industry, strengthen technical equipment support, and vigorously upgrade the comprehensive capabilities to utilize industrial solid waste, scrap metal, and waste electronic and some other products. Besides, we will devote major efforts to developing remanufacturing, such as making high-end remanufacturing for large-scale complete sets of equipment and key components of aerospace engines and gas turbines, etc., using information technology to realize remanufacturing in traditional electromechanical products, and remanufacturing service for electromechanical equipment with old performance, frequent failures, and outdated technology. For the remanufactured products, we need to strengthen and guide its manufacture, further standardize its production, promote its establishment, and realize the international mutual recognition mechanism to make the remanufacturing developed continuously and healthily.

Finally, under the background of green transformation and upgrading of traditional industries, the Belt and Road need to actively build a green manufacturing system. On the one hand, we must vigorously support enterprises to develop green products, conduct ecological design, advance energy-saving products, low-carbon levels, and guide green production and green consumption. On the other hand, we will build green factories and push forward the construction of thousands of green demonstration factories in key industries and explore the green remanufacturing model to achieve remanufacturing of plant density, innocuous raw materials, clean production, waste resources, and low-carbon energy.

6.3.1.2 Establishing a global industrial chain system

Made in China 2025 strategy is the first ten-year plan implemented in the manufacturing industry. If we can seize the opportunity of the Belt and Road Initiative, it will play a positive role in the core competitiveness of Chinese manufacturing companies, especially multi-national companies. China should support the development of a number of multi-national companies and advance its core competitiveness through global resource utilization, business process re-engineering, industrial chain integration, and capital market operations. Also, China should encourage enterprises to carry out mergers and acquisitions, equity investment, and venture capital, establish the R&D center, production and test base, and global marketing service system. Besides, China should facilitate enterprises to make collaborative network design, precision marketing, service innovation, media brand promotion, and establish a global industrial chain system relying on the Internet to improve the international management capabilities and service levels.

Currently, China is the largest manufacturing country. The implementation of the Belt and Road Initiative will provide substantial support for China's manufacturing-related enterprises and provide more cooperation opportunities for regions and enterprises where conditions allow. Through promoting policy guidance and industrial cooperation and extending links based on processing and manufacturing to high-end links such as cooperative development, joint design, marketing, brand cultivation, we will lift the level of international cooperation, develop new models of processing trade, and extend the domestic value-added chain of processing trade to promote the transformation and upgrading of processing trade. In the process of connecting *Made in China 2025* strategy and the Belt and Road Initiative, energy connectivity should be made as a focal point. Oil and gas pipeline equipment will be identified as the first major area. The Belt and Road Initiative can strengthen the cooperation in energy infrastructure and jointly safeguard the channels safety of oil and gas transportation. With the completion of China-Kazakhstan crude oil import pipeline, the China-Pakistan oil pipeline, and the China-Turkmenistan crude oil pipeline, the cooperation between China and the countries and regions along the Belt and Road in oil and gas energy has gradually stabilized. These construction projects of oil and gas channel in China's energy equipment industry provide much room for development. Moreover, power equipment and power engineering should be an important area of development cooperation. China's power generation equipment annual output, power installed capacity, thermal power installed capacity, hydropower installed capacity, and nuclear power unit capacity is among the highest in the world. It can be seen that China has become a leading country in the power equipment manufacturing industry. At the same time, in the field of power engineering, China's large-scale thermal power and hydropower complete sets of equipment, special high-voltage power transmission and transformation equipment lead a series of transmission engineering systems to achieve a high level in the world, which is not only conducive to the domestic power industry in the forefront of the manufacturing industry, while also play an important role in supporting the infrastructure construction.

6.3.1.3 The "Air, Land and Maritime" transporting equipment supporting the Belt and Road Initiative

The area of transportation is a basic area where *Made in China 2025* integrates with the Belt and Road Initiative, and has extensive development prospect with pervasive application areas. Through giving priority to constructing some areas with the Belt and Road Initiative, especially through constructing the key passageways, junctions and projects of transport infrastructure construction, traffic management facilities and equipment of infrastructure connectivity and traffic infrastructure, China's manufacturing will make seamless docking with the implementation of the Belt and Road Initiative from all-round and multi-dimensional "air, land and maritime" area , which will also make China's equipment manufacturing "go global" and reach out to the world.

First of all, we should give priority to the high-speed railway, because as a vital artery of the national transportation industry, it is an essential way for the domestic manufacturing industry to "go global". After more than 60 years of development, China's manufacturing industry of rail transit equipment, equipped with independent research and development, complete supporting, advanced equipment, large-scale operation, has been formed, which integrates with research, design, production, testing, and service. At present, with encouragement and support from the central government, China has established cooperation and negotiation in high-speed rail with many landlocked developing countries in the world. Today, a new wave of technological innovation represented by information network, intelligent manufacturing, new energy, and new materials in the world is emerging, and the leading position of rail transportation facilities will bring about transformation in all aspects. With the advantages of fast speed and high power, China's rail equipment manufacturing industry will rapidly promote the implementation of the Belt and Road Initiative.

Secondly, China's shipbuilding industry and related offshore projects need to be strengthened. Up to now, the domestic shipbuilding industry has occupied a leading position in the world and created unique brand effects and energy-saving, environmental protection and other effects especially in a series of cargo carriers, super-large mineral sand ships, super-large oil tankers and other fields, which is favored in the international market. Also, we have attained breakthroughs in high-tech and high added-value vessels, especially in the high speed to develop marine engineering equipment and the design and construction of deep-sea equipment. With the implementation of *Made in China 2025*, we will develop a number of well-known international brands with independent intellectual property rights in the fields of high-end ships and marine engineering equipment, and gradually master the core design, construction and supporting key technologies, and the digitization, intellectualization and greening level of final shipbuilding will reach the forefront of the world, which supports the implementation of the Belt and Road Initiative.

Finally, we must firmly grasp the development of the most efficient air transportation industry and the manufacturing industry. After decades of efforts, in China, a relatively complete aviation technology system, product lineage, and industrial system have set up, and the manufacturing industry of aviation system develops steadily. From the perspective of the aviation industry, China's aviation product R&D capability, system integration capability, and digital production capacity have been rapidly improved, the self-support capability of advanced weapons and equipment has been continuously enhanced, a number of aviation products and enterprises with certain international competitiveness are gradually forming, and the scale of the industry is expanding rapidly. The successful flight test of China's large aircraft C919 in May 2017 marked the ending of our blank period in the area of large aircraft. The mature technology in this area means that China's aviation manufacturing will become stronger in the international trial production, all of which will lay the foundation for China's international cooperation in the Belt and Road Initiative, especially in the big transport area.

6.3.1.4 Expanding the opening up of the manufacturing industry

To achieve the coordination between *Made in China 2025* and the Belt and Road Initiative, first of all, we need to continue to improve policies to support the financial sector; secondly, we need to deepen the reform of financial industry; finally, we need to push forward technological R&D, and the infrastructure of manufacturing enterprises, and support their export trade through internal security loans, foreign exchange, renminbi loans, equity financing leasing, debt financing, and other measures. We should further expand the demand of manufacturing industry for the outside world, strengthen the legislation of foreign investment and the legal protection for manufacturing enterprises going global, standardize the business activities outside the enterprises, and safeguard the legitimate rights and interests of enterprises. We should support manufacturing enterprises in participating in overseas investment and mergers and acquisitions, and support high-speed railway, power equipment, automobiles, construction, and other equipment and competitive industrial capacity "going global".

We should also establish open service platform for the overseas investment of manufacturing industry and technical trade service platform for export products, improve coordination mechanism and early warning mechanism for dealing with trade frictions and major issues of overseas investment, and create a normative, convenient and safe environment for the overseas investment of manufacturing enterprises.

6.3.2 The "Internet" facilitating China's manufacturing moving to a medium-high level

6.3.2.1 "Made in China + Internet" advancing supply side structural reform in manufacturing

China is currently in a critical period of social transformation, upgrading, and reform. The integration of Made in China and the Internet Plus action plan will boost China's supply-side structural reform, speed up the transformation and upgrading of manufacturing in China and provide a new direction for China's manufacturing industry. We will intensify efforts to promote the integrated development of Made in China and the Internet Plus action plan; build national platforms for innovation in manufacturing; carry out demonstration programs in smart manufacturing; launch projects to build a more solid foundation for industry development, promote green manufacturing, and develop high-end equipment; expedite the depreciation of the fixed assets and carry out major technological transformation and upgrading initiatives. "Cloud computing", "Internet" and "Terminals" have become a new data and communication platform for the manufacturing industry, through which all the elements of the manufacturing industry can be shared and exchanged. For example, the "Internet + Industry" activity carried out by Fuzhou is typical of "Made in China + the Internet". In Fuzhou, there are currently five industrial clusters with RMB100 billion, including textile and chemical fiber, light industrial food, machinery manufacturing, metallurgy, and building materials, and electronic information. What the government should do now is to motivate these enterprises to integrate Internet thinking into technological innovation, management innovation, and business model innovation, such as guiding enterprises to enhance the level of intelligence through the power of the Internet and high technology in enterprise financing, marketing, production equipment upgrading and other aspects.

As the Internet technology develops rapidly, the mode of "Internet + Manufacturing" has become a new manufacturing model where consumers can design products in accordance with their intentions, ranging from mugs to clothes, to home appliances. To conform to the trend of "Internet + Manufacturing", Haier Group has built seven interconnected factories as a model, which can enable global users to customize personalized products through mobile terminals, achieving the best user experience through visualization operation in the whole process of customization, no geographical constraints, no time limited. In the era of interconnection, it is the general trend of the times to achieve high accuracy beyond efficiency and to meet the customized needs of users in time, and therefore, China's manufacturing industry must seize this opportunity to carry out transformation and upgrading.

6.3.2.2 The imperative development of "Made in China + Internet"

On December 17, 2015, the Made in China 1000 Summit 2016, ie., the second "Internet Plus" Manufacturing Summit Forum was held in Shanghai. The forum released the first edition of "China Industry 4.0 Progress Report" in China, in which the all-around aspects such as present situation, existing problems, and opportunities in the development of China's manufacturing industry are manifested for the first time, and the transformation and upgrading of China's manufacturing industry at the macro level are also described. The survey took nearly 100 days and covered a wide range of 22 manufacturing areas in 12 developed cities and provinces in manufacturing, including Beijing, Shanghai, and Guangzhou, etc.

According to the report, more than half of enterprises have a relatively comprehensive understanding of the overall concept of Industrial 4.0, with more than 75 percent starting or being prepared to start investing in Industrial 4.0. Among them, 43.92 percent of the enterprises have already planned to invest in the reform Industrial 4.0, and 32.43 percent of the enterprises have begun to invest in the next three years, a sign of the enthusiasm of Chinese enterprises on Industrial 4.0. The report also shows that there are relatively fewer companies which invest in the vital areas of Industrial 4.0 such as big data, digitization, the Internet of Things, and cloud manufacturing. The lack of talents and R&D innovation capability, as well as the standardization, is a major obstacle to the implementation of China's Industrial 4.0. On February 1, 2016, the conference on the establishment of the Alliance of Industrial Internet was held in Beijing. 143 enterprises, such as the China Academy of Information and Communications Technology (hereinafter referred to as CAICT) affiliated to the Ministry of Industry and Information Technology of China, China Telecom, Alibaba, Huawei and Datang, set up Alliance of Industrial Internet in Beijing, aiming at focusing on and making breakthroughs on the research and development of generic technology, industry standards, security systems and other key areas within the year of 2016 so as to stimulate industrial innovation, improve quality and efficiency through the Internet, and to lay a foundation for China's industry to seize the global industrial transformation. In a word, China's manufacturing industry will have a bright and great future only when it realizes its deep integration with the Internet and replace old growth drivers with new ones. We should continue to strengthen international innovation cooperation and further close cooperation between *Made in China 2025* and "German Industry 4.0". In the golden stage of development during the 13th Five-year Plan period, we will promote and jointly implement the strategies to turn China into manufacturing and network of quality. Make China's manufacturing industry take its wings to move to a medium-high level so as to achieve the Chinese Dream of a strong country in the wave of mass entrepreneurship and innovation.

6.3.3   The initiative of mass entrepreneurship and innovation promoting the quality and efficiency of manufacturing industry

6.3.3.1   Mass entrepreneurship and innovation giving impetus to improving the quality and efficiency of manufacturing industry

At present, China's economic development has entered a new normal that manufacturing industry relies on large-scale investment, and the usual way of relying on low-cost production and export has been hard to maintain. Therefore, the manufacturing industry needs to foster the reform of the old system and strives to move to a high-end level. Mass entrepreneurship and innovation has revolutionized manufacturing innovation and played an active role in increasing effective investment, creating effective supply, leading consumer demand, and boosting the manufacturing industry to rely more on innovation-driven development and change.

Mass entrepreneurship and innovation can tap the potential to develop the traditional manufacturing industry. Compared with the developed countries in Europe and America, China's manufacturing industry is still at the low end of the value chain; traditional manufacturing industry has a vast inventory and more difficulties in upgrading and transforming. However, the traditional manufacturing industry is speeding up its optimization and upgrading by means of new technology, management, and mode of the initiative. "Internet Plus", focusing on consumer demand, will change the production concept of the traditional manufacturing industry, forcing traditional manufacturing enterprises to accelerate innovation based on market demand. Some enterprises, have accelerated the transformation of platform-based innovation organizations, exerted their internal innovation vigor, and produced a large number of new technologies, new products, new patterns, and new product models by innovating organizational structure and management mechanism. Some enterprises have gained access to and have made use of external innovation resources more conveniently through cross-domain and collaborative network innovation platform, which has effectively promoted enterprise design, manufacturing, management, and service. Mass entrepreneurship and innovation also has propelled the transformation of the operation mode of traditional manufacturing enterprise, and the constantly emergence of "design + user" "manufacturing + e-commerce" "marketing + social" and other new models, which has accelerated the development of manufacturing industry towards R&D design, value-added services and other high-end value chain.

Mass entrepreneurship and innovation have sped up the development of the advanced manufacturing industry that is the focus of the innovation and development for the manufacturing industry, and a vital driving force to cultivate emerging industries. The initiative has upgraded the industrial path of global resource integration gradually and offered a rare opportunity to achieve access to the high-end level. In the process of the initiative, a number of open entrepreneurial platforms of global multi-industry are thriving. Through collaborative design and innovation alliances, innovative resources such as enterprises, research institutions, professionals and venture capital have been effectively collected, a number of key technologies have been jointly studied and broken through speedily, which has promoted the development of advanced manufacturing at a high starting point. The initiative has accelerated the deep integration of industrial and information technology across industries, and cloud computing manufacturing, unmanned factories, large-scale customization, and some other new manufacturing models followed, giving impetus to the application of open and smart technologies in the manufacturing industry. The initiative has also promoted the large-scale scientific research facilities such as national laboratories and engineering technology centers to public, reduced the cost of utilizing new technology to research and development new products, and pushed forward the innovation and development of new materials, high-end equipment, biomedicine and other strategic emerging industries to form a new area of growth.

Mass entrepreneurship and innovation have pressed ahead with the service-oriented reform in the manufacturing industry. To adapt to the integration trend of manufacturing and service industries, transforming from the production to the service-embedded producing is an important way to upgrade the manufacturing transformation. The initiative has spurred manufacturing enterprises to innovate in management, mode, and format, to develop personalized customization, lifecycle management, remote maintenance services, and to continue to expand the industrial chain. Technology research and development, technology design, large-scale equipment financing leasing, industry e-commerce, and professional logistics services, are becoming a new business profit point and transformation direction. Some large-scale manufacturing enterprises have sped up the overall transformation of manufacturing, provided system integration and services through the initiative, significantly improving the economic efficiency and management level of enterprises. The initiative has also considerably reduced the cost of service transformation of manufacturing enterprises, accelerated the integration of manufacturing and service industry and promoted their quality and efficiency through information flow, technology flow, capital flow, and logistics integration, while the service-embedded manufacturing is emerging.

6.3.3.2 Mass entrepreneurship and innovation: a new growth drive to facilitate China being a leader in manufacturing

China is at an important moment in the 13th Five-year Plan period, a crucial period for the national economy to promote its quality and efficiency, which requires China's manufacturing industry to start again, adjusting its industrial structure and changing its mode of growth. On the one hand, we need to realize shifting gears without stalling; on the other hand, we should achieve better quantity and quality, so as to lay a solid economic foundation for accomplishing overall well-off society. Mass entrepreneurship and innovation face many constraints, such as the current system and mechanism constraints, inadequate fund dispatch, slow flow of talent and other practical constraints, which need to be optimized while playing an important role in China's manufacturing industry. We are expected to give priority to enterprises when carrying out the initiative of mass entrepreneurship and innovation and make enterprises' innovation the new growth drivers of the development of China's manufacturing industry. To achieve this, our government needs to do a good job in intensifying relevant policies support and improving the development environment of enterprises, and take effective measures to start the engine of entrepreneurship and innovation.

It is conducive to further stimulating the vitality of enterprises by further optimizing the system reform and reinforcing the readjustment of the critical factors like capital and information for the survival of enterprises. It is intended to readjust the market structure, re-tap the market vitality and the innovative ability of talents by promoting mass entrepreneurship and innovation. This calls for a series of relevant systems and policies to escort them. At the same time, we should simplify the government functions and the administrative examination and approval system, perfect the negative list model, and effectively remove barriers for new technology and new products to enter the market, thereby alleviating the pressure on enterprises, reducing the cost of innovation, and making more economic fields as the main direction of entrepreneurship. We also should earnestly advance important fields and key links, facilitate the transfer of the high-quality resources from surplus and inefficient fields to scarce and efficient areas, focus on enhancing the quality and effectiveness of financial support for the real economy, foster and expand venture capital investment and capital markets, guide social capital to converge with manufacturing industries, and provide steady support and promising expectations for the startups and innovation of enterprises. Furthermore, we should re-analyze and restudy the influence of existing social policies on enterprises and whether the current supervision will hinder the development of enterprises. We should revoke the policies launched a long time ago and no longer adapting to the current market in time, and ensure that the newly released system can effectively help the development of emerging enterprises.

The launch of *Made in China 2025* is a reform of the current defects of China's manufacturing industry. Actively advocating mass entrepreneurship and innovation can optimize the existing excess production capacity, provide a driving force for stimulating growth, and strengthen the positive role of innovation in China's manufacturing industry. In terms of the national key strategic principles, we should also attach great importance to the leading part of mass entrepreneurship and innovation playing in the core technological innovation and scientific achievements transformation, especially the innovation role in the main links and special areas. We should pay full attention to the international market mechanism and the innovation resources in the world, and make full use of the positive role of domestic industrial alliances and entrepreneurial platforms, focusing on key technical areas. It is necessary to make a renovation in traditional areas such as quality improvement, energy saving, consumption reduction, and safe production, to accelerate the innovation of technology, process, equipment and production organization mode, and to promote the digitalization, network and intelligent transformation of traditional industries. It is necessary to carry out special actions of mass entrepreneurship and innovation in intelligent and green manufacturing projects, to foster new production modes and industrial models, to enhance the synergistic ability and intelligent level of enterprise in R&D, design, production, management and service from all aspects, to step up efforts to cultivate new products and new formats and create new areas of economic growth.

Due attention should be paid to the important role and the leading part of mass entrepreneurship and innovation play in enterprise innovation so as to gradually establish a number of innovative manufacturing enterprises with independent innovation ability, change the original innovation decision-making and prevention mode, and gradually shape the independent selection mechanism of the market. Attention should also be paid to risk sharing and interests distribution mechanism in the process of technological innovation. We will ensure to fully play the leading role of enterprises and entrepreneurs in the whole process of innovation, especially in technological innovation and achievement conversion. In addition, a good communication platform needs to be set up to normalize the dialogue between enterprises and to ensure that the enterprises can get what they need. The opinions of enterprises with different scales and ownership should be actively listened to in the process of establishing the system and policies in the whole industry. The State's relevant policies should take the interests of the enterprises into account and are conducive to the development of enterprises. Meanwhile, we need to attach importance to the positive role large enterprises play in the initiative of mass entrepreneurship and innovation, encourage to establish various technology and information sharing platforms, and achieve the mechanism of division of labor substituting large for small, whose specific forms involve professional division of labor, service outsourcing, order distribution and so on, thus forming an industrial eco-chain featuring cooperative innovation and win-win cooperation, changing the enterprises' original model of developing alone, and gradually forming a whole industrial chain in which the enterprises develop coordinately and innovate together. We need to perfect the innovation service system for small and medium-sized enterprises, vigorously support the development of professional services such as business incubation, system integration, intellectual property rights and third-party inspection and certification, encourage enterprises to make good use of Internet infrastructure and innovation elements, keep reducing the threshold and cost of innovation for small and medium-sized enterprises, and look for and cultivate a number of invisible technology champions and "little giant" enterprises.

We need to optimize the government's service mechanism further, improve the government's service accuracy, and build a more convenient and soothing platform for entrepreneurship and innovation so as to enable the government to become a servant working for mass entrepreneurship and innovation. It requires to strengthen the government's service functions and to provide an excellent social environment and policy support for mass entrepreneurship and innovation. We need to focus on solving the "last kilometer" of innovative products entering the market, research and develop elaborate innovation support policies and enhance the synergy of different policy measures according to different industry characteristics and business needs. We also need to tighten up the market supervision of the product quality, raise the illegal cost of counterfeit and shoddy goods, and promote the survival of the fittest.

Furthermore, we need to make an investigation into and deal with infringements on intellectual property rights in accordance with the law in order to effectively protect enterprises' rational innovation capability. We need to correctly utilize various types of government resources to build cross-departmental platforms, business exchanges, and cooperation, and boost the integration of innovative enterprises and joint ventures. We need to make efforts to deal with the talent shortage in enterprise innovation by introducing talents and rewarding various forms of innovation achievements. We need to actively promote the accomplishments of technological inventions to be incorporated into economic activities to form commodities and open markets. Moreover, we need to put emphasis on training high-skilled talents and to upgrade the ability of human resource management, ensuring the scale, quality and structure of talents to match with the development of manufacturing industry.

Conclusion

The manufacturing industry is the material foundation of a country's national economy as well as substantial support for the main industry. It is an important power of economic development and an important guarantee of national security. The development of manufacturing industry reflects the comprehensive strength of science and technology, and indicates the level of national economy and comprehensive national strength. Therefore, the manufacturing industry has always been a strategic component of the national economy, in both developed countries and developing countries. In 2010, the output of China's manufacturing industry accounted for 19.8 percent of the world's total output and leaped to the first in the world's manufacturing country. A large number of incentive policies released by the state boosted China's manufacturing industry to grow rapidly. Breakthroughs of some core technologies in fundamental research and key areas have also been made in manufacturing a number of important high-end equipment which had depended on imports and had restricted the industrial safety of our country in a long period of time. Meanwhile, a national-level R&D base centered on universities has also successfully been set up, and many high-tech talents have been trained.

However, China's manufacturing industry is large but not strong. The per capita scale is still less than one-third of the manufacturing powers such as the United States, Japan, and Germany. Problems like outdated comprehensive technology, inadequate innovation capability, excessive national production capacity, low utilization of natural resources, low manufacturing profit and outdated manufacturing additional links and other important problems, are still the obstacles of China's manufacturing industry which need to be overcome. China's economy has entered a "new normal", at which we need to deal with the slowdown in economic growth, making difficult structural adjustments, and absorbing the effects of previous economic stimulus policies. The focus of China's future work will be shifted to optimize the economic structure and upgrade the industrial structure, adjust the economic growth from high rate to medium-high rate with quality and quantity, and change the direction of economic development consumption-driven and innovation-driven. Under such pressure, we must boost green manufacturing to achieve sustainable development of the society.

It should be noted that green manufacturing is a modern manufacturing model that takes into account both environmental impact and resource utilization efficiency, aiming at minimizing the impact of the products on the environment and maximizing resource utilization throughout the product lifecycle in design, manufacture, packaging, transportation, and use to scrap treatment. Green manufacturing is the embodiment of a sustainable development strategy in manufacturing, or it can also be regarded as the sustainable development model of modern manufacturing. Green manufacturing is involved in the whole life cycle of products. In terms of manufacturing environments and processes, green manufacturing mainly involves the optimization and utilization of resources, cleaner production and the minimization and comprehensive utilization of waste. The comprehensive research on intelligent manufacturing technology is the core in high-end equipment manufacturing development and plays an indispensable part in upgrading China from a manufacturer of quantity to one of quality.

Green manufacturing can also be seen as a shift in manufacturing philosophy while inheriting the advantages of traditional manufacturing. Green manufacturing integrates the latest science and technology with processes and concepts to create refined manufacturing from experiential manufacturing. To achieve this, the application of digital, information and intelligent technologies is required to work at the same time, thus intelligent manufacturing in the information age can be realized, the processing fineness, production efficiency, material utilization rate, even the self-diagnosis and smart maintenance of faults can be improved, and the manufacturing concept of the traditional manufacturing industry can be changed. Hence, green manufacturing can help effectively utilize, save and protect resources to the maximum extent, which is an effective way to solve the current shortage of natural resources, and also the best way to achieve sustainable development. Green manufacturing is bound to achieve a rapid development with the help of the two initiatives of the mass entrepreneurship and innovation and the "Internet Plus" initiatives. Today, the launch of the Belt and Road Initiative also puts forward new requirements for China's manufacturing industry. Green manufacturing contributes to the Belt and Road, which is conducive to economic cooperation, political mutual trust, economic integration and cultural inclusion between our country and the countries along the Road, helping establish a community of a shared future and a shared responsibility.

It should also be noted that green manufacturing will become the main mode of production in the future machinery manufacturing industry. In addition, the control of green technology will also become an important way for machinery manufacturing enterprises to occupy the market. In the future market development process, whoever takes the lead in promoting green development will guide the development of the market and increasingly improve the economic and environmental benefits. Considering the environmental impact and resource efficiency, the implementation of green manufacturing technology and green development have become the inevitable route for the development of modern industry. Over the past 30 years, China's economy has made tremendous achievements and become the world's second-largest economy and "world factory". In contemporary China, we should grasp the green trend of industrial transformation to upgrade China from a manufacturer of quantity to one of quality.

Bibliography

[1] Adam Smith, *The Wealth of Nations*, translated by Guo Dali and Wang Yanan, Nanjing: Yilin Press, 2011.

[2] Brian Author, *The Natures of Technology*, translated by Cao Dongming and Wang Jian, Hangzhou: Zhejiang People's Publishing House, 2014.

[3] Bureau of Compilation and Translation of Works of Marx, Engels, Lenin, and Stalin of the CPC Central Committee, *The Complete Works of Marx and Engels* (The 42nd Volume). Beijing: People's Press, 2016.

[4] Guo Yanhua, *Towards Green Civilization*, Beijing: China Social Sciences Press, 2004.

[5] Hao Xiaoyan, Wu Xuehua, "Research and Exploration of Green Manufacturing Mode in Transformation and Upgrading of China's Manufacturing Industry", *Value Engineering*, 2016(4).

[6] Hu Angang, *China: Innovative Green Development*, Beijing: China Renmin University Press, 2012.

[7] Jin Bei, *Made in China 2025*, Beijing: CITIC Press Group, 2015.

[8] Joseph Alois Schumpeter, *The Theory of Economic Progress*, translated by Du Zhenxu, etc., Beijing: China Commercial Publishing House, 2009.

[9] Li Boyang, "Green Manufacturing is a Common Choice in the World", *China Equipment*, 2016(11).

[10] Li Hongwei, "Key Factors in Green Product Development", *Ecological Economy*, 2006(3).

[11] Li Jingwen, Huang Lucheng, "Some Ideas on the Innovation Strategy of China's Manufacturing Industries", *China Soft Science*, 2003(1).

[12] Li Wurong, Hu Debao, "Game Analysis of Credit Deficiency in Consumer Goods Market", *China Development*, 2005(4).

[13] Lin Hanchuan, Wei Zhongqi, "The Latest Definition Standards for Small and Medium-Sized Enterprises in US, Japan, EU, and Its Enlightenment", *Management World*, 2002(1).

[14] Liu Fei, Cao Huajun and Zhang Hua, etc., *The Theory and Technology of Green Manufacturing*. Beijing: Science Press, 2005.

[15] Liu Fei, Zhang Xiaodong, and Yang Dan, *Manufacturing System Engineering*, Beijing: National Defense Industry Press, 2000.

[16] Liu Guangfu, *Green Design and Green Manufacturing*, Beijing: China Machine Press, 2000.

[17] Liu Zhanwei, "Problems in Developing China's Green Consumption and Its Marketing Strategy", *Reformation and Strategy*, 2009(10).

[18] Liu Zhilong, Chen Peng, Ji Li, "Current Situation and Analysis of Small and Medium-sized Enterprises in China", *Market Forum*, 2010(3).

[19] Lu Yongxiang, "Towards Green and Intelligent Manufacturing (Ⅲ): The Road to Manufacturing Development in China", *Electrical Manufacturing*, 2010(6).

[20] Lyu Wei, "Creating an Institutional Mechanism and Policy Environment Favorable to Green Development", *Economic Review*, 2016(2).

[21] Marcus Fairs, *Green Design: Creative Sustainable Designs for the Twenty-First Century*, translated by Teng Xuerong, Beijing: China Architecture and Building Press, 2016.

[22] Meng Qi, "Construction of Manufacturing Global Value Chain Based on One Belt One Road Initiative", *Finance & Economics*, 2016(2).

[23] Peng Shiyi, "A Historical Review and Evaluation of the Definition Standards of China's Small and Medium-sized Enterprises", *Commercial Times*, 2009(32).

[24] Qin Shusheng, "Philosophical Thinking on Ecological Technology", *Science Technology and Dialectics*, 2006(4).

[25] Qu Geping, *China's Environment and Development*, Beijing: China Environmental Science Press, 1992.

[26] Rolston, H., *Environmental Ethics*, translated by Yang Tongjin, Beijing: China Social Sciences Press, 2000.

[27] Su Chang, "The Application of High-tech in the Transformation from Equipment Manufacturing Industry to Intelligent Factory", *Technology and Economic Guide*, 2016(6).

[28] Tao Yong, Li Qiushi, Zhao Gang, "Research on the Green Manufacturing Strategy Oriented to Product Life Cycle", *Forum on Science and Technology in China*,

2016(9).

[29] The Advisory Committee of National Manufacturing Strategy, *An Interpretation of Made in China 2025—Proceedings of the Seminar of Provincial Level*, Beijing: China Industry and Information Technology Publishing & Media Group, 2016.

[30] The Advisory Committee of National Manufacturing Strategy, *Green Manufacturing*, Beijing: China Industry and Information Technology Publishing & Media Group, 2016.

[31] Thomas Piketty, *Capital in the Twenty-First Century*, translated by Ba Shusong, etc., Beijing: CITIC Press, 2014.

[32] Wang Hao, "Discussion on the Implementation of Green Manufacturing Strategy in China's Automobile Manufacturing Industry", *Equipment Manufacturing Technology*, 2009(9).

[33] Wang Songpei, *Management for the 21st Century: Eco-Economic Management*, Beijing: China Environmental Science Press, 1997.

[34] Wu Cheng, *Introduction to Contemporary Integrated Manufacturing System*, Beijing: Tsinghua University Press, 2002.

[35] Xi Daoyun, *Exploration and Practice of Standardization of Green Manufacturing of Equipment in China*, Beijing: Standards Press of China, 2016.

[36] Xiao Xianjing, *A View on Postmodern Ecological Science and Technology*, Beijing: Science Press, 2003.

[37] Xu Bingshi, Zhu Sheng, Shi Peijing, "Innovative Development of Green Remanufacturing Technology", *Welding Technology*, 2016(5).

[38] Xu Binshi, etc., *Remanufacture and Recycling Economy*, Beijing: Science Press, 2007.

[39] Yang Tongjin, *Environmental Ethics: Global Discourses and Chinese Perspective*, Chongqing: Chongqing Press, 2007.

[40] Yang Yonghua, "Study on the Evolutionary Mechanism of 'Adaptive Learning' of Technological Innovation Diffusion—On the Relationship Between Technology Introduction and Independent Innovation", *Modern Economic Research*, 2010(3).

[41] Yang Yudong, "How to Design Topic Investigation Questionnaire by Virtual Situation Questions", *Shanghai Research on Education*, 2010(1).

[42] Yu Pei, Wang Junjie, "Research on the Sustainable Development Path of China's Manufacturing Industry Under the New Normal—Based on a 'Global Factory' Perspective", *Contemporary Finance & Economics*, 2015(7).

[43] Yu Xiujuan, *Industry and Ecology*, Beijing: Chemical Industry Press, 2003.

[44] Zhang Chenggang, *Research on Modern Technological Issues—Technology Modernity and Human Future*, Beijing: Tsinghua University Press, 2005.

[45] Zhang Chunxia, *Research on the Development of Green Economy*, Beijing: China Forestry Publishing House, 2002.

[46] Zhang Jinmeng, *The Ecological Philosophy of Marx and Engels*, Beijing: China Social Sciences Press, 2014.

[47] Zhang Mingzhi, Yu Donghua, "'Made in China 2025' Carbon Emission Reduction Path and Industrial Options in the Context of the New Industrial Revolution", *Modern Economic Research*, 2016(1).

[48] Zhang Weiying, *Game Theory and Information Economics*, Shanghai: Shanghai People's Publishing House, 1998.

[49] Zhang Ye, "A Preliminary Study on the Green Economy", *Review of Economic Research*, 2002(3).

[50] Zhu Qinghua, *Green Supply Chain Management*, Beijing: Chemical Industry Press, 2004.